D0843426

Biracial
Politics

Biracial
Politics

Conflict and Coalition
in the Metropolitan South

Chandler Davidson

LOUISIANA STATE UNIVERSITY PRESS · BATON ROUGE

ISBN 0–8071–0246–6
Library of Congress Catalog Card Number 76–185951
Copyright © 1972 by Louisiana State University Press
All rights reserved
Manufactured in the United States of America
Printed by Heritage Printers, Inc., Charlotte, North Carolina
Designed by Albert R. Crochet

For My Parents

Preface

"The South is changing rapidly. He who writes about it runs the risk that change will occur before the presses stop, no matter how he strives, as I have done, to identify and emphasize elements of continuity." So wrote V. O. Key, Jr., in *Southern Politics* more than twenty years ago. The same holds true today, and perhaps the rate of change is even more rapid now than then. Yet what is remarkable about Key's work is that despite the changes wrought by the succeeding decades, much of his description of southern politics is still applicable. Were he alive today, Key would find the region's social landscape comfortably—or uncomfortably—familiar.

Like Key, I am tempted to apologize for the fact that the passage of time will render my description of racial politics inaccurate. On the other hand, I am skeptical of the claims of "sweeping," "dramatic," "fundamental" changes that are allegedly taking place in the South today. They emanate, more often than not, from the same source as the old predictions of a "New South" following the Civil War: self-seeking publicists eager to convince the rest of the country that the South is responsible enough in racial matters to be free of federal supervision, and economically stable enough to merit the confidence of northern investors.

Changes have occurred, even since the basic field work for this book was being carried out in 1966 and 1967. This is unquestionable. How important they are in transforming the situation of southern blacks—this is very questionable. On the surface some of these changes appear dramatic. In the fall of 1971, for example, Houston's first black councilman was elected to office, along with a Mexican-American city controller. At the same time, a new factional alliance in school board politics composed of Mexican-Americans, Anglos, and blacks swept the board clean of racial conservatives. Two blacks and a Mexican-American now sit on the seven-man board. Significantly all minority and liberal candidates who won office in the fall of 1971 obtained majority votes running at large in the city or school district.

Too, several new pressure groups have risen to local prominence since work on this book began. HOPE DEVELOPMENT, a militant community action group, has grown from its rather shaky beginnings to be a definite force in the black community. Local poverty programs have become a base for several emerging black leaders. The Urban League has now established an office in Houston, as have the Southern Christian Leadership Conference, Operation Breadbasket, and the Black Panthers.

Congressional redistricting in 1971 resulted in the creation of a safe black district in Houston's central city, and state Senator Barbara Jordan will probably become the South's first black congressional representative in the modern era. Legislative redistricting will give Houston four, and possibly five, black state representatives rather than the single one it presently has.

But what are we to make of these changes? Is the rise of new pressure groups, the election to office of a handful of blacks, or the more carefully muted bigotry of some conservative candidates the substance of victory for southern blacks?

My answer, which I elaborate in chapter 5, is no. To believe otherwise is to mistake means for ends. If the electoral changes that have occurred since the high tide of the civil rights movement become effective means for abolishing poverty, dismantling the formidable system of job discrimination that still exists, and destroying the residential segregation of blacks from whites, which is a cause of so many other sorts of inequality—whether in education or food prices or city services—then they will have been as important as prophets of the New South proclaim them to be. But from the vantage point of early 1972, I see no evidence which invalidates my earlier conclusion that the major battle of the war for racial equality—the battle for economic justice—has yet to be fought. If it is not fought soon, and won, everyone who has helped in the struggle for racial equality will have been sold a mess of pottage. And so will we all have been, even if some have made short-term profits from the sale.

Acknowledgments

The following people have contributed in ways helpful to the creation of this book: Robert Althauser, Numan Bartley, Morroe Berger, Jo Bratcher, Barbara Byrd, Sara Craig, Virginia Davidson, Elaine Finley, Chad Gordon, Francis Henderson, Harry Holloway, M. Kent Jennings, Barbara Jordan, Arnold S. Kaufman, Kathy Kobayashi, Duane Lockard, Douglas Longshore, Juan Marsal, Allen Matusow, Clifton McCleskey, Thomas Pettigrew, Barbara Podratz, David Schum, Mary Sheldon, John Strange, and Alana Whitlow.

These are people who come immediately to mind. There are others who will, I hope, forgive me for not mentioning their individual contributions. Among them are the numerous political activists, black and white, who gave generously of their knowledge of Houston politics.

Finally, I would like to acknowledge my debt to Richard Hamilton. Without his persevering criticism and encouragement, this book would never have been written.

Contents

List of Tables

Biracial
Politics

I

Interpretations of the Black Political Experience

The struggle for racial justice in the decade of the 1960s brought undeniable changes in American life. Precisely how these changes should be interpreted, and what further action is called for, are matters of continuing debate. Perhaps even more urgent today than ten years ago, the question remains: Is our political process adequate to the task of bringing about a just society for blacks and other racial minorities?

There are three current answers to this question, and one could classify most Americans according to which response they found acceptable. The "hard liners," who are not as outspoken nor as readily identifiable as they once were, deny that blacks have any special claim to justice. If Negroes are effectively excluded from full and equal participation in the civil life of the nation, it is their own doing, a result of their inferior nature. However, such straightforward racism is out of joint with the times, and even the old-style southern politicians would hesitate to express their feelings publicly in such terms.

A second, more acceptable answer goes something like this: Granted, blacks have been victims of discrimination. But the civil rights movement of the past two decades has given birth to trends in Negro education and employment which, with only minor assistance from the government, will soon lead to full racial equality. The nation can now benefit from a period of "benign neglect" of the Negro question. Further governmental action in behalf of blacks will foment a reaction among whites that would not only arrest Negro progress but also destroy many of the gains they have made.

A third answer is that the progress of blacks in recent years is extremely uneven, that "politics as usual" has so far proven inadequate to remedy their plight, and that new modes of political action are necessary if anything more than token gains are to be registered in the 1970s.

Which position is correct? The first is patently absurd. The second is at least plausible. It combines a very favorable assessment of the results of the civil rights movement with an increasing impatience with blacks for failing to agree with this assessment. In its most optimistic form, the argument is that Negro politics has become an increasingly effective instrument of social change in the North, and once voting rights laws are fully implemented in the South, we can expect the same progress there.[1]

Kenneth Clark's response is typical of the third answer:

> The homicide rate and the delinquency rate in Negro ghettos, which are higher than in most other areas of the northern cities, have not decreased. The ugliness of the ghetto has not been abolished. The overcrowding has increased. Most Negroes are still restricted to ghettos by income and white resistance. Ghetto business continues to be unstable, inefficient, and for the most part controlled by absentee owners. Unemployment and underemployment remain high, particularly among males. The welfare system continues to reinforce family instability and to impose the stigma of charity. The educational system of the ghetto has decayed even further, encouraging extreme restlessness and violence as ghetto parents resort to overt manifestations of their anxieties and their loss of faith in the public school system. . . . The fact is that the

---

[1] For example, in 1964, Oscar Handlin scolded blacks for trying to transplant in northern cities the methods of protest then employed in the South. In the North, he claimed, "Negroes . . . do have legitimate means of making their wants felt." See Handlin, *Firebell in the Night* (Boston: Little, Brown and Co., 1964), 61. Five years later, assessing Negro progress in the 1960s, Handlin was quoted as saying: "If you count the years from the big migration Negroes have advanced far more these ten years than any comparable group did in the past. This has been an extremely prosperous decade." He goes on to warn black militants of the danger of racial polarization and a white backlash, New York *Times*, June 1, 1969.

anti-poverty programs have failed, and part of the reason is the growing identification of the programs with the Negro.[2]

Advocates of this position call into question the belief that the voting rights legislation of the past decade is in itself a vehicle for rapid Negro advancement. They are supported in this by the works of several students of Negro electoral behavior.[3] A fact often overlooked by those who stress the importance of voting is that even if blacks are able to take control of some local governments through effective use of the ballot, they still have little if any influence over the economic institutions which in the long run profoundly affect their chances of obtaining a just share of social rewards. It is one thing to sit on the city council, quite another to sit on the board of directors of a large industrial corporation, where decisions are made affecting the employment status, wages, health care benefits, advancement opportunities, and long-term financial security of thousands of local employees.

But electoral arithmetic provides a basis for skepticism even regarding the claim that Negro voters can soon exercise control over the narrowly limited governmental structures of city and county. The Voting Rights Act of 1965 was primarily intended to help the Negroes in the Black Belt of the Deep South. Negroes in the North and West have generally had the right to vote at least since Reconstruction, and there is evidence that the Negro registration and turnout rates in these areas have not differed greatly during the last few decades from those of whites at similar socioeconomic levels.[4] Yet there, as in the South, the Negro remains isolated from

2 Kenneth Clark, "The Negro and the Urban Crisis," in Kermit Gordon (ed.), *Agenda for the Nation* (Washington: Brookings Institution, 1968), 131, 133.

3 See, for example, Donald R. Matthews and James W. Prothro, *Negroes and the New Southern Politics* (New York: Harcourt, Brace & World, 1966), 480–81; Allen P. Sindler, "Editor's Epilogue," in Sindler (ed.), *Change in the Contemporary South* (Durham: Duke University Press, 1963), 232; John H. Strange, "The Negro in Philadelphia Politics: 1963–1965," (Ph.D. dissertation, Princeton University, 1966), 181; William R. Keech, "The Negro Vote as a Political Resource: The Case of Durham" (Ph.D. dissertation, University of Wisconsin, 1966), 230.

4 Gunnar Myrdal, *An American Dilemma: The Negro Problem and American Democracy* (1944; 20th anniv. ed.; New York: Harper & Row, Publ., 1962), 495–97. The high degree of Negro participation in Chicago is described in Harold F.

the white community and frustrated in his efforts to attain equality.

Those who take an optimistic view of the potential power of the black vote in the South often cite as evidence the remarkable increase in southern Negro registration rates in recent years. The data in Table 1.1 show that progress in participation has indeed been made. Especially noteworthy is the increase in registration between 1964, before the voting rights legislation was enacted, and 1966, when federal registrars were on the scene in many Black Belt communities, and the poll tax as a prerequisite for voting in federal elections had been declared unconstitutional in the last four states which still retained it.

Table 1.1

NEGRO REGISTRATION IN ELEVEN SOUTHERN STATES

Year	Estimated Number Registered	As Percentage of Southern Negro Voting-Age Population
1940	250,000	5%
1960	1,414,052	28
1964	1,907,279	38
1966	2,620,359	52
1967	2,820,000	56
1968	3,112,000	62
1969	3,248,000	65

Source: Southern Regional Council Voter Education Project, Atlanta, Georgia.

Gosnell, *Negro Politicians: The Rise of Negro Politics in Chicago* (Chicago: University of Chicago Press, 1935). See especially pp. 16–17. Whereas Myrdal states that Negroes "vote in about the same proportion as whites," Gosnell adds this qualification: "An analysis of the voting figures shows that the Negroes take about as much interest in voting as do white citizens *of similar economic and social status.*" Italics added. More recently Orum has presented confirming evidence. See Anthony M. Orum, "A Reappraisal of the Social and Political Participation of Negroes," *American Journal of Sociology*, LXXII (1966), 32–46. According to the federal Census Bureau, nonwhite turnout was actually greater than that of whites in the Northeast in 1964 (80 percent to 76 percent), which is all the more remarkable, given the Negro's significantly lower socioeconomic status. New York *Times*, November 3, 1968.

What is less often mentioned is that registration among whites, which in the past has been extraordinarily low in the South when compared to the North, also has been rising. In 1960 slightly more than 59 percent of all voting-age whites were registered. In 1967, a year with no important national contests, approximately 73 percent were. The relative gains of Negroes are therefore much more modest than Table 1.1 suggests. The following table, showing the recent increase in the Negro proportion of the total qualified southern electorate, is more meaningful.

Table 1.2

PERCENTAGE OF ALL SOUTHERN
REGISTERED VOTERS WHO ARE NEGRO

Year	Negro Percentage
1960	10%
1966	15
1967	16
1968	17
1969	17

Sources: Percentages calculated from figures supplied by Southern Regional Council Voter Education Project, and United States Bureau of the Census, *Statistical Abstract of the United States, 1965* (Washington, D.C.: United States Government Printing Office, 1965), 385.

If, by exerting extraordinary effort, southern Negroes are able in the near future to attain a registration rate equal to that of whites, they will still comprise only 20 percent of all registered voters in the region, for only a fifth of the southern voting-age population is black. And as the northward migration of Negroes continues, this fraction will probably diminish. Also, contrary to a widespread belief, Negro adults do not constitute a majority of potential voters in many southern counties. Of 1,136 counties in the eleven southern states, 102 in 1970 had a population whose majority was Negro. Fewer counties had black majorities of voting age.

This suggests that the optimistic interpretation of Negro progress is questionable, at the very least. If this is so, one may well ask whether the political system offers blacks much more in the foreseeable future. Does not the ratio of whites to blacks, even in the South, argue against such a hope? The purpose of this book is to illuminate that question. To do so, the first part of the book focuses upon the theory of democratic pluralism that, in the academic community, has provided a rationale for the optimistic view of Negro political progress. It will be shown that the theory's application to black politics is of little value, as are its practical implications. By means of the case study approach, it will become evident that the pluralist version can be seriously misleading in its account of how ethnic minorities achieve political assimilation in this country. In particular it will be demonstrated that Negro participation in Houston—the largest city in the South and the sixth largest in the nation—has been far greater than most people suppose, while the resultant benefits have been modest indeed. In short, politics has not worked for blacks as pluralist theory predicts.

The problem remains, however, of what form of politics *will* bring about a just society. Violent revolution is one proposed alternative. Black separatism is another. A progressive biracial coalition, based on principles of racial justice and economic reform, is yet a third. The latter has recently been termed impractical by writers who claim to perceive a "white backlash" as a potential barrier to any effective coalition. This backlash is depicted as reactionary on racial matters, and is thought to be located among the blue-collar ethnic enclaves of the North and the poorer whites in the South.

The accuracy of this view is a matter for debate. How much evidence is there that progressive change is no longer possible when the white working class must be depended upon as an ally? This is the question addressed in the latter chapters. The conclusion reached there is that working-class racism has been exaggerated, and that there are many whites from this class who can be persuaded to support political programs which are racially and economically just.

THE CASE STUDY APPROACH

Rather than examine the Negro struggle within the United States as a whole, we have chosen the case study approach. The limitations of this method are well known. The advantages, however, are often overlooked, although in many instances they outweigh the disadvantages. In psychology, the study of a single individual, as in psychoanalysis, is accepted as providing essential data which simply are not accessible in large sample surveys. Systematic surveys and in-depth case studies are recognized as being of comparable value, although providing different kinds of information.

Unfortunately, the same cannot be said in the field of politics, where the nationwide sample survey has acquired such prestige in recent years that case studies are all too often considered to be nothing more than poor approximations of national surveys. It is nonetheless true that in political research, as in psychology, the case study reveals information that cannot be obtained by techniques employed in national sampling. For example, attitude patterns differ from one area of the country to another. Political systems in large cities differ sharply from those in small towns or rural areas. Ethnic voting patterns at the local level often diverge from those reflected in national statistics.[5] Various states have widely differing election rules and party and factional alignments. Yet national surveys are forced to pose standard questions dealing with national issues, so as to have meaning for a respondent in a small town in Nevada, a large city on the East Coast, or a rural county in Mississippi.

5 Raymond Wolfinger mentions an excellent example. Italians in New Haven are strongly Republican and hence are unrepresentative of Italians nationally—who are even more Democratic than the Irish. See Wolfinger, "The Development and Persistence of Ethnic Voting," *American Political Science Review*, LIX (1965), 900.

Matthews and Prothro (*Negroes and the New Southern Politics*, 98) in their study of southern Negroes, were forced to supplement their South-wide sample with case studies of different kinds of counties in order to account for Negro-white differentials in political participation left unexplained by socioeconomic variables.

It is also true that voters often react more intensely to political events at the local than at the national level. "The tangible material rewards at stake in the local election," Robert Lane writes, "combined with a more clear-cut ethnic appeal, evoke responses very different from the broader and more policy-oriented appeals involved in national elections."[6] The 1970 midterm elections, for example, provided several cases of outcomes which were attributed to local issues.[7] The location of a new freeway, the decision to bus children to achieve integration, a bond issue, a rise in the property tax base, or the firing of a police chief are examples of events that are perceived as important to people who are affected by them—more important, in many instances, than who becomes the next secretary of state or whether the prime interest rate goes up or down. The facts of political life at this level are obviously very difficult to gauge using national sampling techniques. For these reasons and others, works such as the Lynds's *Middletown*, Oscar Lewis' *La Vida*, Robert Dahl's *Who Governs?*, Elliot Liebow's *Tally's Corner*, or William Whyte's *Street Corner Society* will never be replaced by national sample surveys.[8] Indeed, the question of whether national surveys or case studies are more reliable is misleading. Both research approaches are necessary for an understanding of the American political system. They are complementary rather than mutually exclusive.

This study centers upon Houston and surrounding Harris County. The city, which properly belongs to the Rim South rather than the Deep South, has had a legally enfranchised Negro electorate since 1944, when the Supreme Court outlawed the white

---

6 Robert Lane, *Political Life* (New York: The Free Press, 1959), 47.

7 See R. W. Apple, Jr., "Political Pros Reject G.O.P. Claim of Election Gain," New York *Times*, November 15, 1970. "As always," Apple writes, "local issues were more important than was generally recognized. The victories of Governor-elect John J. Gilligan of Ohio, Senator-elect Lawton Chiles of Florida, and Senator-elect Lowell P. Weicker, Jr. of Connecticut, among others, were attributed largely to local circumstances."

8 Elliot Liebow's discussion of the merits of the case study is noteworthy. Liebow, *Tally's Corner: A Study of Negro Streetcorner Men* (Boston: Little, Brown, and Co., 1967), 8–10.

primary. Because of the city's Confederate heritage, the entry of blacks into the electorate in a relatively short period of time constituted a challenge to the local status quo, and the results of this challenge can be assessed within a definite time span of about twenty years. Further, the black population is quite large—presently the largest in the South. As this book reveals, Negroes have established a tradition of organized, regular political participation at the grass-roots level that, measured in terms of per capita expenditure of effort, probably rivals or exceeds in many respects that of whites of similar income and education. Thus, it could be argued that unlike the conditions existing in many areas in both the North and South with very small Negro populations, or those existing in some southern cities where enfranchisement is quite recent, the situation in Houston is such that maximum political assimilation should be expected, and it provides an excellent context in which to pursue the questions with which we are concerned.

MAGNOLIA CITY

Whether, and in what sense, Houston is a southern city is a question often discussed by Houstonians themselves. Is it really part of the South? Are generalizations about its politics applicable to other southern cities? The local mass media have tended in recent years to portray the city as more western than southern. The tradition of the cattle-raising frontier is perpetuated by the annual Fat Stock Show and the reenactment, albeit with modern comforts, of the riding of the old Salt Grass Trail. Too, because part of Texas belongs to the Southwest, other areas of the state cash in on the symbolism of the highly commercialized western tradition. Many businessmen in all parts of the state wear Stetson hats as part of their everyday attire. City dwellers who have never ridden a horse wear cowboy boots on the city streets. Texans in all areas and from all walks of life seem eager to accept the spurious but romantic notion of themselves as denizens of the frontier.

Certainly it would be misleading to depict the state as typical of the Deep South. By any standard, Texas belongs to the "peripheral" South or the Rim South rather than to the heart of Dixie.[9] However, there are several reasons for calling Houston a southern city. Foremost among these is its cultural link with the region known as East Texas, which in turn is steeped in the political and social mores of the southern Black Belt dating to pre-Civil War days and continuing into the present.

East Texas can be defined either culturally or demographically. Melvin Banks refers to it as the area from which came "the chief opposition to Negroes [in Texas] enjoying full citizenship" after emancipation. According to Banks: "The Negroes lived principally along the Brazos, Trinity, Neches, Sabine, Colorado, and Red River bottoms, where cotton was first grown on a large scale. The region includes some 70 counties stretching from Lamar County along the Red River down the Texas-Louisiana boundary to Harris (Houston), Galveston, Refugio, and Fort Bend Counties, up the Neches and Trinity River bottoms to Dallas and Ft. Worth. It dips into central Texas along a line from Austin to Waco. Ft. Worth is often advertised as the place where the West begins."[10]

In the southern subcultural typology devised by A. R. Mangus, East Texas and Houston are within the region called "Western Old South," which includes part of Arkansas and Louisiana as well. This region, together with the Eastern Old South and the Mississippi Delta, is embraced by the Cotton Belt.[11] According to Franklin

9 Many students of the South find it difficult to classify Texas. Meyer, for example, admits that both Texas and Arkansas "don't easily fit either the 'Deep', 'Upper', or 'Border' categories." See Alan Samuel Meyer, "The Not-So-Solid South: A Study of Variability in Southern Sentiment in School Desegregation" (Ph.D. dissertation, Columbia University, 1962), 18. Attempts to divide the southern states into relatively homogenous cultural entities include the following: Gunnar Myrdal, *An American Dilemma* (New York: Harper and Bros., 1944), 1071–72; Hugh D. Price, *The Negro and Southern Politics: A Chapter of Florida History* (New York: New York University Press, 1957), 8–9; Gilbert Shapiro, "Myrdal's Definitions of the 'South': A Methodological Note," *American Sociological Review*, XIII (1948), 619–21.

10 Melvin James Banks, "The Pursuit of Equality: The Movement for First Class Citizenship Among Negroes in Texas, 1920–1950" (Ph.D. dissertation, Syracuse University, 1962), 7.

11 A. R. Mangus, *Rural Regions of the Old South* (Washington, D.C.: Works

Frazier, "the plane of living among the farm population in this region was the same as that in the Eastern Old South." [12] Alan Meyer operationally defines East Texas today as "all counties with ten percent or more Negroes except Foard County which is in North Central Texas plus Franklin and Van Zandt counties which have only seven percent Negroes but are in North East Texas entirely surrounded by counties with ten percent or more Negroes." [13]

By all of the above definitions, Harris County, in which Houston is located, falls within East Texas, which in turn is the area of the state where slavery flourished, once it was introduced in the early nineteenth century, and which still today bears witness to the nature of the "peculiar institution." For although slavery came late to Texas, it became firmly established in a short period of time. According to Charles Ramsdell, an historian of Texas Reconstruction: "Slavery had existed in the state ever since the Anglo-Americans had first pushed their way into the wilderness; and climatic conditions, agricultural development, and constant immigration from the older Southern states had contributed to the spread of the institution. It had rooted itself most firmly in the populous eastern and Southeastern counties . . . where the plantation system was in almost exclusive possession of the country and conditions, social and economic, were practically identical with those existing in the older slave states." [14]

There can be no doubt that Houston, although only a small town of 4,845 in 1860, was imbued with the slaveholding traditions of the antebellum South. Frederick Law Olmsted, having visited the "city"

Progress Administration, 1940), 24; cited in E. Franklin Frazier, *The Negro in the United States* (New York: Macmillan Co., 1951), 202.

12 Frazier, *The Negro in the United States,* 202.

13 Meyer, "The Not-So-Solid South," 101n.

14 Charles W. Ramsdell, *Reconstruction in Texas* (New York: Longmans, Green and Co., 1910), 11. Ramsdell, a respected scholar, was nonetheless a product of his time, and many of his observations are clearly biased by his anti-Unionist, anti-Negro attitudes. For a thumbnail sketch of Reconstruction in Texas seen from a very different viewpoint, see W. E. B. DuBois, *Black Reconstruction: An Essay Toward a History of the Part Which Black Folk Played in the Attempt to Reconstruct Democracy in America, 1860–1880* (New York: Harcourt, Brace and Co., 1935), 552–61.

in 1854, wrote in *A Journey Through Texas*: "There is a prominent slave mart in town, which held a large lot of likely-looking Negroes, waiting purchasers. In the windows of shops, and on the doors and columns of the hotel, were many written advertisements headed, 'A likely Negro girl for sale,' 'Two Negroes for sale,' 'Twenty Negro boys for sale, etc.' "[15] Even earlier, in 1839—two years after Houston's founding—an ordinance was passed by the city council setting an eight o'clock curfew for blacks and stipulating that any violator be given ten to thirty lashes. Free Negroes were not allowed in town. Strict laws against intermarriage were enacted.[16] When slavery was threatened by the events leading to the Civil War, most white Texans reacted as Southerners. On February 23, 1861, they ratified the secession ordinance by a popular vote of 46,129 to 14,697. Houston, too, overwhelmingly ratified it. Ironically, General Sam Houston, for whom the city was named, was a Unionist and opposed the Secession Convention. He was forced out of office as governor of Texas and died two years later.

Although the state was not centrally involved in the war, many Texans participated in it and a few engagements occurred in the eastern portion of the state. From one of these, the Battle of Sabine Pass, a Houstonian, Richard "Dick" Dowling, emerged as a minor luminary. Today Dowling Street is the central artery of one of the city's largest ghetto areas. During Texas Reconstruction, Houston was rent by the political divisions which existed in the postwar days throughout the eastern counties. Racial tension in the city was exacerbated immediately after the war when Federal troops were garrisoned there. The first Union troops to enter were Negroes, commanded by white officers. A riot followed shortly. The general reaction of the whites to emancipation is reflected by what must have been extraordinary appeals for moderation by a few Houstonians in this period. Ramsdell writes: "The *Houston Telegraph*

15 Frederick Law Olmsted, *A Journey Through Texas; or, A Saddle-Trip on the Southwest Frontier*, Vol. II of Olmsted, *Our Slave States* (3 vols.; Dix, Edwards and Co., 1857), 363. See pp. 361–63 for a brief but vivid picture of conditions in Houston at this time.

16 B. H. Carroll, Jr., *Standard History of Houston, Texas, from a Study of the Original Sources* (Knoxville: H. W. Crew and Co., 1912), 57.

thought it necessary to warn the people not to allow themselves to develop a feeling of hostility and bitterness toward the blacks, who, although they were doing very many foolish and vexatious things, were 'not responsible for their own emancipation.' "[17] In 1867 the elected mayor of Houston was removed from office by the district military commander, who took "semi-military" control of the local government and appointed a man of his own choosing. In 1868 Governor E. J. Davis, a Radical Republican, appointed another man in his place and made several other changes in the local political structure. In 1870 the governor appointed as mayor T. H. Scanlan, a white Republican, as well as four Negro aldermen. Two years later this slate was elected. However, the newly enfranchised Democrats gained control at the state level the following year, and within two months the city charter was amended to allow Democratic Governor Richard Coke to appoint all city officials. "Scanlan and his Negroes," as another anti-Negro historian of the city referred to them, were turned out.

Following Reconstruction, racial reaction set in, culminating around the turn of the century in Negro disfranchisement. The *Proceedings* of the State Convention of Colored Men of Texas indicate the extent of Jim Crowism in Texas as early as 1883. The delegates to the convention protested against the state miscegenation law, unequal school facilities, the brutal treatment accorded black convicts, segregated public accommodations, and the exclusion of Negroes from juries.[18] Perhaps the most telling index of the condition of Negroes in East Texas at this time consists of the lynching statistics. Between 1882 and 1943 there were 551 lynchings recorded in East Texas, compared with 596 in Mississippi and 571 in Georgia.[19] Harris County recorded 6 Negro lynchings between 1900 and 1931, excluding riot victims.[20]

17 Ramsdell, *Reconstruction in Texas*, 50.
18 *Proceedings of the State Convention of Colored Men of Texas, held at the City of Austin, July 10–12, 1883* (Houston, 1883), reprinted in Herbert Aptheker (ed.), *A Documentary History of the Negro People in the United States* (New York: Citadel Press, 1951), 686–91.
19 Banks, "The Pursuit of Equality," 267.
20 Charles S. Johnson, *Statistical Atlas of Southern Counties* (Chapel Hill: University of North Carolina Press. 1941), 231.

In August, 1917, a race riot broke out in Houston which left sixteen persons dead. As in the case of the riot of 1866, it occurred at a time when Negro soldiers were stationed in the city. A Negro enlisted man had intervened in the arrest of a black woman by a white policeman. Fighting erupted between the Negro soldiers and the police, as well as between the soldiers and their white officers.[21] As a result several Negro soldiers were sent to prison and thirteen were hanged. There was undoubtedly much bitterness during this epoch among Negro soldiers returning from Europe to Texas, where their voting rights had been systematically abridged for almost two decades.

In the 1920s the Ku Klux Klan made deep inroads into state and local government in Texas, bringing with it a new wave of terror and repression. Black delegates to the 1928 national Democratic convention held in Houston were forced to sit in an area separated from the whites by chicken wire.[22] As late as 1930 the newly elected city administration banned Negro clerks from the seafood stalls at the Houston city market, where they had worked for many years.[23] Charles Johnson, collecting data for the Myrdal study in the late thirties and early forties, vividly described the forms of public discrimination in effect then. They included strictly segregated railway facilities, Negro sections on city buses, segregated taxis, and the exclusion of Negro patients from the wings of hospitals in which white wards were located.[24] Many Houston blacks in those days must have harbored the feelings expressed in the letter from a Houston man addressed to Robert S. Abbott, editor of the Chicago *Defender.* "I would like Chicago or Philadelphia," he wrote. "But I don't Care where so long as I Go where a man is a man."[25]

The traditional southern attitude of law enforcement officers

21 See James Weldon Johnson, *Along This Way* (New York: Viking Press, 1933), 321–26; Edgar Schuler, "The Houston Race Riot, 1917," *Journal of Negro History,* XXIX (1944), 300–38.

22 Gosnell, *Negro Politicians,* p. 32.

23 Banks, "The Pursuit of Equality," 208.

24 Charles S. Johnson, *Patterns of Negro Segregation* (New York: Harper and Bros., 1943), 35, 46, 47, 49, 50, 53.

25 Quoted in Charles Silberman, *Crisis in Black and White* (New York: Random House, Inc., 1964), 27.

toward Negroes probably existed even during Reconstruction (although Governor Davis did appoint a number of blacks to the state police). Later the folk singer Huddie Ledbetter, popularly known as "Leadbelly," expressed the itinerant Negro's perception of a well-known Houston sheriff in the following stanzas of his song "The Midnight Special":

> If you ever go to Houston
> You better walk right.
> You better not stagger.
> You better not fight.

> Sheriff Binford will arrest you,
> He will carry you down;
> If the jury finds you guilty
> You are Sugarland bound.[26]

The town's peculiarly southern identification during the present century was indicated by its nickname, "Magnolia City," which persisted into the twenties. Yet even today the spirit of the South continues to be manifested in various ways. Streets and schools—including new ones—bear the names of Confederate heroes. Commercial establishments, from drive-in groceries to casket makers, include the word "Dixie" in their name. The Harris County "Sheriff's Posse," a group of horsemen who perform in rodeos and parades, displays the American and Confederate flags during precision drills. The Sons of Confederate Veterans and the United Daughters of the Confederacy sponsor a "Confederate Ball," which is attended by local social and political dignitaries, including the mayor.

However, several factors temper the city's southern tradition. Among them are sheer size, rate of growth, and the numerous effects of rapid urbanization. Houston, a city of 1.2 million people in 1970, is situated within the country's thirteenth largest standard metropolitan statistical area (SMSA). The Negro population exceeds 300,000, which was approximately the size of Chicago's "Bronze-

26 Quoted in George Fuermann, *Houston, The Feast Years* (Houston: Premier Printing Co., 1962), 9. T. Binford was county sheriff from 1918 to 1937. The state prison is located at Sugarland.

ville" in the thirties when Cayton and Drake undertook their classic study of the black community in that city.[27] Houston lies within Harris County, whose 1.7 million population is the largest in the state and is second in growth rate among the country's most populous counties.

As in the case of the larger community, Houston's Negro population is rapidly increasing (Table 1.3). In 1970, 26 percent of the city's population was black, indicating a continued reversal of a trend that saw the city's black ratio steadily decline between 1900 and 1950. It is presently the largest Negro concentration in the South, exceeding that of either New Orleans or Atlanta. It is the eighth largest black population in the country.

Table 1.3

CITY OF HOUSTON, TOTAL AND NEGRO POPULATION, 1900–1970

Year	Total Population	Negro Population	Percent Negro
1900	44,633	14,608	32.7%
1910	78,800	23,929	30.4
1920	138,276	33,960	24.6
1930	292,352	63,337	21.7
1940	384,514	86,302	21.4
1950	596,163	125,400	21.0
1960	938,219	215,037	22.9
1970	1,232,802	316,992	25.7

Source: United States Bureau of the Census.

An important source of this Negro increase is favorable net migration. Bullock has shown that 87.9 percent of the Negro increase in the city between 1940 and 1950 was the result of migration.[28] A large number of these migrants come from small towns and rural

27 Horace Cayton and St. Clair Drake, *Black Metropolis: A Study of Negro Life in a Northern City* (New York: Harcourt, Brace and Co., 1945).
28 Henry Allen Bullock, *Pathways to the Houston Negro Market* (Ann Arbor: J. W. Edwards, 1957), 31.

areas in Texas and Louisiana. However, the portrayal of this migration as a movement of southern rural inhabitants to the city is oversimplified. Slightly more than 34 percent of the Negro in-migrants to Houston between 1955 and 1960 were from other SMSAS.[29] This is considerably less than the percentage of such urban in-migrants in the northern cities, where the proportion is usually more than 60 percent, but it is higher than that of several other comparable southern ones. In all probability Houston occupies the role of a "stage" city described by the Taeubers: "The redistribution of Negro population from the rural South to northern cities appears to be an indirect process. Few Negroes move directly from Southern farms to Chicago or New York. Negro farmers, croppers, or farm laborers are more likely to move to a nearby southern city. Later they or their children may move to one of the northern cities."[30] As more than 60 percent of Houston's Negro out-migrants in the period between 1955 and 1960 moved to another SMSA, one can reasonably assume that Houston performs the "service" of acclimating many rural blacks to city life before they make their next move to a northern or western metropolis.

Houston Negroes, like their counterparts elsewhere, are highly concentrated in predominantly nonwhite residential areas. In 1960 the city was rated 93.7 on the Taeubers' index of residential segregation. A score of 100 indicates complete segregation.[31] Everett Ladd, borrowing from the terminology of Charles S. Johnson, has distinguished three types of southern residential patterns. In the "back yard" type, Negro residences are distributed uniformly throughout the city. At the other extreme is the "ghetto" pattern,

---

29 Karl E. and Alma F. Taeuber, "The Negro Population in the United States," in John P. Davis (ed.), *The American Negro Reference Book* (Englewood Cliffs: Prentice-Hall, Inc., 1966), 126.

30 *Ibid.*, 129.

31 Karl E. Taeuber and Alma F. Taeuber, *Negroes in Cities: Residential Segregation and Neighborhood Change* (Chicago: Aldine Publishing Co., 1965), 41. The Taeubers (p. 30) explain the index as follows: "The value of the index may be interpreted as showing the minimum percentage of non-whites who would have to change the block on which they live in order to produce an unsegregated distribution—one in which the percentage of non-whites living on each block is the same throughout the city."

with a single intense concentration of Negro residences. A third pattern is that of "urban clusters," involving one to three large concentrations of Negroes, as well as up to twenty smaller clusters scattered across the city.[32]

Houston exhibits the latter pattern. There are three main areas of Negro concentration within the city limits, surrounded by numerous smaller clusters. There is also a fourth major area immediately outside the city's northern limits, which is in many ways integral to the Houston Negro community. A fifth area, much smaller than the other four, completes the five major Negro subcommunities. "These areas are more than sheer aggregates of people," writes Bullock. "They constitute virtual social entities, in which the people have strong loyalties toward the section in which they live and quickly identify with them."[33] There are, in addition to these five main areas, more than twenty smaller ones within the city limits.

As in many other American cities, there has been a large increase in the number of Negroes in the core city. Between 1950 and 1960 the total central city population (Negro and white combined) actually decreased by 34,198, while the Negro population rose by 20,299. The proportion of the core city population which was Negro rose from 23.4 percent to 30.1 percent in the same period.

Although the Fifth, Fourth, and Third wards are within the core city and have a relatively high population density in terms of people per square mile, they are for the most part free of typically eastern slums, which are characterized by aging tenements and stark high-rise apartment complexes. Rather, the core city residential areas consist primarily of mixed single-family and multi-family dwellings. These are accurately described by a City Planning Commission report: "The predominating housing characteristics of these areas are undersized single-family dwellings crowded together, either upon small lots or with several dwellings upon one lot. Where

32 Everett Carll Ladd, Jr., *Negro Political Leadership in the South* (Ithaca: Cornell University Press, 1966), 52–53. See also Johnson, *Patterns of Negro Segregation*, 10.

33 Henry Allen Bullock, *Profiles of Houston Negro Business Enterprises: A Survey and Directory of Their Activities* (Houston: Negro Chamber of Commerce, 1962; mimeo), 16.

larger dwellings exist, they too are frequently crowded together and are often occupied by more than one family. The environment created by this type of residential use is usually substandard."[34]

While a high percentage of Houston's Negroes lives in segregated areas, there is extensive daily contact between the two races in the city. One of the reasons for this is a geographical one. The Negro areas are gradually expanding into a north-south belt, cutting the city in half. Movement of whites from one half to the other often requires that they cross through a Negro area. White traffic is particularly heavy through the Third Ward—which lies directly southeast of the main business district—and the Fourth Ward, which is an enclave in the older central business area.

Another reason for this interracial contact is that the Negro community is not economically self-sufficient. The Fifth, Fourth, and Third wards each have an important main street occupied by many small commercial establishments catering to blacks. But the large department stores, banks, theaters, and parks are outside these areas. Further, there is not an old, established Negro commercial and financial district in the city, such as exists in Atlanta or Durham. There is only one Negro-owned bank, opened in 1963, and one Negro savings and loan association, chartered in 1959. Each had less than four million dollars in total assets in 1966. The total resources of the Houston area's banks (not counting savings and loan associations) were more than five billion dollars.

A third reason for extensive interracial contacts lies in the work patterns of the Negro labor force. Most domestics must go outside the ghetto to work. The same is true for Negroes engaged in lawn care, manual labor, industrial enterprises, and the small but growing white-collar endeavors. Thus, while the majority of white Houstonians do not often pass through Negro residential areas, they meet blacks every day on the city streets, in stores and restaurants, in their own segregated neighborhoods, and of course as servants and laborers in their homes.

To summarize, Houston's history gives evidence of the city's

34 Houston City Planning Commission, *Population, Land Use, Growth* (Houston, 1959), 78.

strong identification with the traditions and values which are peculiar to the former slaveowning states who fought against the
Union more than one hundred years ago. This is not to deny that
the southern mystique is gradually dissipating under the impact of
urbanization and the integrating bonds of nationalism. Nor does it
contradict the fact that Houston, lying on the periphery of the
South, has developed regional loyalties to the Southwest as well.
The thesis that Houston is a southern city does imply however that
the barriers of caste are a little stronger, the exercise of white power a
little more brutal and unashamed, and the intransigence of officials
and voters alike to the demands for Negro equality somewhat more
unyielding than is the case in the North and West of this nation
today.

II

The Organizational Weapon

From Tocqueville on, observers of the American scene have been struck by the importance of voluntary associations in the political life of the nation. The pluralists, who can justly claim Tocqueville as their most imaginative and influential theorist, incorporated the celebrated propensity of Americans to join organizations into an explanation of how our political system works. This explanation had the good fortune to be introduced at a time of growing dissatisfaction with individualistic, atomistic theories to account for the new political parties and mass movements of the nineteenth century.

The organized group as the central feature of American political life continues to dominate pluralist thought today. According to this school, American society is "fractured into a congeries of hundreds of small 'special interest' groups, with incompletely overlapping memberships, widely differing power bases, and a multitude of techniques for exercising influence on decisions salient to them."[1] These groups, while not all equally powerful, share in influencing the major decisions of government and manage to see at least some of their interests served. There is genuine competition among them. Furthermore citizen participation through voting and adherence to internally democratic voluntary organizations, including parties, is adequate to insure grass-roots support for the legitimacy of the system. The pluralist model does not entail even a rough individual

1 Nelson Polsby, "How to Study Community Power: The Pluralist Alternative," in Roderick Bell, David V. Edwards, and R. Harrison Wagner, *Political Power: A Reader in Theory and Research* (New York: The Free Press, 1969), 34.

equality of wealth, income, status, and political power.[2] The widely distributed right to vote and citizen membership in numerous overlapping groups moderates the inequalities among individuals.[3] In particular the "organizational weapon" of the less affluent majority countervails against the weapons of wealth and personal influence.[4]

Thus it is the *organized* power of the lower orders that successfully confronts the resources of wealth and status. There are two major problems, however, which beset this view. First, how many people actually belong to effective political interest groups? Second, how easy is it for such groups to form and successfully function, especially when they recruit primarily from the lower social classes? Richard Hamilton, a critic of pluralist theory, cites the results of several nationwide surveys as evidence for his assertion that "a large part of the American [adult] population—close to half in three of the studies and more than half in a fourth—have no voluntary association connections."[5] Moreover many if not most of these associations which proliferate among Americans are not even vague-

2 Indeed Robert Dahl, in his book *Who Governs? Democracy and Power in an American City* (New Haven: Yale University Press, 1961, p. 3) sets for himself the task of answering the question, "How does a 'democratic' system work amid inequality of resources?"

3 Arnold Rose, another pluralist, also cites the alleged "ever changing" nature of the "elite" as a factor which mitigates inequality of resources. Rose, *The Power Structure* (New York: Oxford University Press, 1967), 485

4 Thus, Dahl argues that "few groups in the United States who are determined to influence the government—certainly few if any groups who are organized, active, and persistent—lack the capacity and opportunity to influence some officials somewhere in the political system in order to obtain at least some of their goals." Quoted in William E. Connolly (ed.), *The Bias of Pluralism* (New York: Atherton Press, 1969), 9. Rose writes: "While money in the hands of rich people opens special opportunities ... these [political] processes are by no means closed to poor people. A volunteer campaign worker for a congressman will have more influence on him than most lobbyists." Rose, *The Power Structure*, 491.

5 Richard Hamilton, *Class and Politics in the United States*, in press. See also Herbert H. Hyman and Charles R. Wright, "Trends in Voluntary Association Memberships Of American Adults: Replication Based on Secondary Analysis of National Sample Surveys," *American Sociological Review*, XXXVI (April, 1971), 191–206. Hyman and Wright present data which suggest an increase in the percentage of adult membership in voluntary organizations in the 1950s. The percentage of adults reporting membership in no organizations (exclusive of labor unions) dropped from 64 in 1955 to 57 in 1962. The percentage of families reporting membership in no organizations (inclusive of labor unions) dropped from 47 in 1953 to 38 in 1958.

ly concerned with politics. Membership in political voluntary associations decreases with income and social status. One might argue therefore that the pluralist model is more applicable to the upper echelons of society than to the lower ones. In response the pluralists are likely to claim either that one's failure to become organized into a politically instrumental group signifies general acquiescence in governmental policy, and hence constitutes a vote of approval; or that the "reserve army of the unrepresented" is declining at a satisfactory rate.[6] A corollary which often accompanies this latter hypothesis is the proposition that new interest groups will be assimilated with relative ease into the system of already competing groups. Earl Latham seems to imply something of the sort in this passage: "[In] the classic struggle of farmers against business enterprise ... the latter at first [were] more efficiently organized, and able (before the farmer became 'class conscious') to gain advantages which the farmers thought exorbitant, under conditions which the farmers found offensive. But organization begets counterorganization. The farmer organizes in the American Farm Bureau Federation or the National Grange ... But the organized farmer pays little attention to the tenant and the sharecropper, and they in turn experience an impulse to organize for their own advantage."[7]

6 David Riesman's term for the unrepresented—"the not yet grouped," those "unorganized and sometimes disorganized unfortunates who have not yet invented their group"—seems to imply that they are in process of organization. See Riesman, *The Lonely Crowd* (New Haven: Yale University Press, 1950), 213–14. Riesman's chapter 10 contains an influential discussion of pluralism, relying on the concept of "veto groups." David B. Truman, another pluralist, phrases the fact of underrepresentation in this rather delicate fashion: "Despite the tremendous number of interest groups existing in the United States, not all interests are organized." Truman, *The Governmental Process* (New York: Alfred A. Knopf, Inc., 1951), 510. Dahl's rhapsodic hymn to the alleged crumbling of status barriers is a variation on this theme. "Sailing, skiing, riding, and fly-fishing become the pastimes of clerk and butcher's helper, and the man with the new swimming pool turns out to be a carpenter with a working wife," he writes. Dahl, *Who Governs?*, 236. Several works appearing in the 1960s questioned the theory that wealth and income—both correlated with status—have become significantly more equally distributed in America in recent decades. The first systematic attack on this theory was Gabriel Kolko, *Wealth and Power in America* (New York: Frederick A. Praeger, Inc., 1962).

7 Earl Latham, "The Group Basis of Politics: Notes for a Theory," *American Political Science Review*, XLVI (1952). Reprinted in H. R. Mahood, *Pressure Groups in American Politics* (New York: Charles Scribner's Sons, 1967), 37.

Ethnic groups are often taken as the paradigm of newly formed interest groups in process of assimilation into the political system.

Yet, here again, the pluralists encounter difficulties. Studies have revealed that assimilation of ethnics—even those of European stock —has been extremely uneven.[8] Jews on the whole have done quite well, although they are still excluded from the upper reaches of corporate and financial power. The Irish have managed to occupy prominent political offices, but without bringing notable benefits to the Irish community as a whole.[9] Italians and Poles have done poorly both politically and economically.[10] Even in the New Haven described by Dahl, a leading pluralist, the average estimated period of political assimilation for white ethnics is three-quarters of a century, while for Negroes the process is far from completion.[11]

Latham should have gone on to point out that although the tenant and the share-cropper may have "experienced an impulse" to organize, they never did, and they succumbed to technological forces beyond their control following the depression, as did most of the farmers, organized or not.

8 For example, Nathan Glazer and Daniel Patrick Moynihan, *Beyond the Melting Pot* (Cambridge: M.I.T. Press, 1963).

9 This fact causes Moynihan to comment that "the relevant question is not how the Irish have succeeded, but why they have not succeeded more." *Ibid.*, 256.

10 Nathan Glazer, "The Negro's Stake in America's Future," New York *Times* Magazine, September 22, 1968, p. 94.

Stanley Lieberson's study of ethnic occupational assimilation in large cities found that while it is true that, on the average, second-generation members of ethnic groups are in occupations more similar to those of native whites than to those of first-generation ethnics, second-generation white ethnics in some cities have nonetheless experienced a *decline* in occupational status. Lieberson, *Ethnic Patterns in American Cities* (New York: The Free Press, 1963), 173–75. The data are from the 1950 census and apply to males between the ages of twenty-five and forty-four.

Otis Dudley Duncan and Peter M. Blau point to some difficulties in interpreting "foreign stock" data recently collected. One is that the occupational pattern of entering immigrants before and after World War I has changed considerably. Another is that few "foreign born" today were among the great pre-World-War I immigrant waves. For these reasons sample survey data do not tell us very much about mobility patterns of immigrants before the first World War. However, the authors, in their analysis of a national sample collected in the 1960s, claim that "the occupational achievements of the second generation are superior to those of native whites among men who stayed close to their birth place *but not—at least, not consistently—among migrants.*" Duncan and Blau, *The American Occupational Structure* (New York: John Wiley and Sons, Inc., 1967), 233. Italics added.

11 Dahl, *Who Governs?*, 36. The criteria for successful political assimilation of ethnics are not clear. While Dahl stipulates (p. 35) that in the final stage of assimilation, "large segments are assimilated into the middling and upper strata," his data reveal that three ethnic groups comprising more than half his New Haven

Surely American history provides ample reason for skepticism of ethnic "ease of assimilation" theories. The sharp rise in racism accompanying the growth of slavery in the seventeenth century, the dramatic reversal of the Negroes' social and political progress following Reconstruction and their relative economic decline during the Depression, the steady decline in Irish political preeminence throughout this century, the sudden increase in virulent anti-Semitism in the 1890s, the nativist ground swell leading to the restrictive immigration laws in the 1920s, the internment of the Nisei during World War II—these reactionary phenomena are as much a part of American ethnic history as are the rapid spurts of progress and the occasional rags-to-riches success stories.

Indeed it has long been recognized that numerous factors are associated with the ease of assimilation and that they are distributed unequally among those groups seeking entry into the political system.[12] One of the most important obstacles to successful group

---

sample—Negroes, Italian Catholics, and other European Catholics—had work forces which were 76, 61, and 58 percent manually employed, respectively, as compared with 27 percent for the native American Protestants (p. 60). As Dahl did not include service workers in his "manual" category this tends to underrepresent the blue-collar work force. (Some sociologists have assigned the service worker a rank, in terms of occupational prestige, midway between skilled and semiskilled workers. See, for example, Lieberson, *Ethnic Patterns*, 172.) Moreover Dahl's sample was drawn from voters, who tend to have a somewhat higher socioeconomic status than the general population.

12 Wallace Sayre, writing in the 1930s, argued that "the rapidity with which an immigrant group rises to power and influence within one of the national parties, and the degree of that power and influence, depend upon several factors," which include not only size and distribution of the group, but "less obvious factors" such as the tensions within the party system at the time assimilation is attempted, absence or presence of a language barrier, cultural and political similarity or dissimilarity, the ability to adapt to the going economic system, and the degree of group cohesion. Sayre, "The Immigrant in Politics," in Francis J. Brown and Joseph Slabey Roucek (eds.), *Our Racial and National Minorities* (New York: Prentice-Hall, Inc., 1937), 644–45.

Glazer and Moynihan demonstrate the extent to which differences in family structure, religion, economic experience and attitudes, education and political outlook account for the relative success of Jews, Germans, and English in New York, and the difficulties of Irish and southern Italian peasants, Puerto Rican slum dwellers, and southern Negro in-migrants. Glazer and Moynihan, *Beyond the Melting Pot*, 14–16, 154, 311ff.

Thus, the much debated question of whether the experience of blacks is analogous to that of "assimilated" immigrant groups is misleading in an important sense:

formation is the resistance of those groups already within the system, whose values and power are threatened by the emerging group. The violent history of the labor movement illustrates this point eloquently. At least as serious as external barriers, however, are the internal difficulties which beset any fledgling political organization, but are most pronounced in the formation of associations by the poor, the uneducated, the manual laborers, the newcomers. Several conditions must be met in order for a voluntary organization to become an effective pressure group. It must be able to support a full-time leadership cadre. (Or, if it cannot support one financially, it must be able to recruit full-time personnel who have the income and leisure to serve without pay.) It must have an effective propaganda machine, with ready access to the mass media. It must have a strong network of internal communication that can quickly mobilize the members. Most important, the membership must have a sense of the organization's political efficacy—an attitude that develops only with time, after some initial success.

All of these conditions are more likely to be met in a middle-class organization than in a working-class one.[13] Financial support for a central administration is easier to obtain in the middle class, especially if a few wealthy individuals or corporations can be recruited into the dues-paying membership. People with professional training, such as attorneys, are more likely to provide sophisticated leadership, as they have the connections and the know-how to get things done. The better educated are also more adept not only at writing political propaganda but also at distributing it. In a recent Houston campaign, for example, a well-financed group was able to influence

---

it masks the striking differences in assimilatory success achieved even by these latter white ethnic groups. It is usually assumed that if the analogy between blacks and white ethnics is correct, then there is reason for an optimistic assessment of Negro progress and for a favorable assessment of the resilience of the American political system. But there are grounds for believing just the opposite. If the Negro can do as well but no better than many white ethnic groups have been able to do in the past hundred years, his "eventual" assimilation into the political system may not occur until far into the twenty-first century, if then.

13 Glazer and Moynihan have demonstrated the importance of the role of the "business class" in ethnic assimilation in New York City. Glazer and Moynihan, *Beyond the Melting Pot*, 30–44.

a bond issue referendum by hiring a group of off-duty telephone operators to make individual calls to a large segment of the probable electorate. The operators' expertise and the technical facilities at their disposal enabled them to make at least four calls in the length of time required by an amateur to make one. Finally, voter studies provide overwhelming evidence that middle-class people have a greater sense of political efficacy than do working-class people, in part no doubt because they do have greater efficacy, and in part also because they are socialized to believe in the effectiveness of political activity.

How, then, does the Houston case bear upon the theory of the organizational weapon as a resource in political assimilation? There are in this city four types of voluntary associations through which Negro activists attempt to exert influence. These include locally based affiliates of national civil rights organizations, such as the NAACP; purely local Negro organizations with political or civil rights aims; Negro community institutions whose primary purpose is not political; and white-dominated political organizations. An examination of each of these types will provide an answer to this question.[14]

The local chapter of the NAACP is by far the oldest and most respected of the Houston civil rights organizations. It was founded in 1912 and by 1918 it had more than four hundred members. In the thirties and forties, it handled the legal actions challenging the white primaries. It later took the case of Heman Sweatt, a Houston mail carrier suing for entrance in the University of Texas law school, resulting in the *Sweatt* v. *Painter* decision in 1950, an important precedent for the *Brown* v. *Board of Education* decision four years later. In 1956 the state attorney general, John Ben Shepperd, encouraged by Governor Allan Shivers, filed eight charges against the organization, of which the main one was barratry—the practice of soliciting lawsuits. Although the organization was enjoined from any activities other than those of an "educational and charity" nature, the outcome of the trial was considered a victory for the

14 Most of the field research for this chapter was completed in early 1968. Minor changes, including a few hopeful developments, have occurred since then, but the overall situation is pretty much the same in 1972.

NAACP, as no new restrictions were placed upon it, and the executive secretary of the Houston branch was not forced to make public the organization's membership roll. Under vigorous leadership in the fifties, the local chapter attained a membership of about nine thousand, making it one of the largest in the nation. But as the tempo of the civil rights movement increased, the NAACP went through a period of leadership crisis, popular support declined, and it lost much of its effectiveness. What prestige it has today is due in large measure to its earlier reputation and its affiliation with the national organization. The latter is able to give aid when the need is especially great. The local chapter, for example, collects defense funds for civil rights litigation, while the national organization furnishes lawyers, as well as additional money.

There have been numerous charges that the local NAACP is ineffective. In 1961 a columnist for a Negro newspaper claimed that the local branch had fewer than 200 active members; in 1963 the same newspaper charged that it was "stagnant and fruitless."[15] Two years later the chapter was reorganized into eight area branches under the jurisdiction of the Houston Metropolitan Council of Branches. A spokesman said at the time that the total membership was 2,869. In 1967 an official said that membership had increased to "over 3,500."[16] Yet monthly branch meetings were attended by only a handful of people. At a typical one a quorum of 5 was not present and the meeting had to be held informally.[17] An executive of the central office, who also belongs to one of the branches, said: "Our branch has three or four hundred paid members. If there's a crisis, you can expect a crowd. Otherwise, ten or fifteen members show up. There's some deadwood, of course. But in a crisis, even the 'dead' come alive. The NAACP doesn't go out looking for problems, but will work on a problem once it comes."[18]

15 *Forward Times*, July 22, 1961, and January 12, 1963.

16 Interview conducted by the author.

17 This is based on observations by the author, who attended some of the branch meetings held in 1967.

18 The above quotation from an anonymous source, like other quotations in this chapter, is taken from transcriptions of interviews of both black and white political activists conducted by the author. Anonymity was guaranteed the respondents, and hence their identification is not possible. See Appendix B.

In the 1960s the organization was more successful in preventing civil rights militants from demonstrating than in influencing white officials. One mass-based demonstration was sponsored by PUSH (People for Upgraded Schools in Houston), led by a group of "young turks," mostly black professionals in their twenties and thirties, who were angry with the school board's grade-a-year desegregation plan. PUSH had begun in the spring of 1965 as an NAACP project. In early May Reverend William Lawson, a popular Baptist minister, led a crowd of more than two thousand to protest a school bond referendum, one of whose effects was to provide money to reinforce patterns of *de facto* segregation. This came after a one-day school boycott by more than ten thousand Negro children. Marches and rallies involving thousands of persons took place in June and July, and negotiations were held with the school board, eventually resulting in minor concessions. However, from the beginning strong pressure was exerted upon PUSH by the regional office of the NAACP in Dallas, reportedly at the behest of local old-guard members who felt that the NAACP was not receiving adequate credit. The regional office was against the protest, it said, because all other legal recourse had not been exhausted.[19] When the leaders of PUSH went ahead with the demonstrations, the NAACP withdrew its backing, including legal counsel and public support. The movement lasted scarcely two months, and it is not clear whether its demise was primarily a result of the loss of enthusiasm of its supporters or the pressure of the NAACP. One PUSH leader said: "We had a good thing going, but . . . ultimately, we couldn't fight our fathers and our grandfathers on this issue. Out of deference, we had to back down."

When the problem became one of pressuring city government rather than the young militants within its own ranks, the NAACP was less successful. A dramatic confrontation between the organization and the mayor occurred in 1966, as a result of the killing of an

---

19 "Symbolic" protests were approved by the NAACP's old guard. Two months previous to the PUSH affair, the local chapter had called for a demonstration in front of the city hall asking for federal intervention in Selma, Alabama. An NAACP spokesman predicted a turnout of "several thousand." A few hundred participated.

unarmed Negro by a policeman under questionable circumstances. On the afternoon of February 24, Eugene "Lucky" Hill bought a loaf of bread at Mixon's Supermarket, a grocery owned and run by whites in the predominantly Negro Third Ward. According to one account, Mrs. Mixon suspected that Hill was concealing a barbecued chicken under his coat and called the police after he left the store.[20] A white policeman arrived soon afterward and found Hill drinking beer in a lounge nearby. He searched Hill and then asked him to accompany him outside. A few minutes later the police officer fired three shots, two of which hit Hill at close range. He died later that day. Several witnesses gave conflicting reports of what happened.[21] Some corroborated the testimony of the officer, who said Hill resisted arrest and tried to take his gun from him. Others said Hill had not turned on the officer, but had simply raised his hands to defend himself against a blow.[22] A crowd of angry blacks soon gathered, as did numerous policemen and patrol cars. Pickets were thrown up around the supermarket (which was forced out of business in a matter of days), and handbills were soon on the streets, asking Negroes not to patronize the store.

Reverend D. Leon Everett, a local black Baptist minister, appeared on the scene soon after the shooting, assumed command of the picketing, and became the group's spokesman.[23] Although not an NAACP official, he got the approval of a few of the organization's notables and for the next several days, he was referred to in the press as representing the NAACP "and other interested citizens."

Everett sent night letters to the mayor and the chief of police, "respectfully requesting" an audience with them. The next morning he and five other Negroes were allowed to meet with the police chief. According to one of those present, the chief defended the actions of the officer who killed Hill and emphasized the fact that

20 This is an account in *Forward Times*, March 5, 1966. Another account, in an article by Larry Lee, "Black Houston," *Texas Observer*, May 13, 1966, reported that Mrs. Mixon had doubted that Hill had paid for the bread he carried out of the store in a paper sack. He didn't have the receipt, but he told her he had paid for it and told her where he would be if she wanted to call the police.

21 Houston *Post*, February 25, 1966.

22 *Ibid.*

23 *Ibid.*

Hill had had a criminal record. However, he admitted that there was no evidence that Hill had stolen anything.[24]

Everett went before Mayor Louie Welch and the city council the following Wednesday, along with about forty other blacks and a few concerned whites to demand a full hearing of the "Lucky Hill" incident, as well as to request a change in the police department's attitude toward Negroes. Everett specifically asked for (1) the initiation of a "buddy system" in patrol cars to replace the practice of segregating the forty-three Negro patrolmen on the force; (2) a human rights court of inquiry to investigate all cases of alleged police mistreatment of citizens; and (3) a program instructing the police officers in the "psychology of human relations." Mayor Welch asked that representatives of the Negro groups meet with him in closed session the following day. At the second meeting, Welch seemed conciliatory and admitted that the police and "some white politicians" had "failed miserably" in communicating with blacks.[25] But Everett's requests were refused. As for the review board, Welch said that a grand jury, with subpoena powers, was the proper instrument for investigation of the incident, despite the objection that the police department prepares most of the material which goes before it. The grand jury met on March 11 and the patrolman was exonerated.[26] The "Lucky Hill" affair was dropped. Relations between the city's Negroes and its police force remained as tense and hostile as before, if not more so.[27]

In summary the NAACP has not in recent years been successful in bringing effective pressure on city and school officials. It is still a sounding board for moderately critical Negro activists, but it has no easily identifiable mass support in the community. Its most important function is as a source of legal and financial support for civil rights litigants.

Throughout the "decade of protest," there were demonstrations

---

24 Confidential interview with one of those present at the meeting.

25 Confidential interview with one of those present at the meeting. Also, see Houston *Post*, March 3, 1966.

26 Houston *Post*, March 11, 1966.

27 Following violent incidents in the summer of 1967, the police department finally instituted a mandatory "community relations" course for its officers.

by small groups of Negroes with very limited goals. These were sporadic and of short duration, with the exception of the important Progressive Youth Association protests, which succeeded in de-segregating lunch counters and movie theaters before the passage of the Public Accommodations Act. The groups usually began as spontaneous reactions to police actions, evictions, school board de-cisions, and so forth. Typically the participants met in a neighbor-hood church, chose a spokesman, and carried picket signs to city hall or the county courthouse. Their views were presented and the group dissolved.

Here are some examples of this pattern of action:

Houston Citizens' School Committee. Formed to fight the seg-regation of the San Jacinto Technical High School. The leader, E. Stearnes, met with United States Attorney Woodrow Seals. A number of Negro notables gave Stearnes their support.

Shriver Protest Group. When Sargent Shriver, then head of the Office of Economic Opportunity, arrived in town to tour the pov-erty areas, he was met by a group of Negro and Mexican-American activists who were critical of local antipoverty efforts. The group never organized formally.

The Egalitarians. A group of high school and college students picketed a bank for discriminating against Negroes. Picketing con-tinued for two weeks. An adult "advisory committee" was formed. The organization disappeared.

Gentry Eviction Protest. Mrs. Gentry, a pregnant woman, was allegedly manhandled and forced to dress in front of two deputy constables who served her with an eviction notice. A group of her neighbors protested to the "war on poverty" headquarters and later to county officials. The charges were denied by the latter and the group disbanded.

Between 1960 and 1970, many Negroes participated in such pro-test activities, with little success. There was no long-range planning, no serious attempt to apply sanctions, no solidarity fostered by lengthy participation within a single organization fighting for clearly defined goals. In many cases the protested wrongs were not judged by other Negroes as affecting the interests of the entire black community.

With the dissipation of the civil rights movement and the advent of "black power" as a slogan, a small nucleus of young, aggressive black activists began serious efforts to mobilize the Negro poor—the stratum which had hardly felt the impact of recent civil rights legislation and judicial decisions. In 1966 a group called ENRICH set up a ramshackle office in one of the seamiest areas of the Third Ward. It attempted to coordinate the welfare services available to Negroes and inform the ghetto community about these services. Although its leaders were advocates of "black power," whites were recruited to work within the organization. It disappeared several months after its founding.

A second group was formed in the summer of 1967. Called HOPE Development, Incorporated, it was led by Reverend Earl Allen, a militant black minister. Allen had been employed by the Office of Economic Opportunity as the local community development director, at an annual salary of fifteen thousand dollars. His views clashed sharply with those of his superiors, however. Allen felt that his community organizers should attempt to politicize the people in the poverty areas by making them aware of their interests and willing to confront the "white power structure" with demands and sanctions. Unable to put his ideas into effect while working within the federal agency, Allen finally resigned in protest and founded HOPE, a private antipoverty foundation.[28] The group has had a difficult existence, however, because of a scarcity of funds with which to pay full-time organizers. The mayor, the newspapers, the police, and conservative Negro leaders have all been antagonistic to Allen and his group. Whether HOPE will succeed in establishing a wide power base among the poor remains to be seen.

Houston's Negro professional circles are extremely small. In 1960, of a male Negro labor force in the county of 54,916, there were only 1,460 professional, technical, and kindred workers, and only 1,433 managers, officials, and proprietors.[29] A small proportion

28 Houston *Post*, August 2, 1967.
29 Calculated from figures in United States Bureau of the Census, *U.S. Census of*

of them is actively involved in politics. Two professional groups in recent years have played a minor role in the city's political life, without having any noticeable impact. One prominent member of the Business and Professional Men's Organization, who is himself politically active, said, "I seldom attend their meetings anymore. They are totally out of touch with reality—a real 'black bourgeois' organization." According to another activist member, "You can describe their activities in one sentence: The group just meets and eats." The main type of political activity of the group seems to be sending letters to the newspapers. One such letter urged defeat of a 1965 school bond issue. A letter in 1967 denounced the mayor and the police for their handling of a racial confrontation at predominantly black Texas Southern University, a state-supported school. The group had earlier tried to mediate between the University's administration and the campus radicals, but its offer was not accepted.

A group that caters to the business and professional people is the Twentieth Century Organization. It was founded in 1961 to help finance local sit-ins. It was reportedly composed of members of the Business and Professional Men's Organization after the latter had refused to give support. Since those early days, however, it has not attempted nor accomplished anything of political importance. Some of its members, nevertheless, were strong supporters of the United Political Organization, the Negro group backing conservative Democrat John Connally in his campaigns for governor in 1962, 1964, and 1966.

Negro churches have long been recognized as a source of grass-roots political power. Harold Gosnell pointed to the key role they played in Chicago Negro politics in the twenties and thirties. He wrote: "It is not uncommon on a Sunday morning during a primary or election campaign to see a number of white candidates on the platform ready to present their claims for support at the polls as

---

Population: 1960, General Social and Economic Characteristics, Texas, Final Report PC(1)-45C (Washington, D.C.: United States Government Printing Office, 1962).

soon as the regular service is over and before the congregation is disbanded."[30] Hugh Price, writing in the fifties, claimed that in the South: "The Negro minister, the church organization, the fraternal orders, and the community morticians have generally declined in political influence, especially in the larger cities. . . . With the growing acceptance of the Negro voter and competition between candidates for Negro support the need is no longer for a quasi-religious crusade but for hard headed political bargaining and door-to-door organizing work."[31]

Ladd, on the other hand, found in his recent study of Winston-Salem and Greenville that "the clergy continues to play a central role."[32] Of the forty-nine black political activists systematically interviewed for the present study in Houston, nine were ministers, and at least three of them had been influential. Negroes in the South are still by and large a church-going people; and while the image of an all-powerful preacher leading his obedient flock in political matters is a gross caricature, it is true, as one local observer pointed out, that "the Negro preacher still speaks directly to more people in the black community than any other single business or professional man." This indicates his potential influence, whether or not he decides to use it.

Gosnell's description of white candidates sitting on Negro church platforms applies to many of the larger black churches in Houston during campaign time. None of the ministers interviewed refused to let candidates speak at his church, although none admitted to soliciting candidates to do so, or taking money for this service. One said: "We let candidates speak at our church. Others do the same. The Negro church is a social or religious institution of subtle and yet tremendous impact in the Negro community. . . . If a pastor makes an endorsement, I would say it *does* have influence. Usually, though,

---

30 Harold F. Gosnell, *Negro Politicians: The Rise of Negro Politics in Chicago* (Chicago: University of Chicago Press, 1935), 96. See pp. 94–100.

31 Hugh D. Price, *The Negro and Southern Politics: A Chapter of Florida History* (New York: New York University Press, 1957), 68–69.

32 Everett Carll Ladd, Jr., *Negro Political Leadership in the South* (Ithaca: Cornell University Press, 1966), 238.

I just hammer away at the need to vote, whoever the candidate. Occasionally I have made endorsements, although not too often, as this can be dangerous."

But another pastor said he thought that "ministers as a whole in Houston don't exercise influence, though little camps of them do." This is plausible for there are many local Negro churches. Professor Henry Allen Bullock estimated in 1961 that there were two hundred fifty non-storefront Negro churches in the city. A black minister estimated in 1967 that there were more than seven hundred preachers. Many are only part-time ministers, uninterested in politics. But there are a few large churches whose pastors encourage their congregations to become involved.

Two extremes in ministerial leadership are exemplified by the late Reverend L. H. Simpson, a Negro long influential in city politics, who died while the present study was in progress; and Reverend William Lawson, a younger minister who first took a leadership role in the 1960s.

Simpson, until his death, was the pastor of Pleasant Hill Baptist Church, a congregation in Houston's Fifth Ward. It is the largest Negro church in the city, and one of the largest in the South.[33] Simpson, who was once a janitor, founded his church and the Negro Baptist Ministers' Association in the twenties. He remained pastor of the church and president of the association until his death more than forty years later. Simpson became a close personal friend of Oscar Holcombe, who occupied the mayor's office for more than half of those forty years. Although he had been an NAACP official, he was not a militant. In his role as a friend of city hall, and as a preacher who could usually deliver votes in two or three precincts around his church, he was able to achieve occasional welfare goals. "He may seem like an Uncle Tom," one activist told the author, "but Reverend Simpson got Lyons Avenue paved back in the days when nobody else in the Fifth Ward could."

Besides the power Simpson wielded over his congregation, he was

33 I owe this fact, as well as some others about Simpson, to an unpublished manuscript by Saul Friedman on Negroes in Houston, written while Friedman was a reporter for the Houston *Chronicle*. The newspaper refused to publish it.

influential with members of the Ministers' Association. According to one informant who was a member, Simpson was able single-handedly to get the association to endorse a candidate. "He has a 'screening committee' which often doesn't endorse anybody, but when it recommends an endorsement, it is accepted by the association. And he controls the screening committee." What sanctions was he able to apply to keep the association in line? There were allegations that money changed hands, although he denied it. The same informant quoted above said: "He works behind the scenes, telling people his opinion, asking them to do one thing or another. He's a very persuasive person. [Pause] The preachers in the association who won't go along will not get very far as Baptist ministers in this town." An observer attending one of the association's meetings was sure to be struck by the deferential, if not fearful, attitude most of the other fifty or so ministers exhibited towards the diminutive Simpson, who presided with a great deal of authority.

One Baptist minister who was not a member of Simpson's association was Lawson. He has done work toward a doctorate at the University of California and is an articulate and popular speaker. He is pastor of a small congregation in the Third Ward, near Texas Southern University. Most of its members are middle-class, and their religious attitudes are far removed from the other-worldly fundamentalism of Simpson's flock.[34] Lawson moved to Houston in 1955 and has engaged in numerous civil rights and political activities, including campaigns for Negro candidates, speeches before Negro and white audiences, support for the Council on Human Relations and the PUSH protest movement, writing in *Forward Times*, a Negro newspaper, mediation between students and administration at Texas Southern, and get-out-the-vote drives. Unlike Simpson, Lawson refused to become identified with city hall. Such a link would be disastrous for any popular Negro leader today. Yet, in one respect the two ministers' styles were similar. Both demonstrated an uncommon ability to get along with other Negro activists and outlive the constant factional feuds and internecine warfare

34 A study conducted by Professor William McCord and Blair Justice of Rice University in 1967 ascertained this fact.

within the black leadership ranks. Both men—Simpson, until his death, Lawson still today—have been able to converse freely with members of the white power structure and even, at times, to bargain effectively with it. Yet when the issues are clearly drawn and compromise requires the white officials to relinquish some power to the Negro community, Lawson hardly seems better equipped than Simpson ever was to press successfully the Negroes' claims. PUSH, the organization he built to fight the school board, had little direct effect upon school desegregation or the outcome of the referendum to float bonds that strengthened the patterns of *de facto* segregation.

Of the white-dominated organizations, the Houston Council on Human Relations is on the periphery of politics. It is staffed and supported by upper middle-class whites, including numerous Jews, and a sprinkling of Negro notables. As one Negro described it, with a trace of sarcasm, "It's composed of a lotta good white folks, and a few Negroes." (A *Forward Times* account of an annual banquet estimated that no more than 10 percent of the crowd was black.) The council sponsors low-key programs designed to foster good "race relations." But, as another Negro respondent pointed out: "Effective politics and effective race relations are sometimes at cross purposes. Negroes in the South today can sometimes help keep 'good relations' between the races by keeping their mouths shut and maintaining the status quo."

In the 1960s the Negro community received few direct benefits as a result of the council's activities, even though one of its brochures quoted the executive director of the Southern Regional Council as saying: "The Houston Council is a magnificent study of success—undoubtedly the best in the South and likely in the nation." It has supervised VISTA workers, conducted occasional studies of job opportunity and housing, and produced plays such as "Raisin in the Sun" and "In White America." In 1966 it sponsored a "Meet the Mayor" program arranging for the mayor to talk to residents in Negro neighborhoods and listen to criticism and questions.

The image of the council in the eyes of Negro activists was tarnished when a former president, a white minister, left his post to become head of the Houston-Harris County Economic Opportunity

Organization, an arm of the Office of Economic Opportunity. Many Negroes were angry because a white with little knowledge of the Negro community was chosen for the position rather than a black. He was extremely unpopular in the poverty agency and was replaced by a Negro when the organization was merged with another one in the summer of 1967. Part of his unpopularity undoubtedly rubbed off on the council itself.

However, there are other explanations for the ineffectiveness of the council and these derive from the nature of biracial committees in general. Lewis Killian and Charles Grigg, as a result of their study of southern race relations organizations, suggested the following reasons: (1) By becoming part of a team whose purpose is interracial harmony, the Negro members are under strong pressure to subordinate "race" goals to "harmony" goals. (2) The purpose of a biracial committee is generally to forestall open conflicts, or to "depoliticize" issues, some of which are preeminently political and can best be resolved through conflict. (3) The whites on a biracial committee are seldom important leaders in the white community, and thus the decisions of the committee have little impact upon a racially conservative white power structure.[35] The committee, in other words, has no political brawn for implementing its decisions and hence must rely almost totally upon moral suasion. The Houston council, like biracial committees in many other cities, is consulted by white officials in periods of crisis and its recommendations for bringing about a cooling-off period are sometimes accepted. But when the trouble has passed, the organization is usually forgotten.

A more effective group, operating clearly within the political sphere, is the Harris County Council of Organizations. In a sense it is misleading to place it under the rubric of "white-dominated" groups, for in the past it has been relatively successful in resisting this domination. But today, although its personnel are still Negro, it is drifting more and more under the influence of the local liberal coalition. The Harris County council was formed to unite the coun-

35 Lewis Killian and Charles Grigg, *Racial Crisis in America* (Englewood Cliffs: Prentice-Hall, Inc., 1964). See chapters 2 and 3, pp. 29–80.

ty's Negro voters and to reduce the attempted vote selling which arose following the *Smith* v. *Allwright* decision in 1944. Over the years it has been fairly successful in both aims. There is no evidence that vote selling is widespread in Houston today. Interviews failed to turn up more than a few isolated charges of venality. In fact only four names were consistently mentioned, and the high degree of consensus among the respondents on these four suggests that the practice of accepting money to deliver votes is rare. Opinion is mixed as to whether they are actually able to deliver. No one believes that their influence extends over more than a few precincts. One of the men is reputed to be close to Mayor Welch. He is thought to be in trouble for having been unable to deliver his own precinct. One informant said: "He'll be finished in two years. He is traditionally against the Negro. He'll take money from whites of any persuasion, ultra-liberal or ultra-conservative." Others felt that he would be able to make a comeback. "He still has influence in his area," one said. "When he backs a candidate, he gets lots of ladies out doing precinct work." Another of the reputed vote sellers is said to donate part of the money to an orphanage. He also keeps groceries under padlock to distribute to needy neighbors on request.

In the past the Harris County council has managed to build up its influence by spearheading voter education projects and registration drives. On occasion it has sent representatives to the city hall or county courthouse to protest policies. Its reputation for honesty has been important, too. Until recently the membership has consisted solely of groups. In 1967 more than sixty civic clubs, churches, Negro labor unions and other associations were affiliated, and delegates attended regular monthly meetings. During campaigns a screening committee meets to hear candidates who come before it seeking endorsement. Once the screening committee approves a candidate, the recommendation is made on the floor at the meeting, and a two-thirds vote is necessary for the organization's endorsement. Generally the screening committee's recommendation is accepted, but sometimes it is not. According to its president, the council does not accept money from candidates, except as expenses for campaign material. Usually when a candidate is endorsed, his name appears on the council's slate card. This card is thought to be influential, as evidenced by its frequent counterfeiting, with one or two name changes.

On the other hand, some people have claimed that the council's endorsement is a kiss of death for white candidates. A member of the screening committee denied this. "Our endorsements are always public," he said. "We ask a candidate who is before the screening committee if he wants it known that we have endorsed him. If he says no, he's had it." The eagerness of many white candidates to get an endorsement seems to have increased in recent years. There was a particularly hard-fought battle for it between gubernatorial candidates in 1962 during the first Democratic primary campaign.[36] The screening committee had recommended Don Yarborough, the most liberal candidate. But there were several partisans of Attorney General Will Wilson on the floor, and they argued against the recommendation on the grounds that Yarborough had made segregationist statements as a student official at the University of Texas in 1950. The conservative Connally forces were led by Hobart Taylor, Sr., a wealthy Negro who is a personal friend of Lyndon Johnson. They were well organized and had planned their strategy in advance. Although Connally stood no chance of endorsement, his forces on the floor tried to persuade the Wilson partisans to side with them and block Yarborough's endorsement. They succeeded and Yarborough lost by 3.5 votes, although Barbara Jordan, then a first-time Negro candidate for the legislature, gave an impassioned plea for his endorsement. Nevertheless, in the second primary campaign, which featured Yarborough and Connally in the runoff, the council endorsed Yarborough. Feelings ran so high in this crucial contest that a number of member groups refused to abide by the rule that all members must support the endorsed candidate or remain inactive in the campaign. The split was so deep that it almost destroyed the organization.

There is a frequently expressed opinion among activists that the

36 The account that follows was reconstructed from interviews with some of the participants. Also helpful were accounts in *Forward Times*, April 14, May 26, and August 18, 1962.

influence and autonomy of the council is declining. Probably the most accurate assessment is the following, from an interviewee: "About 60 or 70 percent of the Negro voters pay attention to the council as a rule. This percentage has probably declined a little bit the past few years. The effects of the council, however, are most visible when there are clear-cut issues. . . . There has also been a gradual coming together of the council and the liberal coalition, and the latter has taken over some of the functions which the council performed earlier."

The Harris County Democrats, which is the focal point of the liberal coalition in the county, is predominantly white and its role is controversial among Negro activists. Since its founding in the early fifties, labor has come to play a stronger and stronger part in the way the group is run.[37] Not only Negroes, but many "independent liberals" and Mexican-Americans as well are resentful of labor influence. One reason for the uneasiness of the labor-Negro alliance is that with the exception of the Teamsters, who only recently have entered the coalition formally, the local trade unions are for the most part racially segregated.[38] Another reason is that labor precincts have not given enthusiastic support to black candidates. Moreover, despite the populist ideology of the organization, which stresses the open caucus and the absence of policy making in "smoke-filled rooms," many blacks believe that Harris County Democrats is un-

37 In 1968 part of organized labor split off from the Harris County Democrats following the latter's endorsement of Eugene McCarthy for President.

38 Throughout this work the terms "liberal" and "conservative" appear. It is of course an oversimplification to characterize people as either liberals or conservatives, as almost everyone harbors some beliefs of both kinds. For our purposes, two kinds of liberal-conservative differences can be distinguished. As used here, an *economic* liberal usually supports the labor union movement, believes in tax policies which place the heaviest burden on the rich and on corporations, and advocates such measures as a minimum wage, industrial safety laws, and antipoverty programs. A *racial* liberal usually favors school integration, more widespread and effective political participation by Negroes, efforts to foster interracial friendship, and governmental action to create equal job opportunities for minorities. Both economic and racial liberals in Texas usually backed Roosevelt, Truman, Stevenson, Kennedy, and Johnson in presidential elections, and statewide leaders such as Ralph Yarborough or Bob Eckhardt. In 1968 they were split between Humphrey and McCarthy. The conservative, as here defined, opposes the liberal's views on these issues and candidates. It is important to recognize that one may be an economic conservative and a racial liberal, or vice versa.

duly influenced by a small clique of whites, most of whom are connected with labor or with the town's leading labor law firm.[39]

In the last fifteen years the group has infused new life and organization into the local liberal forces. Its blockworker plan, involving intensive cultivation of voters at the precinct level, has benefited black precincts as well as white ones. The liberals identified with the organization who have been elected to office have been more sympathetic to the Negro cause than have other politicians. Further the organization has offered an institutional base for Negro candidates running for state and county office. This includes advertising and money, which are no small matters in a county of more than a million people. Yet, as James Q. Wilson discovered in Chicago, when blacks join white allies in search of broader support and more adequate financing, "white allies tend to become senior partners."[40] Among all the Negro respondents connected in some way with the Harris County Democrats, few had unqualified praise for the organization. Some were ambivalent, and a few, who continue to work within the coalition's ranks and even to fraternize occasionally with the whites, were bitter and talked of pulling out of the organization altogether. They felt that although blacks have contributed disproportionately to the support of white liberal candidates, so far the spoils of victory had been few. The following incident demonstrates how Negroes come to feel slighted.

A white member of the coalition, "Jim Smith," obtained an important governmental post and appointed a promising young black as an assistant. Later a higher level job became available and it was logical that Smith should use his influence to secure it for his assistant because his work under Smith had made him more qualified than anyone else to fill it. It would have been an important promo-

---

39 Several blacks who belonged to Harris County Democrats expressed this belief in confidential interviews. The author, himself a participant-observer in the organization, corroborated their belief by watching the decision-making process in 1966–1967. The organization seems less cliquish in the early 1970s than it did then. And in fairness, it should be added that minority-group access to influence within Harris County Democrats is probably easier than in any other biracial political organization in the area.

40 James Q. Wilson, *Negro Politics: The Search for Leadership* (New York: The Free Press, 1960), 154.

tion for the Negro, putting him in line for Smith's job in the future, as it was known by insiders that Smith would be moving up the ladder shortly himself.

Several Negro activists who were also connected with the Harris County Democrats learned that Smith, meanwhile, was seriously considering a white for the job. They obtained letters from a member of the administration in Washington, requesting Smith to appoint his Negro assistant to the job. One informant described it this way:

> We had letters from —— and —— and others saying they would support ——'s [the Negro's] appointment. He had seniority over any other candidate for the job. But Smith appointed —— [the white], and frankly admitted that he had to pay off a political debt. There were Jewish friends who had backed Smith financially in previous campaigns. Smith is still far above many white liberals in my book; but he yielded to political pressure. Of course, we never backed him up against the wall and said, "Look here, appoint him or else." But, well, now we're looking askance at blindly following HCD. The organization has largely taken care of whites, even in the last few years, when many patronage jobs have been opening up, and there were qualified Negroes to fill them. . . . Negroes have been given token jobs—but the most important jobs, and the most remunerative ones, have gone to whites. This is a matter of growing concern with us.

One other point of criticism is often directed at the group, but it comes from Negroes outside the organization rather than from those within. As one respondent put it, "HCD is dealing with a lot of old pseudo-leaders." Many of the younger black activists (and some white ones as well) feel that the liberal organization consists of people who are preoccupied with outdated issues.

In 1968 a Negro became chairman of the organization for the first time, but even this event was viewed by some as a fluke. The black, William L. Wood, a twenty-six-year-old attorney, had been recommended by the nominations committee for the job of vice-chairman, to balance the slate. The chairman was a union official. But shortly after the election, the chairman was transferred to another area and Wood became the new chairman automatically. He did not become an influential member of the organization's power structure.

There is no functional equivalent of the Harris County Democrats which unites the diverse interests and goals of the conservative faction of the party through a formal organization. However, in recent years United Political Organization, a small group of conservative Negroes, mostly wealthy businessmen, has worked at the state level to carve out a slice of the Negro bloc for the conservative Democrats. Specifically the organization has been the instrument of one man, John Connally. It was formed in 1962, when Connally first ran for governor against Don Yarborough. Its members take credit for the relatively unimpressive showing that the liberal Yarborough made among the state's Negro voters. According to several black political activists interviewed by the author, including one member of United Political Organization, a considerable amount of money was given to the group by the Connally organization that year, which went into advertising and block work. The forces managed to prevent the Harris County Council of Organizations from endorsing Yarborough in the first primary. Members who were interviewed gave various reasons for backing Connally, who is not only economically but also racially conservative. One man said the governor "was a businessman. He was just more experienced than Yarborough. And I knew him personally. He's a fine man." Another was rather uncomfortable about Connally's having publicly denounced President Kennedy's Civil Rights Bill in the summer of 1963. But, he reasoned: "Negroes are handicapped by always picking a loser. They are tied to the liberals, but the liberals usually lose. I think something is to be gained by aligning oneself with a man who wins office."

The United Political Organization was amply rewarded for its steadfast allegiance to Connally. Most of the governor's Negro appointments went to its members or to Negroes designated by the organization as being deserving. For example, in 1966 there were six blacks on the ten-man board of regents of Texas Southern University. The board was appointed by Connally. Of the six Negroes, at least five were important United Political Organization officers. Only one of the six Negroes on the board was a Houston resident— S. M. Nabrit, then president of Texas Southern University. This suggests that the Houston branch of the organization is much less effective than those which do not have to compete with liberal Negro organizations.

Several informants believed that the United group was given the task of compiling invitation lists of Texas Negroes who attend important honorific functions, such as the White House Conferences on Civil Rights. A well-known Houston activist said: "M. J. Anderson [the state president of UPO] is called 'the black governor of Texas.' . . . I was invited to the White House Civil Rights Conference in 1965. At one point I arose and criticized Katzenbach, who was the attorney general then. . . . After the meeting Anderson and some of his boys came up and raked me over the coals for speaking out like that. . . . I wasn't invited to the '66 conference, although it was much bigger and less selective than the first one."

During Lyndon Johnson's administration, the United Political Organization assumed the additional role of acting as a liaison between Negro influentials in Washington and Texas. Thus, in 1966 the organization set up a meeting between George L. P. Weaver, a Negro in the Department of Labor, and a handful of important Houston Negroes. Weaver was touring the state, trying to drum up support for Waggoner Carr, a conservative Democrat who was attempting to unseat Republican Senator John Tower. Carr had refused, when questioned, to say that he would have supported the 1964 Civil Rights Act had he been a senator then, and he had been unable to get the backing of most Negro organizations. According to one of those present at the meeting, Weaver argued that President Johnson was concerned only about the possibility of three victories in the fall of 1966: Reagan in California, for obvious reasons; Brooke in Massachusets, which might decrease Negro support for the Democrats in 1968; and Tower in Texas, which could be interpreted as a repudiation of the President in his home state. Few of the Negroes at the meeting were enthusiastic and none openly supported Carr. This illustrates the limits of the United Political Organization's power. Operating without mass support, and solely as an arm of the conservative Democratic organization, the group has no effective sanctions with which to force popular Negro leaders into taking a position which could damage their image among Negro voters.

The institutional bases for Negro activists, we noted above, are the following: the local chapter of the nationally based NAACP; the small local organizations, composed primarily of Negroes, that have no national connections or support; the Negro community institutions, such as churches, civic clubs, and voluntary organizations whose primary purpose is not political; and white-dominated organizations.

The all-Negro local organizations have demonstrated serious shortcomings. They generally have operated on an *ad hoc* basis, and hence it has been impossible for them to develop strong solidarity, a fund of common political experience, and adequate financing. Too, many of the aims of the more ephemeral pressure groups have been hastily formulated during a crisis situation, and this results sometimes in unrealistic demands, or in demands which are so specific that the support of the larger Negro community cannot be obtained.

"Divisive leadership," "lack of organization," "apathy"—frequently cited reasons for the lack of efficacy of these organizations—are inadequate explanations or, rather, they in turn require more fundamental explanations. They go back finally to the general poverty and low educational level of the Negro community. David Riesman and Nathan Glazer have written that

the lower-class adult will find himself limited in his political activity by his class position, in subtle as well as obvious ways: he is apt to be more tired in the evening, and cannot take time off for meetings in the afternoon (unless he is a shop steward); he does not have a secretary, even if he is a leader in a local union, to type memoranda and make appointments; indeed, he is often ill at ease in handling such middle-class routines as telephone calls and memoranda; lower-class women with children find it of course still more difficult to be active politically.[41]

Houston Negroes, even many of their leaders, are for the most part "lower class" in the sense that they lack the economic and professional skills, as well as the leisure, to participate in politics with the ease that the white middle class does. For the mother or grandmother who is a maid in a white home on the other side of town, or for the father who puts in a hard day at manual labor, the mere act of voting, which may involve standing two hours in line outside a voting booth, is an arduous chore. Active participation in other sorts of political activities is in some cases even more difficult. There is no doubt that the Negro pressure groups which exist in Houston could be improved. But given the "underdeveloped" nature of the black community, there are limits upon this improvement, without significant contributions of expertise, money, and good will from the whites.

The primarily nonpolitical organizations have in some cases contributed to whatever political power Negroes in Houston now have. The church, much maligned by latter-day militants, has figured importantly among them. But all such institutions are obviously handicapped by their very nature: politics is only a subsidiary purpose for the pastors and the congregations. At some point the militant minister must make a choice between devoting most of his energies to politics or to religion. And it is hardly surprising when he chooses the latter. So it is with the business and professional groups. One must be relatively well off before he can devote a good deal of his time to politics. And few members of the Negro bourgeoisie have attained this degree of affluence. For example, in 1959 only 1,418 nonwhite families in Harris County had incomes of ten thousand dollars and over. There were 54,176 white families in this category.[42] This was at a time when the Houston black population

41 David Riesman and Nathan Glazer, "Criteria for Political Apathy," in Alvin Gouldner (ed.), *Studies in Leadership: Leadership and Democratic Action* (New York: Harper and Bros., 1950), 533.
42 United States Bureau of the Census, *U.S. Census of Population: 1960.*

was larger than the entire population of Charlotte, North Carolina, Jacksonville, Florida, or Richmond, Virginia.

The white-dominated organizations, on the other hand, have the expertise and money that are lacking in the Negro groups. But in politics above all other endeavors, the man who pays the piper calls the tune. The tune that the whites call is a moderate one. Moreover the rewards that are distributed by the white-dominated organizations go primarily to whites. Thus, at a time when Negroes are becoming more and more sensitive to the limited commitment of white liberals, these organizations may be losing their appeal, even to the middle-class, "respectable" Negro activist.

These facts are difficult to reconcile with the "ease of assimilation" thesis. The unassimilated and the unorganized are more often than not the least able to make use of the political resource which pluralists claim is their most useful one—the organizational weapon. Thus, many blacks in America, like poor people in general, are expected to perform feats of political skill that are far more difficult than those required of middle-class whites. Negro politics is not simply, as it has sometimes been described, "the search for leadership." No leaders, even those as talented as Martin Luther King or Malcolm X, are adequate to the task. The search is rather for a form of political power that the poor and the near poor can effectively use. The rise of black separatism is essentially an expression of the profound skepticism among younger Negroes that such a form of power is possible in this country today.

III

The Vote:
Antidemocratic Contrivances

The vote, along with the organizational weapon, occupies a crucial role in pluralist theory. It is employed to explain the paradoxical fact that modern democracies, which describe themselves as governments by the people, are nonetheless run by a minuscule proportion of citizens. The argument is that in any large political unit such as a nation state, decisions must of necessity be made by political experts. Therefore even a democracy is elitist, in a manner of speaking. Town meetings or referenda are inadequate methods for deciding how to meet an imminent military threat or an economic slump. The vote, however, allows the entire electorate to participate indirectly in the affairs of state. When there is universal suffrage, an informed electorate, a meaningful choice of policies, and widespread participation, the vote allows the citizenry a chance to evaluate past policies and remove elected officials. In a system wherein the direct participation of the elite is supplemented with the indirect participation of the masses, democracy genuinely exists, according to the pluralists.

"It would be difficult to overstate the significance of popular elections for democratic theory and practice," write Angus Campbell and his colleagues in their influential work *The American Voter*. While it is true that "no democratic state has ever been governed by direct democracy," popular election "combined with representation has greatly expanded the distribution of political power."[1] The vote, which Robert Dahl calls "the most widely

1 Angus Campbell, Philip E. Converse, Warren E. Miller, and Donald E. Stokes, *The American Voter* (New York: John Wiley and Sons, 1960), 4–5.

distributed political resource," is the weapon of the many in restraining and guiding the few who have access to the controlling machinery of state.

When pluralists focus more narrowly upon the competition among interest groups, the vote is seen as a resource of every group in its struggle against the rest, and as the most effective resource of the less affluent groups, who have the greatest numbers. It is thought to be the resource par excellence of the ethnic group struggling towards political assimilation. According to this theory, once the leaders of the group have inculcated in the rank and file the habit of regular voting, once the machinery of voter education and voter turnout has been established and set in motion, the organizational weapon finds its most effective expression through the franchise. And as Negroes constitute the largest of the identifiable ethnic minorities in this country, the vote is assigned special importance in their case. By the same token, if any group is not successful in its efforts to enter the political mainstream, it is assumed that the group has not learned to use the vote effectively, that the members are apathetic and ignorant of the subtleties of electoral politics, and easily victimized by their leaders. It is assumed, in other words, that any group, however destitute of other political means, has—at the very least—ready recourse to the ballot.

Scholars, however, have begun to take a hard look at the assumption that the vote is an effective instrument for the expression of political preference. What has come to light, as a result, is a complex system of electoral rules and practices that serve as interlocking devices contrived to neutralize the power of marginal groups. The American practice of putting the burden of voter registration on the citizen rather than the state is a case in point. An investigation by Stanley Kelly and his associates involving one hundred four major American cities revealed that 78 percent of the variation in the proportion of the voting-age population that voted could be accounted for by the percentage of that population which was registered. Registration requirements were deemed to be "a more effective deterrent to voting than anything that normally operates to deter citizens from voting once they have registered, at least in presidential elections."[2] The local variation in registration rates, in turn, reflects local differences in systems of registration rules. The authors point out that in the latter half of the nineteenth century, when the turnout of eligible voters was exceedingly high (even in the South), there were no registration requirements in many parts of the country, and in other parts automatic registration was the rule. But in the period from 1896 to 1924—the era which began with the demise of Populism as a biracial, class-based movement and ended with the final legal consolidation of Negro disfranchisement (the white primary became law in Texas in 1923)—voter turnout declined steadily, and state after state enacted registration laws, typically requiring registration annually and in person.[3] They also point to the high turnout rates of countries such as Britain, France, and Canada which place the burden of registration on the state rather than the citizen.[4] Their findings lead them to take issue with the view that the size and shape of the electorate are a product of socioeconomic forces, pure and simple. Electorates, they argue, "are much more the product of political forces than many have appreciated . . . [and] to a considerable extent, they can be political artifacts. Within limits, they can be constructed to a size and composition deemed desirable by those in power."[5] Their findings were applicable to northern cities as well as to those in the South, where the artifactual nature of electorates has long been appreciated.

The standard arguments against permanent registration—that it permits fraud, is cumbersome and costly, weeds out those who are uninterested, and so on—have been successfully refuted not only in theory but in practice.[6] Apparently the sole reason for retaining

2 Stanley Kelly, Jr., Richard E. Ayres, and William G. Bowen, "Registration and Voting: Putting First Things First," *American Political Science Review*, LXI (1967), 362.

3 *Ibid.*, 374.

4 *Ibid.*

5 *Ibid.*, 375.

6 See, for example, Janice C. May, "The Texas Voter Registration System," *Public Affairs Comment*, XVI (July, 1970), 4, 5; Kelly *et al.*, "Registration and Voting," 375; Richard M. Scammon, "Electoral Participation," in Bertram M. Gross (ed.), *Social Intelligence for America's Future* (Boston: Allyn and Bacon. Inc., 1969), 90.

a restrictive registration system in many locales—especially in the South—is to manipulate the electorate. There is a growing body of evidence, too, that other sorts of rules have served to erode the power of ethnics and lower-income groups at the municipal level. Many of these rules that have become effective as a result of "good government" reform movements have in fact resulted in "the reduction of governmental services, have benefited the well-to-do at the expense of the poor and the Negro, and have removed numerous issues from the political arena thus benefiting proponents of the status quo."[7] Among the "reforms" with these consequences are the small, unpaid city council, city-wide election districts, nonpartisan city elections, and the establishment of blue-ribbon advisory boards and commissions. It is necessary, therefore, to look carefully at some of the rules and practices which characterize racial politics in Houston. How do they affect Negro participation? Who is responsible for them? Answers to these questions will provide a better understanding of the configuration of power in the city, and the status of marginal groups within it.

THE REGISTRATION SYSTEM

The poll tax as a qualification for voting went into effect in Texas in 1904, with the intention of restricting the suffrage of Negroes and poor whites alike.[8] However, contrary to practices in the Deep South states until very recently, Texas tax assessors dispensed poll tax receipts to most if not all of those Negroes who were willing to pay.[9] In Houston one was indeed required to pay

---

7 John Strange, "Representation in Local Government—Old Dogma Reappraised" (unpublished address given at 74th Annual Meeting of National Municipal League, New Orleans, December 3, 1968), 4.

8 This was probably a reactionary response to Populism. However, as Key has shown, a sharp drop in voter turnout occurred in Texas after the high tide of Populism in 1896 but before the poll tax went into effect in 1904. Thus, the poll tax cannot have been responsible for the decline of Populism. However, the tax may have been instituted to discourage its resurgence. See V. O. Key, Jr., *Southern Politics in State and Nation* (New York: Alfred A. Knopf, Inc., 1949), 533–35.

9 Stephen J. Pollack, an attorney in the Civil Rights Division of the Justice Department, told the Baytown Human Rights Council in 1966: "In our search [of

his $1.50 poll tax at the same time he rendered his property taxes. This requirement was dropped soon after the *Smith* v. *Allwright* decision striking down the white primary in 1944, for it had the effect of automatically making Negro property holders eligible to vote in the primaries. As a prerequisite for voting in national elections, the poll tax was retained in Texas until 1964, when it was invalidated by a constitutional amendment. It was struck down by a federal court order in 1966 as a requirement for voting in state and local elections as well.

The effect of the poll tax in earlier years must have been significant. In Houston, as the tax was originally imposed, it was undoubtedly a barrier to the poor of both races. According to James Weinstein, the $2.50 tax eliminated seventy-five hundred voters from the city's potential electorate of twelve thousand.[10] Most certainly many of these were white. Exactly what effect the tax had on discouraging voter registration in recent years is not known. "A priori," Clifton McCleskey wrote shortly before the tax disappeared, "it would seem that improved economic conditions and inflation have robbed the tax of most of its deterrent value, but those who have participated in poll tax drives insist that in lower-income areas there is resistance to payment because of economic hardship, and in support of that contention they point not only to a generally lower rate of payment but also the tendency for the tax to be paid for only one person in the family, usually the husband."[11]

In the fifteen-day period following the 1966 decision, more than a hundred thousand voters were added to the registration rolls in

---

records in preparation for the government's anti-poll tax case] we did not find any overt instances of the use of the poll tax to deny the vote as we have in other states." Houston *Post*, May 26, 1966. Harry Holloway has argued that one reason for this apparent leniency among rural East Texas registrars was the ability of white influentials to manipulate the Negro vote. See Holloway, "The Negro and the Vote: The Case of Texas," *Journal of Politics*, XXIII (1961), 526–56. Holloway says (p. 545) that "white paternalism means that the white community encourages Negroes to register and to vote in the normally well-founded belief the vote will be a friendly one."

10 James Weinstein, "Organized Business and the City Commission and Manager Movements," *Journal of Southern History*, XXVIII (1962), 177.

11 Clifton McCleskey, *The Government and Politics of Texas* (2nd ed.; Boston: Little, Brown and Co., 1966), 52.

Harris County alone. And in 1967 voter registration rates for both whites and Negroes were significantly higher than in previous odd-numbered years in the 1960s, as Table 3.1 demonstrates.

Table 3.1

VOTER REGISTRATION RATES, BY RACE
HARRIS COUNTY, RECENT ODD-NUMBERED YEARS

Year	Negro Adults	White Adults
1961	37%	47%
1963	38	46
1965	36	39
1967	47	57

The 1967 increase over the average rate for 1961, 1963, and 1965 was slightly greater for whites (29 percent) than for Negroes (27 percent).[12]

As soon as the poll tax was declared illegal in 1966, a battle developed between liberal and conservative factions in the state over whether to require annual or permanent registration. The assumption shared by both groups was that an annual registration would discriminate against lower-income persons. As is the case in most pitched battles between conservatives and liberals in the legislature, the liberals lost. Governor Connally's forces were able to pass a bill that set the annual registration period from October 1 to January 31, ending at least three months before the state primaries and at least nine months before the November elections.[13] This was the same as the old poll tax payment period, which required one to register long before campaigns were under way. The Connally faction further succeeded in incorporating the annual system into

12 Unless otherwise indicated, all local voter registration statistics used in this book were obtained from the office of the county tax assessor-collector's office. Local voting statistics were calculated from official returns, obtained either from city hall (in municipal elections), the county clerk (in primary and general elections), or the secretary of the school board, in school trustee elections.

13 Houston *Post*, January 13, 1967. Also see *Texas Observer*, February 18, 1966.

the state constitution by submitting a vaguely worded constitutional amendment to a referendum.

Two essential features of the old poll tax system—annual registration and an early cutoff date—were therefore salvaged in 1966. As Janice May observed afterwards, "perhaps the single most important generalization that can be made about the current registration system is that it is very similar to the poll tax system, minus the poll tax."[14] Until the system of annual registration, along with the early cutoff date, were invalidated by a federal court in 1971, Texas was one of the most illiberal in this respect of any state in the Union, including those in the South. As it was conceived and implemented by the Bourbons who dominate state politics, it discriminated against the poor of both races. As such, like the poll tax, it was a class barrier as well as a racial one. It is significant that support for an anti-poll tax referendum in 1963 received somewhat greater support from lower-income white precincts in Houston than from the more affluent ones. We shall return to this point in chapter 7, when we examine the theory that southern Bourbons are the most likely allies of blacks.

Another rule operative in Houston that is often mentioned as placing special burdens on blacks and poor people generally is the residence requirement. Although no systematic evidence is locally available, there is reason to believe that people in lower socioeconomic classes in general change residence more often than those on higher levels, thus making it more difficult for them to register.[15] The county tax assessor-collector estimated in 1971 that 20 to 25 percent of Harris County residents move annually.[16]

ELECTION RULES

A second means of restricting Negro voting power consists of rules that make it more difficult for a Negro candidate (or a

14 Janice C. May, "The Texas Voter Registration System," 2.

15 James Q. Wilson, "The Negro in American Politics: The Present," in John P. Davis (ed.), *The American Negro Reference Book* (Englewood Cliffs: Prentice-Hall, Inc., 1966), 432.

16 Houston *Post*, June 6, 1971.

white liberal) to win. Five in particular have this effect in Harris County: those requiring at-large elections, "place" voting, a majority vote to win, nonpartisanship, and the unit rule.

AT-LARGE ELECTIONS

Approximately 23 percent of the total Houston population was Negro in 1960. For Harris County the figure was 20 percent; and for the school district, probably between 20 and 25 percent.[17] Yet a tiny proportion of all officeholders during the 1960s was Negro. One reason for this is the at-large election, in which all the voters in a governmental unit such as a city or school district or county vote for the same set of candidates. This is the opposite of the ward-based system, in which the governmental unit is divided into a number of districts or wards, and the people in each district vote for different candidates to represent them on a governing body. In the ward system, district lines can be drawn to enable Negroes to elect a proportionate number of their race to office, even without the support of white voters. (On the other hand, lines can be drawn to prevent Negroes from doing this.) In a governmental unit in which Negroes constitute a small minority of the total population, and white allies are difficult to find on election day, a ward system offers one of the few possibilities of electing Negroes to office.

A Negro ward, however, is not necessarily advantageous. If most of the blacks in a city are enclosed in a single ward, this has the effect of removing them from other wards, where they might have some effect upon electoral outcomes. Furthermore it is possible to "pack" a Negro ward in such a way as to neutralize large numbers of black votes. In a city like Houston, a political unit which is 40 percent black is for most practical purposes black controlled, because Negroes can count on a minority of friendly whites to give a black candidate the remaining votes he needs to exceed the 50 percent mark. Thus, any Negro ward that is more than 40 percent black will contain an excess of black votes needed for a black candidate.

17 United States Bureau of the Census, *U.S. Census of Population: General Population Characteristics, Texas*, Final Report PC(1)–45B (Washington, D.C.: United States Government Printing Office, 1961).

Packing a Negro ward by making it, say, 90 percent black means that 50 percent of the ward's black voters are of no use to a black candidate. That 50 percent could be very valuable in another predominantly white district, by helping defeat a racially conservative candidate.

Nevertheless, in the South generally, white lawmakers have preferred at-large elections, pure and simple. This is true in Houston for most county and all municipal and school board elections.

Among the most important county political offices that are voted on county-wide are those of county judge, clerk, treasurer, district attorney, a host of judgeships, and the chairmen of both the county Democratic and Republican executive committees. (The committeemen of the county Democratic executive committee, however, are elected in each precinct, and hence the predominantly Negro precincts elect Negroes to represent them.) Until 1965 the county's twelve state representatives and one state senator were also elected county-wide.

All trustees of the school board are elected district-wide and have been since before the 1944 Supreme Court decision. Prior to a city charter revision in 1955, five of the eight city councilmen were elected from wards, and the others were elected at large. Since then all councilmen have been elected on an at-large basis, although five of them are required to live in the district they are said to "represent."[18]

Attempts to change the at-large system in the municipality and the school district have so far met with little success. A blue-ribbon charter-revision committee appointed by Mayor Louie Welch recommended that four of the eight city councilmen be elected from wards, which would give both Republicans and Negroes a better chance for representation on the city council. Since then, the rec-

18 There is no indication that Mayor Roy Hofheinz, who advocated this change in the 1955 charter revision campaign, was racially motivated. Indeed, according to a former member of his administrative staff, the abolition of wards resulted from the naïve belief of Hofheinz and other reformers that at-large elections would curtail "ward politics" in the councilmanic districts. The Negro precincts gave strong support to the measure. The revision, however, did little to change the complexion of council politics.

ommendation has been quietly buried because of the incumbent councilmen's opposition, described as ranging from "very much" to "vigorous."[19] In 1967 Curtis Graves, as a newly elected Negro legislator, introduced a bill that in its amended form provided that five trustees of the Houston school board would be elected from districts and that the remainder would be elected at large. In the vote to suspend the House rules to consider the bill, Graves was unable to muster even a simple majority—much less the two-thirds required. Among the Harris County delegation, the liberals backed Graves and the conservatives voted against him.[20]

Graves also introduced a bill that would increase the size of the city council from eight to ten and require eight to be elected from districts. This, too, failed, meeting opposition not only in the legislature but also from the city council. One councilman, Arthur "Curley" Miller, was particularly upset by the bill. Miller had been opposed by a black candidate in 1969 and narrowly won reelection. He lost in the district in which he resided. Calling the bill a "return to the horse and buggy days," Miller charged that if it became law, his and another councilman's district would be dominated by blacks, and "the white people would be like the Negroes are now."[21]

PLACE VOTING

The at-large system does offer one possibility for a Negro's being elected. Suppose, for example, that there are four positions on the school board open for contest in an election. Twenty candidates, one of whom is Negro, are vying for these offices, and the top four candidates will be declared winners, each obtaining one of the four seats. Each voter will have a chance to mark his top four preferences. The Negro leaders get together before the election and decide that it will be to their interest, given that the other candidates are unappealing, to vote only for the Negro candidate, and to withhold their other three votes. This takes away votes from

19 Houston *Post*, October 30, 1966.
20 Houston *Post*, May 26, 1967.
21 Houston *Post*, February 24, 1971. Miller was defeated in November, 1971, by his black 1969 opponent, Judson Robinson, Jr.

the other candidates and increases the votes of the Negro candidate relative to the others, assuming that the Negro bloc is agreed upon who their candidate is. In other words, if they are unified in their choice, they are privileged not only to cast a vote for their single candidate, but to withhold a vote from three others. They have, in a sense, two votes instead of one, although they relinquish their right to help decide which of the other candidates are elected. This is the practice of "single-shot" voting.

Single-shot voting has been used by Negroes occasionally in the South, with varied success. To guard against this eventuality, a system known as place voting has been established in many communities. Rather than simply declare the top four candidates winners of the four seats, as in the example above, the place rule requires that each candidate must declare himself to be running for a specific seat or "place." Thus, all the candidates running for, say, four school board seats are no longer in competition with all the other candidates. They are only in competition with those candidates running for the same place. In this situation the voter does not get to list his four top preferences for office. He is merely allowed to vote for his favorite candidate in each of the four races. By withholding votes from three of the four and voting only for one, the voter no longer takes away from the others. Single-shot voting is hence a useless tactic. Roy Young has demonstrated the logic behind single-shot voting in regular at-large elections by constructing a hypothetical example which is represented in Table 3.2.

The use of the place system was introduced in Texas as early as 1905, according to Young.[22] The same Terrell Election Law which paved the way for the white primary made place voting mandatory in all primary elections. Since that time its use has become widespread in other types of elections as well, and it serves to "protect" the white population from Negro or Mexican-American officeholders. In many cases this clearly has been the intention of the lawmakers who established place voting. Young says:

22 Roy E. Young, *The Place System in Texas Elections* (Austin: Institute of Public Affairs, University of Texas, 1965), 2. Young's book presents a lucid account of the role which place voting plays in state politics.

A member of one city charter commission admits that the place system was written into the charter "to prevent minority groups from voting against all candidates but one in order to ensure their man got the most votes." An individual who helped draft another charter candidly acknowledged that the place system was selected so that the Negro minority in this city would be unable to elect a councilman.

Such candor is rare, however.... But there seems no doubt that the growing political power of Negro and Latin American citizens in Texas has resulted in efforts to dilute or offset it. The place system has been one weapon available to those seeking this aim.[23]

As Young points out, this is not the sole reason for the advent of the place system, for it has been adopted in cities which have no sizable ethnic minorities. Yet it is by far the most credible single explanation. As mentioned above, the use of place voting in party primaries is as old as the Terrell Election Law. Its use in the school board elections dates back to 1941, when the state legislature passed laws requiring it in three Texas school districts, one of which was Houston's.[24] Place voting in municipal elections is of more recent vintage, having been inaugurated along with the change from ward-based to at-large voting in 1955. It continued to be employed in 1966 in the three Harris County multimember legislative districts, as it had been before redistricting the previous year.

THE MAJORITY REQUIREMENT

It was not by chance that the first Negro elected to office in Harris County since Reconstruction won by a plurality, rather than by a majority of the votes. Neither Mrs. Charles E. White, elected to the school board in 1958 and 1962, nor Asberry Butler, elected to the board in 1964, was able to obtain an absolute majority of the votes cast. Mrs. White came close. She received 47 percent of the total in both races mentioned above, running against two white opponents the first time and five the second. Butler received 39 percent of the total vote in a race against two whites. Had the majority requirement existed at that time, both Mrs. White and Butler would

23 *Ibid.*, 21.
24 *Ibid.*, 10–11.

Table 3.2

RESULTS OF A HYPOTHETICAL ELECTION FOR A FIVE-MEMBER GOVERNING BODY WITH AND WITHOUT SINGLE-SHOT VOTING

Candidate Number	100 Voters' Count	50 Single-shot Count	Situation A With Single-Shot Voting		Situation B All 150 Voters Casting 5 Votes	
			Total Votes	Results	Total Votes	Results
1	100	——	100	Elected	125	Elected
2	95	——	95	Elected	120	Elected
3	90	——	90	Elected	115	Elected
4	60	——	60	Elected	84	Elected
5	50	——	50		73	Elected
6	40	——	40		66	
7	30	——	30		55	
8	20	——	20		47	
9	10	——	10		10	
10	5	50	55	Elected	55	
Total	500	50	550		750	

Source: Roy E. Young, *The Place System in Texas Elections* (Austin: Institute of Public Affairs, University of Texas, 1965), 19, Table III (with slight modifications).

have been forced into a runoff against a single white candidate. It is probable that neither Negro would have won such a contest. C. W. Thompson, a Negro, obtained a plurality opposing five white opponents for the city council in 1963. In the runoff he faced a white who won, 116,826 to 43,857.

Elections for most major offices in Harris County and Houston have long required a majority to win. Runoff elections have been required in state primaries since 1918.[25] They were instituted in city elections in 1955. Thus, in 1965 the school board was the only governmental body of importance in the county which did not require a majority vote—general elections for state and county office constituting the obvious exceptions.

School board politics since the Supreme Court decision of 1954 has borne the stamp of a single, ever-present issue: school desegregation. Prior to 1969 the last "liberal" majority to sit on the board had failed to meet the issue squarely and, after much temporizing and ineptitude, was ousted in 1956 by a strongly conservative slate that vowed, along with most southern politicians at the time, "Never!" In 1964, however, the majority's six-man margin was cut sharply to one, when Asberry Butler, a Negro, and Mrs. Howard Barnstone, who is Jewish, joined Mrs. White on the board. (Mrs. Barnstone was also elected by a plurality.) There was immediate speculation that in two years there would be a strong possibility that a liberal majority would take over, for only one liberal—Mrs. White—would be up for reelection, while two conservatives would have to defend their seats on the board. Much public money had been spent by the conservative majority between 1956 and 1964 in lawsuits designed to impede school desegregation. The goals of the segregationists would have been imperiled by a new liberal majority.

In the spring following the 1964 November elections, a bill was introduced in the Texas legislature by Representative Henry Grover of Harris County to change the law in two respects. First, it stipulated that the date of school board elections in Houston be changed from even years (coinciding with state and national general elec-

25 *Ibid.*, 10.

tions) to odd-numbered years (coinciding with the municipal elections). Grover's ostensible reason for this change, according to a memorandum attached to the bill in the school board files, was that "it would relieve the crowded condition of the ballot on the general election date. . . . The ballot in Harris County has become so long with so many candidates appearing on it that it is not only confusing to the voters, but presents a real problem to the election officials to be able to get on the ballot all of the matters to be voted on at the general election." The second proposed change contained in the bill provided for a runoff in any school board race in which no candidate received a majority. The above-mentioned memorandum was discreet enough not to mention the reason for this. The Grover bill encountered opposition in the house from approximately twenty liberals, including three Harris County legislators. It passed, however. As it was a local bill, the opposition from the sole senator from Houston at that time would have been sufficient to kill it. But he let it pass and the bill became law.

At the end of the legislative session, Grover, a history teacher in the public schools, was given an administrative post, the salary for which, under the terms of the twelve-month contract, was to be $11,273. This contrasted with the $6,000 under a nine-month contract he would have earned had he continued to teach history. Mrs. White publicly charged that Grover got the promotion as a payoff from the conservative board members for his aid in getting the election laws changed. Grover denied her allegation. She also questioned the propriety of Grover's receiving both his salary as a legislator and as a school district administrator.[26]

Running for reelection in 1967 against a single white opponent, Mrs. White was defeated. Ironically the new majority requirement was not needed to remove her from office. The segregationist faction, covering all bets, dissuaded all potential white opponents but one from entering the first race against her, and a runoff proved unnecessary.

Mrs. White's case is only one of many examples of the bending of election laws by the business-dominated legislature for its own pur-

26 Houston *Post*, July 21, 1965.

poses. After Senator Ralph Yarborough won a special senatorial election in 1957 with 37 percent of the vote, the legislature changed the law to require a majority vote in subsequent special elections. Indeed anti-Yarborough forces in the legislature attempted to change the law before the election. As Yarborough entered the race in April, the bill that was introduced in the house to require a runoff came after the cutoff date for normal consideration, which meant that a two-thirds vote was necessary for passage. After falling eight votes short, the bill was brought back by parliamentary maneuver, and following some especially effective arm twisting, the house passed it. The senate, however, refused to go along, at least until the election was over. In 1964 the legislature conveniently changed the law to allow Lyndon Johnson to run both for vicepresident and senator that year. Texas Bourbons leave very little to chance in electoral politics.

In short the three requirements—at-large voting, the place system, and the majority rule—have worked to the disadvantage of Negroes in Houston politics. In rare cases Negro candidates have been able to surmount one or two of these barriers and win elections. But in only three instances has a Negro candidate won election when all three barriers were in effect simultaneously.

NONPARTISANSHIP AND THE UNIT RULE

Two other electoral rules in Houston probably work a hardship on blacks. One requires nonpartisan elections in municipal and school board politics. James Q. Wilson and William Banfield have argued that nonpartisan politics works against all minority group candidates. In partisan elections, where there are often ethnically balanced slates, "a minority-group member 'adds strength to the ticket' because his being on it causes members of his group to vote for it without causing other persons who are indifferent to, or mildly hostile to, his group to vote against it."[27] But in nonpartisan elections, so it is argued, ethnically balanced slates will not work, because the voter does not feel loyalty to the organization—as opposed

[27] James Q. Wilson and William Banfield, *City Politics* (Cambridge, Mass.: Harvard University Press, 1966), 158.

to a "real" party—and, as it cannot discipline him, he picks and chooses candidates to suit his tastes.

The unit rule has long been in effect in Democratic Party conventions, from the precinct level on up to those at the statewide level. The assumption has been that among the quite small percentage of the total electorate which attends precinct conventions on primary election night, voters from lower economic levels with liberal proclivities will be underrepresented. Thus, as the precinct convention elects delegates to the senatorial conventions, which in turn elect delegates to the state meetings which, in presidential election years, send delegates to the national convention, it is possible, through use of the unit rule—which requires that all delegates to a convention vote with their unit's majority—for the conservative head of a delegation to deliver votes *en bloc*, effectively excluding any dissenting liberal votes. This has the effect of sending to national conventions a Texas delegation headed by a conservative governor, such as John Connally, who is able to deliver (as in 1968) all 104 Texas convention votes to the candidate of the governor's choice.

The governor, of course, does not actually have to coerce the delegates at the national convention. The unit rule has already produced an overwhelmingly conservative delegation in state and local conventions. That blacks, Mexican-Americans, and unaffluent whites are severely underrepresented goes without saying. But middle-class liberals are also in scarce supply. An Associated Press poll of two-thirds of the Texas delegates at Chicago revealed that only one planned to support Eugene McCarthy if released from his pledge.[28] A few liberals, however, were munificently included in the delegation. Frank Erwin, a national committeeman and Connally crony, candidly explained why to the rules committee: "We put them on there because we knew we could control them under the unit rule."[29]

The Democratic national convention in 1968 proscribed the use of the unit rule at any step in the process by which delegates to the party's 1972 convention are elected—a fact that undoubtedly added

28 Houston *Post*, August 24, 1968.
29 *Ibid.*

to Connally's disenchantment with the national party. As one conservative state party official commented at the time, "This crumbles the whole foundation of our control."[30] Yet, while this will give blacks a better chance for representation at national conventions, it does not abolish use of the unit rule in elections within the state.

POLITICAL CARTOGRAPHY

The county commissioners court is the most important local body whose members are elected on a ward basis. Actually only the four commissioners are elected from wards, or "commissioners precincts" as they are called. The presiding officer, the county judge, is elected county-wide. Until 1972 three congressmen were also elected from separate districts, as were five state senators. Nineteen state legislators were elected from three multimember districts in the county.

The commissioners precinct boundaries were established in 1857, and were only redrawn in 1967 when, as a result of unequal population growth, one precinct contained more than half the county's inhabitants. Harris County formed a single congressional district until 1958, when it was split into two. In 1965, as a result of the "one man, one vote" decision handed down by the Supreme Court in 1962, it was divided into three districts. Also in 1965 the Texas legislature was forced to reapportion the state representative and senatorial districts. Where the county had previously had a single multimember representative district, it was given three. And instead of one single-member senatorial district, it was given four and a portion of a fifth.

The redrawing of these voting districts is of great political importance. By deciding upon one set of boundaries rather than another, legislators or other persons responsible for redistricting can limit or enlarge the voting strength of various segments of the electorate. Andrew Hacker has called this practice of gerrymandering "the art of political cartography," the aim of which "is for one

30 Houston *Post*, August 31, 1968.

party to obtain the maximum voting advantage at the other's expense."[31] In the strictest sense, gerrymandering refers to the practice of "political cartography" by a party—for example, the Democrats or the Republicans—at the expense of another party or parties. But more generally it connotes such practice by any political group in power at the expense of its political opponents. The case studies of redistricting which follow concern the effects of political cartography on blacks. We shall first examine 1965 congressional redistricting. Table 3.3 shows the percentage of voting-age nonwhites (as of 1960) in each district before and after reapportionment.

In the 1966 elections a Republican was sent to Congress from the newly created Seventh District, while a liberal Democrat was elected from the Eighth District, and a conservative Democrat from the Twenty-second District. It is doubtful that the liberal, Bob Eckhardt, would have been elected had not the conservative congressman from the old Eighth District, Albert Thomas, died shortly

Table 3.3

PERCENTAGE OF VOTING-AGE NONWHITES BEFORE AND AFTER
CONGRESSIONAL REDISTRICTING IN 1965

District Number	Before	After
7	——%	14.4%
8	24.7	26.0
22	14.2	16.5

Source: United States Bureau of the Census, *Congressional District Data Book* [*Districts of the 87th Congress*] (Washington, D.C.: United States Government Printing Office, 1961), 64, 146, 147. United States Bureau of the Census, *Supplement to Congressional District Data Book: Redistricted States* [Congressional District Data Book Supplement No. 21] (Washington, D.C.: United States Government Printing Office, July, 1966), 10, 13, 16, 19.

before the spring primaries. The class and ethnic composition of the old and new district was not changed appreciably by redistricting,

31 Andrew Hacker, *Congressional Districting: The Issue of Equal Representation* (rev. ed.; Washington, D.C.: Brookings Institution, 1964), 54–55.

and Thomas, a long-time officeholder, would have been difficult for any contender to beat.

In terms of the proportion of Negroes in the districts alone, one could argue that the situation was worse for Negro candidates after rather than prior to 1965. Before there was one district of the two in which a Negro had at least a small chance of winning; afterwards there was one of three. And the increase in the percentage of voting-age Negroes in the Eighth District was only from 24.7 to 26.0.

The new Eighth District was one of the few in Texas where a Negro might conceivably have won. If one had tried, he would have had to run against Eckhardt, whose liberal credentials were impeccable. A similar situation existed following the change in state representative boundaries. Prior to 1965 the entire county constituted a single district, and twelve representatives were elected at large. The legislature created three representative districts coterminous with the three new congressional ones. The results of this change are shown in Table 3.4.

Table 3.4

PERCENTAGE OF VOTING-AGE NONWHITES BEFORE AND AFTER
STATE REPRESENTATIVE REDISTRICTING

District Number	Before		After	
	Percent Nonwhite	No. of Reps.	Percent Nonwhite	No. of Reps.
Harris County	18.8%	12	——%	——
22	——	——	14.4	7
24	——	——	16.5	6
23	——	——	26.0	6

Source: *Ibid.*

The short-run effects have been beneficial to Negroes. The campaigns of a black, Barbara Jordan, in 1962 and 1964 for a seat in the legislature dramatically illustrated the difficulty of a Negro's winning in an at-large election. Neither time did she make the runoff. Yet in 1966, 1968, and 1970, Curtis Graves, another black, was elected. In the other two new districts, however, the chances of a Negro victory were smaller than in the old county-wide district. The Negro voting-age population in the Twenty-second and Twenty-fourth districts was 14.4 percent and 16.5 percent, respectively, as compared to 18.8 percent in the county. Furthermore a smaller percentage of working-class whites lived in these two districts than in the former, which further reduced a Negro candidate's chances of election in the party primaries, where economic issues tend to polarize the white voters by class. The results, in terms of blacks elected to office, were hardly spectacular in the years following redistricting. Under the old system, none of the county's twelve representatives was black. Under the new one, there was one Negro in the county's nineteen-member delegation.

The effect of redistricting upon state senatorial elections can be seen in Table 3.5.

Table 3.5

PERCENTAGE OF REGISTERED NEGRO VOTERS IN EACH SENATORIAL
DISTRICT IN 1966, BEFORE AND AFTER REDISTRICTING

District Number	Before	After
County	18.8%	———%
6	———	11.9
7	———	15.5
11	———	43.2
15	———	3.8
17	———	Combined with out-of-county district

Source: Computed using precinct-by-precinct estimates.

Whereas there was almost no possibility of a Negro's being elected from the pre-1965 district, the new Eleventh District became a safe constituency. Thus, one senator out of five was a Negro. As about a fifth of all residents in the county were Negro as well, it can be seen that the senatorial redistricting was the one case which allowed "proportional representation" for black voters, so to speak.

The clearest case of recent gerrymandering occurred when the county commissioners precincts were redrawn in 1967. The commissioners court is the most powerful governing body in the county. Among its main functions are supervision of county courthouses and jails, the hiring of county personnel, appointments to fill vacancies in elective and appointive positions, and the determination of county tax rates. The court also serves as board of equalization for state and county tax assessments, lets contracts in the name of the county, builds and maintains roads and bridges, and establishes hospitals and parks.

Negro and white liberal leaders argued strongly in favor of a plan that would lump a relatively high percentage of Negroes in one district, so that either a Negro or a liberal would have a safe constituency. Actually, in old Precinct Three about 36 percent of the qualified voters were Negro before redistricting. However, the incumbent, who had announced he would retire in 1968, was a virtually undefeatable racial conservative. The liberal faction, led by Bill Kilgarlin, an attorney who was a past chairman of the county Democratic executive committee, submitted a plan which would provide for one precinct with about the same percentage of Negroes as the old Precinct Three. After a spirited fight, which was well covered in the press, the choice of redistricting plans was narrowed down to two. One was the "Collier Plan," named after its author, Everett Collier, an editor of the Houston *Chronicle*. It was similar in many respects to other plans submitted by conservatives and was enthusiastically endorsed by both daily newspapers. The second was the "Kilgarlin Plan." Table 3.6 shows how the two proposed plans differed with respect to the Negro proportions in the four commissioners precincts.

With the Precinct Three commissioner's office up for grabs in 1968, there was a good possibility under the Kilgarlin Plan that a popular Negro candidate with liberal coalition support could have won a seat on the court. The liberal plan did not pass, however. The majority of the redistricting committee were conservative members

Table 3.6

PERCENTAGE OF REGISTERED NEGRO VOTERS IN 1966
IN COUNTY COMMISSIONERS PRECINCTS UNDER
TWO PROPOSED REDISTRICTING SCHEMES

Collier Plan		Kilgarlin Plan	
Precinct Number	Approximate Negro Percentage	Precinct Number	Approximate Negro Percentage
1	16.0%	1	14.4%
2	22.8	2	6.5
3	12.3	3	36.8
4	16.5	4	5.6

Source: Precinct-by-precinct estimates. These are very rough estimates and should be treated cautiously.

of the city's business elite and they approved the Collier Plan. Table 3.7 shows the effects of the redistricting, based on 1966 registration figures. The Negro percentage in Precinct Three, the only one before redistricting in which a Negro could have been elected, was diluted with whites; and while the percentages of Negroes in the three remaining precincts were raised slightly, the changes were negligible. Negroes in Harris County are now virtually barred from office on the commissioners court in the foreseeable future.

Table 3.7

PERCENTAGE OF REGISTERED NEGRO VOTERS IN 1966 COUNTY
COMMISSIONERS PRECINCTS BEFORE AND AFTER REDISTRICTING

Precinct Number	Approximate Negro Percentage	
	Before	After
1	12.9%	16.0%
2	22.5	22.8
3	36.2	12.3
4	5.9	16.5

Source: Precinct-by-precinct estimates

BARRIERS TO CANDIDACY

The barriers to full Negro participation, it now becomes obvious, are myriad. They are placed, like hurdles on a race track, at many different points. Some barriers are thrown up to make voter participation difficult. Other barriers are erected to minimize the influence of those voters who actually turn out on election day. Another set of obstacles must be overcome in order for the aspiring officeholder to be certified as a candidate. The most formidable legal restriction on candidacy has been the exorbitant filing fee (Table 3.8) that, like so many other barriers, discriminates against the poor—and the not-so-poor—of whatever ethnicity. (This was ruled unconstitutional in 1970.)

The significance of these figures should not be ignored. The filing fee for all state and county offices in the party primary, with the exception of state representative and county surveyor, has been at least $1,000 and usually much more. The fees were higher for a statewide candidate, who had to pay filing fees in every county in which his named appeared on the ballot. The filing fee for mayor was $1,250, and for councilman $500. The fees for some county offices were above the Negro median family income in 1960.

Another obvious means of discouraging blacks from actively seeking election is harrassment and intimidation of candidates and elected officials. This has been a tactic widely used throughout the South in recent years. Interviews with Houston blacks who are politically active did not bring to light a systematic pattern of intimidation by violence or threatened violence. Only one Negro candidate, out of more than a dozen who had run for office recently, claimed that serious physical intimidation had occurred during his campaign. In this case he had been fired upon from a moving car. Most of the candidates admitted that they had received a few crackpot telephone calls but minimized their importance or danger.

Yet it would be a mistake to conclude that blacks do not feel sensitive to other sorts of intimidation. In recent years at least three black political activists have encountered difficulties that many peo-

Table 3.8

FILING FEES IN PARTY PRIMARIES IN HARRIS COUNTY

Office	Fee
United States senator, governor, lieutenant governor, attorney general, comptroller, state treasurer, land commissioner, agriculture commissioner and railroad commissioner	$1,000
United States congressman	4,250
State senator	1,000
State representative	500
County commissioner	2,970
Court of criminal appeals, presiding judge and judge	1,000
Court of civil appeals judge	1,300
Judge, county court at law	3,150
Judges, district court, juvenile court and domestic relations court	4,200 (for Democrats) 3,900 (for Republicans)
Probate court judge	3,420
County clerk	2,772
District clerk	2,772 (for Democrats) 2,706 (for Republicans)
County treasurer	2,484
County surveyor	115
Justices of the peace	
Precincts 5 and 6	1,800
All other positions	2,160
Criminal court at law	2,100
County, 133rd district court	2,800

Source: Houston *Post*, February 2, 1970

ple have construed as harrassment purposely designed to discourage blacks from assuming positions of political leadership. One of the three, who will be called Jack Jones, was ruined politically and financially as a result of events that he and his supporters believed were at some point politically motivated. Jones ran for a position on the school board in the early 1960s. To everyone's surprise he won, becoming the second Negro to gain elective office in the county and the second one to sit on the board. A native Houstonian, Jones was an attorney, having received his law degree locally from Texas Southern University. Before settling in Houston to practice law, he had worked in the General Service Administration real estate section in Washington and Chicago and as an agent of the Internal Revenue Service in Philadelphia. After returning he became active in the NAACP and eventually was elected president of one of the Houston branches. He did not ally himself with any political organizations in town and was not known as a "politician" before he tossed his hat in the ring. During the campaign his views were not widely known even in the Negro community. Political observers at the time saw him as just another candidate without money, grass-roots backing, or ideological alliances, who had suddenly been bitten by the political bug and decided to run. Hence there was every reason for surprise at his election. He soon made it clear that his loyalties on the school board were with the liberals.

According to Jones, he had become aware shortly after the November election that certain people were unhappy with his success. A prominent Negro friend called him on the phone one morning and told him, "You're being investigated." In the next few months, Jones received letters from friends and relatives in widely scattered parts of the country saying that private investigators were looking into his past. He also began getting calls from present and former clients, saying that a well-known private detective had been interviewing them. At one time word came to him that a forgery case was being built against him. Every one of his past accident clients had been interviewed, he claimed, some of them at late hours of the night for lengthy periods of time. At another point Jones received word via the "grapevine" that an attempt would be made to indict him for bigamy. He had previously been married to a woman who had left the country after their divorce, during which proceedings there had been irregularities. But nothing came of this either. Later, according to Jones, he was informed that a statement had been obtained from a fourteen-year-old girl charging that he had committed statutory rape previous to his election. Through his own private investigator, Jones was able to find out the girl's name. He had never met her, but he invited her and her mother to his office and was able to get a tape-recorded statement saying that she had been paid to make the charge.

In October, 1965, Jones was brought before a grand jury. The district attorney attempted to have him indicted for subornation of perjury, or inducing a client to commit perjury. The district attorney himself appeared before the jury to argue for the indictment. Jones was no-billed. In November of the same year, he was indicted by a grand jury for filing fraudulent insurance claims. Less than a month later, he was indicted on another felony theft charge, that of obtaining money by illegal means from another insurance company. Both charges were for alleged actions that occurred prior to his election. In January, 1966, a year after he had been in office, Jones was indicted on a third count—subornation of perjury. This indictment grew out of the same charge that the district attorney's office had made in October, and for which the grand jury at that time had refused to indict him. In the interim a new grand jury had been impaneled, and Jones was indicted by it. In Texas, such a practice is legal, but it rarely occurs. It is so rare, in fact, that the assistant district attorney in charge of the grand jury division, stated to a reporter (almost two years after Jones was first indicted): "There have been some cases where I felt that a grand jury was mistaken. . . . However, there have been none to my knowledge [i.e., no persons] who have been indicted [for the same charge] after a prior grand jury has no-billed them."[32] He had apparently forgotten the Jones case.

Shortly after his indictment, a legal defense committee for Jones formed, consisting of prominent Negroes and white liberals. The two Negro newspapers came out strongly in Jones's behalf, and it seemed at first as though his case would become a *cause célèbre*. However, the initial enthusiasm soon died down. Jones's law practice ceased. The district attorney who had become the target of

32 Houston *Post*, August 13, 1967.

hostility among Jones's supporters resigned to run for Congress. In the summer of 1966, Jones was convicted of subornation of perjury and given a suspended sentence of six years. In 1967 he was found guilty in one of the felony theft cases and given ten years probation. Both convictions were appealed and lost, and the district attorney subsequently decided not to prosecute the remaining theft case.

Jones's political and professional careers collapsed. In the fall of 1967, he appeared in court to ask the state to pay the cost of the trial transcript in his second conviction, for use in his appeal. He said that his law practice had declined to the point that he had taken a job driving a truck. He estimated that his income had dropped from $1,000 a month in 1965 to $175 two years later. He was unable to pay his own lawyers and claimed that efforts by his defense committee to raise money in either the white or Negro community had failed. The Houston Legal Foundation—a poverty agency—as well as the Peace Corps and the Texas Employment Commission, had turned down his application for a job because of his felony convictions. A few months later, after his convictions had been sustained in a higher court, Jones left the city to try to rebuild his shattered career somewhere else. One question never answered in the case was that of who paid the private detective who spent several months uncovering incriminating evidence. Early speculation was that the conservative members of the school board were the source of funds. They denied this under oath during Jones's first trial. The detective himself later testified that he had done it as a public service.

A crude, and unsuccessful, attempt to smear black Representative Curtis Graves occurred in the summer of 1969. In early May a large number of "mug shots" of Graves were circulated among legislators in Austin. The photographs, showing the usual side and front views, bore a Houston police identification number and the date "2-27-61," the date Graves was arrested for participating in a sit-in in the city's Union Station. Houston police records showed that Graves's police record and photo were furnished by the police department to a Harris County assistant district attorney on April 22, 1969. The latter told reporters that he picked up the file at the request of District Attorney Carol S. Vance, but Vance denied having any knowledge of the affair. The matter ended as abruptly as it had begun. Representative Graves, with characteristic humor, expressed the wish that the pictures had been enlarged, "so they'd be better for autographing."

The most celebrated case of racial intimidation recently in Houston has concerned a civil rights militant rather than an elected official or a candidate for office. But the significance of this case cannot be separated from the others. Lee Otis Johnson, who was associated with the Student Nonviolent Coordinating Committee on the Texas Southern University campus in 1967, made headlines in the Houston papers at the time for his "black power" pronouncements and his involvement in several skirmishes with the police. At one point, as a result of a demonstration his group mounted after being barred from the university, Johnson was arrested and placed under a peace bond of $25,000 by a local judge. This was later reduced to $1,000 after strong protests from blacks and civil libertarians. Johnson's notoriety as a black militant consequently made him the object of intensive police surveillance. (He had previously served time in prison for auto theft.)

Following the assassination of Martin Luther King in the spring of 1968, Johnson was one of several speakers at a memorial meeting held in a public park. He expressed strong criticism of the mayor and his police chief, both of whom were roundly disliked by many in the Houston black community. Shortly thereafter Johnson was indicted for possession and sale of marijuana, and arrested. The indictment alleged that he had sold a marijuana cigarette to a black undercover officer more than a month prior to the indictment. Actually Johnson simply gave a marijuana cigarette to the agent, but in Texas law this act constitutes selling it. The length of time between the act and the indictment was explained as necessary for the protection of the undercover agent's safety.

Johnson's case was argued by the district attorney himself. A request for a change of venue was denied, even though Johnson's name had appeared in local newspapers more than a hundred times in the preceding eighteen months. Ten people on the jury panel admitted that they had heard Johnson's name previously, but the judge refused his attorney's request to examine the panelists separately and in private, to determine if what they had heard about Johnson was prejudicial. The judge also refused Johnson's lawyer a continuance until the mayor and police chief (who were out of town and could not be subpoenaed) were available to testify. Johnson's lawyer contended that they had conspired to harass and entrap his client in order to prevent "his further exercise of his rights of free speech and assembly." An all-white jury, after hearing the testimony of three policemen, found Johnson guilty and handed down a thirty-year prison sentence. At this writing he is still in prison.

The conclusion that many Houstonians have drawn from these three cases is exemplified by the comment of a black attorney interviewed by the author: "Any Negro in this city who runs for office has to have an absolutely clean record. If there are any skeletons in the closet which he doesn't want the entire city to know about, he sure as hell better not run. And even if he doesn't have any skeletons, he better think the matter over carefully, anyhow. They can always plant one, if they want to get rid of you bad enough."

SUMMARY

What are the combined effects of the rules, institutions and patterns of behavior examined in this chapter? Clearly the answer is a formidable barrier to effective political participation on the part of lower-income people in general and Negroes in particular. This did not come about by chance. If chance were involved, some of the restrictions, at least, would adversely affect the wealthy more than the poor and those with middling incomes. But this is not the case. The poll tax was regressive. The present voter registration system banks upon the less intense political interest which characterizes those in lower socioeconomic categories. The majority rule, the at-large election, and the place system work to the disadvantage of ethnic minorities, as do nonpartisanship and the unit rule. The extremely high filing fees have worked against all but the most affluent, or those who have access to extraordinarily plentiful coffers. Gerrymandering is most often done at the expense of blacks.

These facts play havoc with the pluralist model, which relies heavily on the concept of "dispersed inequalities" and the role of the vote in insuring this dispersion. For in the pluralist scheme, the vote is preeminently the poor man's political resource to balance against the wealth and status of the elite. Yet the Houston case provides evidence that the game of electoral politics consists of rules that give numerous advantages to those who are accustomed to winning other sorts of games as well. Indeed the restrictive laws have been enacted by governmental bodies controlled by wealthy conservative businessmen—not "rednecks"—who view the political potential of lower-income whites with almost as much disquiet as that of blacks. It is quite natural that they should utilize their lawmaking capacity in this manner. Such a fact should not come as a surprise to anyone acquainted with the history of the battle for the franchise in western countries. The manipulation of electoral rules and electoral qualifications has long been recognized by opponents of democracy as an efficient means of limiting the effects of popular opinion when some form of suffrage has already been granted.[33]

33 Carl E. Schorske, *German Social Democracy, 1905–1917* (Cambridge, Mass.: Harvard University Press, 1955). Schorske's account of the devices employed by Imperial Germany to limit the growing strength of the working-class movement at the turn of the century demonstrates the purposes to which election rules have been put in that country.

IV

The Vote:
How Blacks Use It

Given the difficulties placed in the path of the Negro electorate, one might expect even the most resourceful and determined group to despair of the vote as a political weapon. But there are other reasons as well for expecting a poorer electoral performance of blacks, especially in a southern metropolis such as Houston. Many are new to the city, having migrated from rural areas of East Texas and Louisiana. They occupy a much lower socioeconomic position, in general, than whites. The tradition of voting is relatively recent. Hugh D. Price, in his study of Florida Negroes in the 1950s, wrote that they "have not been subjected to decades of civil exhortations on the virtues of voting *per se*. In fact, their very right of participating in elections at all is still politically controversial, even though legally settled. As a result, most Negro voters go to the polls only when there is a contest that presents a choice of direct meaning to them. And once in a voting booth, Negro registrants are still quite likely to indicate a choice only in the contest or contests that have particularly attracted their interest."[1] The findings of Philip E. Converse, based on the University of Michigan's Survey Research Center data, provide a further basis for pessimism. He described the majority of southern Negroes in the 1960 survey sample as "extremely ignorant, disoriented, and in the most utter confusion about politics."[2]

[1] Hugh D. Price, *The Negro and Southern Politics: A Chapter of Florida History*, (New York: New York University Press, 1957), 77.
[2] Philip E. Converse, "On the Possibility of a Major Political Realignment in the South," in Angus Campbell, Philip E. Converse, Warren E. Miller, and Donald

83

Do these depictions of other southern Negroes fit Houston's blacks? To answer this, it is first necessary to sketch in broad strokes the recent history of racial electoral politics in the city. For Houston blacks, as for many Negroes in the Rim South, regular political participation began with the abolition in 1944 of the so-called "white primary," an institution that excluded Negroes from voting in the Democratic primaries, the most important elections in the state. The years following Reconstruction had witnessed the gradual erosion of black strength within the Republican Party. Early in the present century, as a result of the attempt by the Populists to weld an alliance between white farmers and the black poor, Negroes were disfranchised through such measures as the poll tax and the white primary. Consequently formal participation by blacks was nonexistent until the 1940s, although pressure groups such as the NAACP and various local civic clubs provided money and encouragement for civil rights litigation.

Whites in Houston took the news of Negro enfranchisement in April, 1944, with relative calm. No racial incidents were recorded. Of the estimated 5,000 registered Negroes, about half voted in the July primary, compared with a third of the 158,000 registered whites in the county. In that year, although blacks constituted about 20 percent of the voting-age population, they made up only 5 percent of the electorate. Two years later the first steps were taken to integrate Negroes into the political structure. Black delegates were elected to attend the Democratic county convention. Others were deputized to "write poll tax" in the Negro wards. A few black precinct chairmen were elected from Negro wards.[3] These developments led to attempts by conservative Democrats to buy Negro votes. The Negro leadership, keenly aware of the dangers inherent in this practice, established the Harris County Council of Organizations, a loosely structured federation of Negro civic

---

E. Stokes, *Elections and the Political Order* (New York: John Wiley and Sons, 1966), 234.

3 Donald S. Strong, "The Rise of Negro Voting in Texas," *American Political Science Review*, XLII (1948), 513.

clubs whose intent was to discourage venality and to educate and mobilize the Negro electorate. The first tentative steps were taken toward an alliance between Negroes and "liberal-loyalists," so called because of their identification with the national Democratic Party rather than the state Bourbon machine, which often prefers Republican presidential candidates.

In the 1950s Negroes continued to strengthen their ties with the liberal faction, which by 1953 had formed an organization with the dual aims of fostering allegiance to the national party and providing support for liberal candidates at the state and county level. Numerous attempts were made to desegregate municipal facilities and obtain more and better jobs for Negroes in public employ. At the same time, the issue of school desegregation became a focal point of school board politics. A long struggle between segregationists and integrationists began that today continues to influence the nature of the city's racial crisis. This struggle was dramatized by the election of a Negro school teacher to the board in 1958—the first black elected to public office in Harris County since Reconstruction. Since then a handful of Negroes have held both elective and appointive positions in Houston and more than fifty have campaigned for office.

The confrontation tactics of the civil rights movement in the early 1960s were employed in Houston as they were throughout the South. The sit-ins led to significant desegregation of public facilities in downtown areas of the city. School boycotts and mass protests were less effective, and token integration of the public schools came about only after federal court order. Protest turned to violence in the summer of 1967 when rebellious students at Texas Southern University confronted several hundred policemen on the campus in a fracas growing out of a series of unconnected racial incidents. Sporadic gunfire was exchanged between the two groups, leading to the death of an officer. The source of the fatal bullet was never discovered. When the policemen broke into the men's dormitory from which gunfire had been issuing, they destroyed several thousand dollars worth of students' personal property. The failure of the mayor to discipline the police for this led to a growing hostility between city hall and the Negro community.[4]

As the decade waned, Negro political participation extended to new areas. Struggle for control of newly formed poverty agencies involved the efforts of many local groups, and sometimes pitted the older civil rights organizations against the new militants. Community action groups espousing the philosophy of black power were established in the ghetto areas. The mayoral race of 1969, which saw a liberal black legislator running against the white incumbent, reflected the new aspirations of Houston Negroes. Although the Negro lost, it marked the first time in twenty-five years of electoral participation that the city's top elective post was declared fair game for a black challenger.

We can now turn to an analysis of Negro voting in Houston. One of the most important indices of this type of activity is voter registration. Table 4.1 reveals that, as predicted, white registration rates have consistently been higher than those of Negroes.[5] More important, however, is the fact that in two decades since the death of the white primary, Negro registration has risen steadily, so that the gap of 41 percentage points in 1944 had narrowed to 15 by 1964.

An examination of the period from 1960 to 1967 suggests, moreover, that a comparison of rates during presidential election years is misleading, because the difference between Negro and white rates is greatest then. The gap narrows on congressional off-years

4 The most credible eyewitness account of the TSU incident, including the destruction of property and the treatment of students by policemen, is contained in an article by Reverend William Lawson, "A Second Look at the 'TSU Riots,'" *Forward Times*, May 27, 1967. An investigation after the incident is reported in Bill Helmer's "Nightmare in Houston," *Texas Observer*, June, 1967. Various estimates of the cost of the damage to student property have been given. One figure, mentioned by a former dean of students at TSU while testifying before the Senate permanent investigations subcommittee in November, 1967, was thirty thousand dollars. Houston *Post*, November 4, 1967. A detailed description of the damage done to students' personal effects is contained in the New York *Times*, May 18, 1967.

5 It should be borne in mind throughout this chapter that both registration and voting figures are estimates, based on aggregate statistics, and the most conservative estimates of Negro participation are consistently reported. Thus, the gap between whites and blacks is probably smaller in some cases than the figures indicate.

Table 4.1

Negro-White Voter Registration, Harris County, 1944–1967

Year	Total Registered		Whites Registered			Negroes Registered		
	Number		Number	As Percent of White Adults		Number	As Percent of Negro Adults	As Percent of all Registrants
1944	163,000		158,000	47%		5,000	6%	3.0%
1956	339,669		297,669	57		42,000	35	12.3
1958	311,131		265,131	48		46,000	36	14.7
1960	392,121		343,871	59		48,250	35	12.3
1961	339,813		286,520	47		53,293	37	15.6
1962	353,783		298,230	47		55,553	37	15.7
1963	354,443		296,065	46		58,378	38	16.4
1964	464,319		393,572	59		70,747	44	15.2
1965	334,710		273,547	39		61,163	36	18.2
1966	479,078		400,644	56		78,434	45	16.3
1967	503,600		418,047	57		85,553	47	16.9
AVERAGE 1956–67:				51.5			39.0	

and decreases still further on odd-numbered ones (Table 4.2). In short, Negro-white registration rate differences have decreased dramatically in the last two decades. In odd-numbered years there has been little difference at all, amounting to an average of 7.7 points since 1961. In 1965 there was a gap of only three points.

Table 4.2
AVERAGE NEGRO-WHITE REGISTRATION DIFFERENCE
BY TYPE OF YEAR, 1960–1967

Type of Election Year	Average Difference in Percentage Points
Presidential (1960, 1964)	19.5
Off-Year (1962, 1966)	10.5
Odd Year (1961, 1963, 1965, 1967)	7.7

Table 4.3 contains a number of indices of actual Negro-white voter turnout. Table 4.4 summarizes the data by type of election. Low voter turnout is a well-known characteristic of southern politics. In none of the elections analyzed, including the Johnson-Goldwater contest in 1964, did the total vote cast for a major office exceed 50 percent of the voting-age population. The Negro turnout rate was lower than that of whites. But the average racial difference between 1960 and 1966 was only 8.7 percentage points. As in the case of voter registration, the difference is decreasing rapidly —from 30 to 14 in presidential elections between 1952 and 1964 (Table 4.5).

Once again the gap is greatest in presidential elections. It is much smaller in primaries, averaging only 5.2 percentage points in the four May primaries between 1960 and 1966. There was only a two-point difference in the 1961 mayoral race. Negro and white rates are probably similar in school board races in which a popular Negro candidate runs, although in other elections the Negro vote drops.

Table 4.6 shows that the Negro turnout, as a percentage of the total vote, was 21.2 percent in 1962, when Mrs. Charles E. White, a popular black, was a candidate. The Negro proportion of the total voting-age population in the school district probably did not exceed 25 percent in this period.

Table 4.3

NEGRO AND WHITE VOTER TURNOUT, HOUSTON
AND HARRIS COUNTY, 1960–1966

Year and Election	As Percent of Voting-Age Population			As Percent of Registered Voters		
	White %	Negro %	Difference	White %	Negro %	Difference
1960						
Primaries[a]	25%	13%	12	42%	40%	2
President	48	27	21	81	77	4
School board	—	—	—	61	46	15
1961						
Municipal	18	16	2	40	40	0
1962						
Primaries	21	19	2	52	50	2
Governor[b]	29	21	8	63	56	7
School Board	—	—	—	43	47	−4
1963						
Municipal	—	—	—	50	53	−3
1964						
Primaries	25	20	5	43	46	−3
President	49	35	14	83	80	3
School Board	—	—	—	46	31	15
1965						
Municipal	—	—	—	46	43	3
1966						
Primaries	19	17	2	35	39	−4
Governor[b]	29	16	13	51	37	14
AVERAGE:	29.2	20.4	8.7	52.5	48.9	3.6

[a] There was no Republican primary in 1960. The figures for subsequent years include both primaries.
[b] General elections.

Table 4.4

AVERAGE DIFFERENCE IN TURNOUT RATES, BY TYPE OF ELECTION
HARRIS COUNTY, 1960–1966

Type of Election	Average Negro-White Difference
Presidential (1960, 1964)	17.5
Gubernatorial (1962, 1966)	10.5
Primaries (1960–66)	5.2
Mayoral (1961)	2.0
School Board	No Data

Table 4.5

NEGRO-WHITE TURNOUT FOR MAJOR PARTY PRESIDENTIAL
CANDIDATES, HARRIS COUNTY, 1952–1964

Year	Percentage of Voting-Age Population		Differences in Percentages
	White	Negro	
1952	51%	21%	30
1956	43	20	23
1960	48	27	21
1964	49	35	14
AVERAGE:	47.7%	25.7%	22.0

Negro-white turnout differences can also be measured in terms of the percentage of registrants who vote. In this case the racial disparity decreases even more. The average difference is only 3.6 percentage points for the fourteen elections in Table 4.3 above. Dan Nimmo analyzed the voting behavior of a random sample of registered voters in Harris County in 1964. He classified them ac-

Table 4.6

NEGRO PERCENTAGE OF TOTAL VOTES CAST IN
HOUSTON SCHOOL BOARD RACES

Year	Percentage
1960	12.1%
1962	21.2
1964	13.3

cording to how many of the three elections they voted in that year. Of the total sample of four thousand, Negroes comprised 15 percent. Yet of all persons sampled who voted in none of the elections, only 13 percent were Negro. And of those persons voting in all three—first and second primaries and the general elections—16 percent were Negro. In other words a disproportionately small percentage of Negro registrants were in the "lowest participation" category, and a disproportionately high percentage of Negroes were in the "highest participation" category. According to these measures, Negro registrants actually exhibited a higher degree of voter participation than whites in the presidential election year of 1964 (Table 4.7). Further, Table 4.3 shows that the qualified Negro electorate had a higher turnout than their white counterparts in four of the fourteen races analyzed. Of these four, two were party

Table 4.7

NEGRO-WHITE VOTER PARTICIPATION, RANDOM SAMPLE OF
4,000 REGISTRANTS, HARRIS COUNTY, 1964

Race	Registrants as Percentage of Sample	Percent of Sample Voting in No Elections in 1964	Percent of Sample Voting in All Three Elections in 1964
Negro	15.42%	13.25%	16.13%
White	84.58	86.75	83.87
Total	100.00	100.00	100.00

Source: Dan Nimmo, "Comparison of the Potential, Qualified, and Actual Electorates in Harris County, 1964" (Department of Political Science, University of Houston; unpublished tabulations).

primaries, one was a school board contest, and one a municipal election. Significantly there were Negro candidates in all four.

It is clear that if the adults of the two races are compared, the whites have a higher average turnout rate. However, in each of these voting-age populations there exists a smaller set of participants who constitute the registered electorate. The white group consists of a larger proportion of the white voting-age population than does the group in the Negro community, but the difference is decreasing. Negro registrants are on the average almost as active as whites and sometimes turn out in larger proportions. The number of white registrants who vote fluctuates greatly in a four-year period. The number of the Negro registrants is more stable and has increased steadily since 1960. In the interim between presidential election years, a large number of inactive whites do not bother to register. They usually do not vote even in the presidential year primaries, but only in the November election. It is this pool of occasional voters in the white community that contributes to the disparity between Negro and white rates. The Negro "regulars" have no such reinforcements.

To summarize: Negro participation rates, conservatively estimated, are not far behind those of whites, and the difference between the two has steadily decreased. If the fact that only 20 percent of all adult Negroes voted in the 1964 May primaries constitutes grounds for scandal, so does the fact that only 25 percent of the whites did. Considering the importance of socioeconomic factors in determining electoral participation, the small difference between Negro and white rates is surprising. In 1959 the median income of white families in Harris County was more than $6,100. That of Negro families was $3,386, or only 55 percent as much.[6] Yet the average Negro registration rate between 1956 and 1967 was three-quarters as great as that of whites. The average Negro turnout rate in the nine races analyzed between 1960 and 1966 was 70 percent that of whites. If Negroes and whites at the same income levels had

6 United States Bureau of the Census, *U.S. Census of the Population: 1960, General Social and Economic Characteristics, Texas,* Final Report PC(1)–45C (Washington, D.C.: United Stated Government Printing Office, 1962).

been compared, Negroes would probably have been found to participate at equal or greater rates.[7]

However, a marksman is not measured solely by the number of rounds per minute he can fire. Nor is the effective use of the ballot determined by the proportion of voters an ethnic group can muster. In theory Negroes could vote in great numbers without voting intelligently. An examination of partisan and factional voting preferences reveals a number of surprising facts—surprising, at any rate, to those who hold the popular myth about Negro confusion at the ballot box. The preference of blacks for the national Democratic Party has been an established fact for many years. In Texas there was deep disenchantment with the Republicans even before Roosevelt's election in 1932.[8] Harris County Negroes have conformed to this pattern (Table 4.8) and have in fact given greater support to the Democrats than have Negroes at the national level (Table 4.9).

Harris County Negroes' support for the Democrats in these four elections averaged 11.5 points higher than the Negro support nationally. Moreover this strong preference is remarkable even in comparison with other southern cities (Table 4.10).

One reason for this high degree of Democratic presidential support in Houston may be the virtual absence of an established Negro social aristocracy based on the inherited wealth of two or three generations, such as that in New Orleans, Atlanta, Durham, Chi-

7 See Donald R. Matthews and James W. Prothro, *Negroes and the New Southern Politics* (New York: Harcourt, Brace and World, 1966), 89. "A vast majority of Negroes at the lowest income levels appear to be frozen completely out of southern political life. But those with reasonably decent family incomes— $4,000 or above—get into southern politics as voters in proportions as great as do whites, and as political activists in greater proportions than do whites." The authors find, (p. 90), that if occupational status and educational attainment, as well as income, are held constant, the participation gap between the races is further reduced. Bradbury Seasholes, in his study of Winston-Salem and Durham, concludes that Negroes and whites in the same income category participate at almost the same rate. See Seasholes, "Negro Political Participation in Two North Carolina Cities" (Ph.D. dissertation, University of North Carolina, 1962), 74–77. Similar findings for northern Negroes are reported by Anthony Orum, "A Reappraisal of the Social and Political Participation of Negroes," *American Journal of Sociology,* LXXII (1966), 40.

8 Melvin James Banks, "The Pursuit of Equality: The Movement for First Class Citizenship Among Negroes in Texas, 1920–1950" (Ph.D. dissertation, Syracuse University, 1962), 201.

Table 4.8

NEGRO-WHITE SUPPORT FOR DEMOCRATIC PARTY
HARRIS COUNTY, 1952–1964

Year	Percentage of White Voters	Percentage of Negro Voters	Difference
1952	42%	94%	52
1956	38	66	28
1960	47	86	39
1964	60	99	39

Table 4.9

NEGRO SUPPORT FOR THE DEMOCRATIC TICKET
NATIONALLY AND IN HARRIS COUNTY, 1952–1964

	1952	1956	1960	1964
Harris County	94%	66%	86%	99%
United States	79	61	68	94

cago, and other older cities. Another reason may be the alliance between white liberal Democrats and Negroes in the city and state, and the almost total absence of Texas Republicans who have expressed any sympathy with Negro aspirations. In the northern cities, liberal Republicanism exists. In most southern cities, organized white racial-economic liberalism is minimal. Houston has differed in these respects from both northern and other southern cities.

When the Harris County Negro presidential vote is compared with that of whites, the difference is striking. Table 4.8 shows that the majority of whites usually vote Republican. Although the Negro Democratic vote was not large enough to swing the county from the Republican to the Democratic column in any of the analyzed presidential elections, the high degree of unity among Negroes increased the magnitude of the role they played in supporting Democratic candidates. Whereas they constituted 15 percent or less of the total presidential turnout, they amounted to about a third of the Democrats' total support, when the white vote split down the middle.

Table 4.10

NEGRO PERCENTAGE VOTING FOR EISENHOWER IN
SELECTED SOUTHERN CITIES, 1952–1956

City	Percent for Eisenhower	
	1952	1956
Atlanta, Ga.	30.9%	85.3%
Charlotte, N.C.	16.3	38.5
Chattanooga, Tenn.	20.5	49.3
HOUSTON, TEXAS[a]	10.5	34.8
Jacksonville, Fla.	15.7	40.9
Knoxville, Tenn.	29.7	40.9
Memphis, Tenn.	34.4	54.0
New Orleans, La.	20.2	55.1
Richmond, Va.	21.9	73.0

[a] The 1952 figure, calculated by Moon, is about four points higher than the one in Table 4.8, which is based on this author's calculations.

Sources: Henry Lee Moon, "The Negro Vote in the Presidential Election of 1956," *Journal of Negro Education*, XXVI (1957), 224. Cited in James Q. Wilson, "The Negro in American Politics: The Present," in John P. Davis (ed.), *The American Negro Reference Book* (Englewood Cliffs: Prentice-Hall, 1966), 441.

Table 4.11 demonstrates that the preference of Harris County Negroes for the Democratic candidate holds true in recent gubernatorial elections as well. No candidate for governor on the Democratic ticket received less than 88 percent of the Negro vote in Harris County. In part this is a function of the Negro's tendency to vote the straight ticket. It is important to note that even when the Democratic candidate in the general election was an economic and racial conservative, he received the Negro bloc vote. This was the case with both Price Daniel and his three-term successor, John Connally. In the May Democratic primaries held in the four election years under examination, the majority of the Negro vote went to liberal opponents of Daniel and Connally. But in November the conservative Democratic candidates could count on a large Negro majority and (with the exception of 1966) a sizable Negro turnout as well. Price Daniel as a senator had signed the Southern Manifesto. Connally, in the summer of 1963 on statewide television, denounced in vigorous terms President Kennedy's civil rights bill then pending in Congress.

Table 4.11
GUBERNATORIAL TWO-PARTY VOTE BY RACE
HARRIS COUNTY, 1960–1966

Year and Party	Percent of Two-Party Vote	
	Whites	Negroes
1960		
Democrat	65%	88%
Republican	35	12
1962		
Democrat	42	95
Republican	58	5
1964		
Democrat	64	99
Republican	36	1
1966		
Democrat	65	97
Republican	35	3

This does not necessarily reflect confusion among Negro voters. Without exception, the Republican gubernatorial candidates pitted against the Democratic conservatives in the above four elections offered Negroes no alternatives. The liberal wing of Texas Republicanism is almost nonexistent, and the dominant elements in the party have hewed to an ultraconservative line which is sometimes to the right of the Democratic conservatives. Houston blacks, like many of their race throughout the South today, are often faced with a choice between Bourbon Democrats and rock-ribbed Republicans, indistinguishable in their political philosophies. But even in this situation—a travesty of the pluralist electoral model—many Negroes are sensitive to subtle distinctions between the Tweedle Dees and the Tweedle Dums.

The congressional race of Republican George Bush in 1966 provides an illustration of shifts in the Negro vote that even hairbreadth differences between candidates produce. Bush, an oil millionaire, had unsuccessfully challenged liberal incumbent Ralph Yarborough in the 1964 United States Senate race. His opponent in 1966 was Frank Briscoe, a conservative Democrat who had left his post as district attorney to run in the newly created Seventh District, one of the wealthier ones in Texas. It had a Negro population of 15 percent. Neither Bush nor Briscoe was a racial liberal, but Bush's image, as it came over in the mass media, was slightly less conservative than his opponent's. Both were strongly opposed to the open-housing section of the 1966 civil rights bill, as well as to the newly created poverty program. They both made "rioting and lawlessness" one of the main issues. In his 1964 campaign Bush had attacked Senator Yarborough's vote for the Civil Rights Act of that year, and was a supporter of Goldwater. Briscoe was widely perceived in the Negro community as having taken a personal interest in bringing criminal indictments against a black school board trustee.

Nonetheless, Bush made subtle appeals to the Negroes that his opponent did not. Since his defeat in 1964 he had attended Negro political and social functions, getting his picture in the Negro newspapers—a distinct departure from the Texas conservative tradition. The *Congressional Quarterly* said he "took a substantially more liberal stand than his opponent by promising 'to work with the Negro and white leadership to root out the causes' of civil disturbances and rioting. At another point, Bush said, 'I think the day is past when we can afford to have a lily-white district. I will not appeal to the white backlash.'"[9] Briscoe, on the contrary, attempted to make an issue out of the fact that Bush had once sponsored a Negro girls' softball team. He accused Bush of "appealing to the Negro bloc."

As the campaign neared its climax, the Negro newspaper, *Forward Times*, which two years previously had lambasted Bush in his race

9 *Congressional Quarterly*, December 2, 1966, p. 2947.

against Yarborough, endorsed him in glowing terms. ("Measured by any standard, [he] is one of the finest young men in the nation . . . a fine and upright gentleman.") Several Negroes, Republicans and Democrats, worked hard to get out the black vote for Bush. He beat Briscoe by a landslide of 53,756 to 39,958. However, the hoped-for Negro defections from the Democratic candidate did not fully materialize, as Table 4.12 confirms.

Table 4.12

BIRACIAL VOTE IN BRISCOE-BUSH RACE
SEVENTH CONGRESSIONAL DISTRICT, 1966

	White		Negro	
Candidate	Number of Votes	As Percent of 2-Party Vote	Number of Votes	As Percent of 2-Party Vote
Briscoe (D)	36,562	41%	3,396	66%
Bush (R)	51,985	59	1,771	34

While 59 percent of the white voters in the district supported Bush, only 34 percent of the Negroes did. But, if one measures Briscoe's Negro support against that of the Democratic gubernatorial and senatorial candidates in the Negro precincts of the Seventh District, Bush fared well (Table 4.13). Connally and Carr both received at least 90 percent of the Negro vote in the district. Both men, moreover, were racial and economic conservatives who had made minimal appeals to the Negro voters. But in their case there was no appreciable difference between their own position on the race issue and that of their Republican opponents. This suggests that a Republican who is perceived to be less conservative racially than his Democratic opponent stands a good chance of carving out a large slice of the Negro vote. If a Republican who was clearly liberal on race issues were to run against a conservative Democrat, he could undoubtedly make even stronger inroads into the Negro electorate.[10]

10 Negroes in Arkansas, for example, gave overwhelming support to Republican Winthrop Rockefeller in his campaigns against race-baiting Democrats.

Table 4.13

NEGRO SUPPORT FOR THREE CONSERVATIVE DEMOCRATS
SEVENTH CONGRESSIONAL DISTRICT, NOVEMBER, 1966

Candidates	Percent of Negro Vote
Connally (Governor)	95%
Carr (Senate)	90
Briscoe (Congress)	66

The discipline and perceptiveness of the Negro electorate can also be measured by analyzing their preferences in factional conflicts within the Democratic Party. These conflicts, between liberals and conservatives, have assumed major dimensions since the rise of Negro voting in the 1940s. Actually it is helpful to think of three "factions" in Harris County politics: liberal Democrats, conservative Democrats, and Republicans. Often the same persons belong to the two latter groups. There is no law against crossover voting in Texas, and it is common practice for conservatives to vote in the Democratic primary in the spring, and to vote for Republican candidates—especially presidential ones—in the fall. Although there are of course borderline cases, it is usually possible to distinguish the "liberal" candidate by whether or not he receives the support of the liberal coalition's organization, Harris County Democrats. Especially when this group provides enthusiastic support, the candidate will be more or less sympathetic to organized labor and Negroes. In any Democratic primary, many voters in the county, with the aid of the mass media, can correctly identify the major candidates as either liberal, conservative, or middle-of-the-road. The white liberal candidates in recent years have been careful to ask for the support of Negro political leaders, and they usually are invited to speak in Negro churches and at rallies in Negro precincts. If possible they secure the endorsement of the Harris County Council of Organizations, the Negro screening group. Ideally they are introduced to

Negro gatherings by a popular Negro candidate or elected official.

In order to determine what kind of support Negroes give to white liberals opposed by conservatives in the Democratic primaries, several races are examined in which major offices were at stake, and the factional issues were extraordinarily clear cut. All candidates were running county-wide, and the liberals were endorsed by Harris County Democrats. The pattern of Negro support is seen in Table 4.14. In no contest did liberals receive less than 53.9 percent of the Negro vote. The highest percentage, 89.5, was received by Senator Yarborough in 1964. The average support was 74.5 percent.

Despite this impressive evidence of Negro solidarity in factional politics, some disgruntled white liberals have charged the Negro

Table 4.14

NEGRO SUPPORT FOR WHITE LIBERAL CANDIDATES,
DEMOCRATIC PRIMARIES, SELECTED RACES, HARRIS
COUNTY, 1960–1966

Year	Candidate	Percentage of Negro Votes	Negro Percent of Total Turnout in Race	Percent of Liberal's Total Vote Received from Negro Precincts[a]
1960	Eckhardt	87.4%	9.1%	13.4%
1960	Kilgarlin	80.4	8.7	16.2
1962	D. Yarborough	68.0	16.3	30.6
1962	D. Yarborough (*runoff*)	65.7	15.7	18.8
1964	R. Yarborough	89.5	15.6	24.2
1964	D. Yarborough	61.0	16.4	27.2
1966	Spears	76.9	No data	No data
1966	Spears (*runoff*)	88.0	16.8	29.0
1966	Woods	53.9	17.2	29.8
AVERAGE:		74.5%	14.4%	23.6%

[a] In 1960 Negroes comprised 18.8 percent of the county's adult population.

voter with "roll-off" voting—the practice, more pronounced among low-income participants, of voting in the most important races at the top of the ballot and leaving the rest of the ballot blank.[11] A controversy on this issue has led occasionally to serious strains within the liberal coalition. Negroes complained in 1962 and 1964 that organized labor had not contributed a substantial bloc of voters to the Negro legislative candidate, Barbara Jordan. Some liberals, on the other hand, claimed that Negroes voted for Miss Jordan, but ignored races in which a white liberal opposed a conservative.

The results of the May Democratic primary in 1966 shed light on this question. Negro support for the two black legislative candidates is compared with their support for eight white liberals running for fairly important offices. All ten candidates had the backing of the liberal coalition. As Table 4.15 shows, a greater proportion of registered Negroes turned out for Miss Jordan's race. Of those Negroes voting, moreover, a higher percentage voted for her than for any other candidate listed in the table. At the other extreme, only 32 percent of the qualified Negroes in the county voted in the gubernatorial race, and of those, only 54 percent supported the liberal candidate, Woods.[12] Thus, only 17 percent of the county's registered Negroes supported him. These two cases, however, represent extremes. Kilgarlin, a white congressional candidate running against a racially conservative incumbent, ranked second after Jordan, receiving 32 percent of the registered Negro vote. This was a larger proportion than Graves, the other Negro candidate, received.

Table 4.15 demonstrates clearly that Negroes did not ignore white liberals on the same ballot with Negro candidates. But more than this, Negro candidates were not even assured a higher degree of

11 There are some grounds for believing that Negroes do tend to vote more regularly in races at the head of the ballot and to ignore lesser ones. This is not necessarily irrational or a sign of apathy, for it often happens that these minor contests do not offer Negroes (or any voters) a significant choice.

12 One reason for this low support may be that his campaign was considered to be largely symbolic. No seasoned observer gave him a ghost of a chance against the extremely popular incumbent, Connally. Some Negro respondents told the author that they perceived a greater benefit to be gained from Negroes' backing the winner, of whatever political stripe, than a sure loser, however commendable his racial views.

Table 4.15

NEGRO SUPPORT FOR NEGRO AND WHITE LIBERAL CANDIDATES
FIRST DEMOCRATIC PRIMARY, SELECTED RACES, HARRIS COUNTY, 1966

Candidate (Negroes' names in italics)	Office	Number of Opponents	Percent of Registered Negroes Voting in Race	Percent Voting who Supported Negro or Liberal
Jordan	State Senator	1	42%	98%
Brooks	State Senator	1	27	84
Spears[a]	Attorney General	2	23	77
Woods	Governor	2	32	54
Kilgarlin	Congressman	1	34	95
Eckhardt	Congressman	2	34	67
Graves	State Representative	2	29	92
Cruz	" "	4	28	80
Allen	" "	1	25	83
Williams	" "	2	25	81

[a] Returns from three Negro precincts are missing in this race; thus, the above figures in Spears's race are slightly low.

support than white liberals. It is true that the average Negro support for the black candidates was greater than that for the white liberals. But it should be remembered that both Graves and Jordan were also economic liberals. They were also outspoken advocates of civil rights—more so than any of the white candidates. Both had campaigned hard in Negro precincts. Jordan, who had run unsuccessfully twice before, had attended innumerable teas, picnics, and other social gatherings, and was a sought-after speaker. Graves had led well-publicized civil rights protests.

A popular, relatively militant Negro candidate will probably fare somewhat better in the black precincts than a white liberal, running in the same constituency for an office of roughly equal importance. But in every case in Table 4.15 for which data were available, the Negro percentage of the liberals' total support was disproportionately high, when compared to the proportion of Negroes in the adult population.

The relevance of the statistics presented in this chapter to pluralist theory is considerable. They indicate, first of all, that Negroes have voted at only slightly lower rates than whites in recent years, and in several elections black participation was probably higher than that of whites of similar social position. Their lower income, education, length of time in the city, and social status make the performance of blacks in Houston in the 1960s truly remarkable. According to pluralist theory, they have successfully met the first criterion of electoral efficacy. By overcoming the numerous difficulties that confront a severely disadvantaged minority, they have come close to rivaling whites in voter turnout.

How can we square this fact with the tendency among so many observers of Houston politics to play down the extent of Negro participation? Robert Blauner's concept of "neo-racism" is helpful here. "Where conventional racism is expressed in brutalities (lynching, police harrassment) and in outright exclusion," Blauner writes, "neo-racism 'includes' black people only when they meet standards that are not applied to whites."[13] In the Houston case, those who minimize Negro voter participation tend to measure Negro turnout as a percentage of the Negro population, without comparing it to white turnout.

Even more important than voting rates, however, is the sophistication of the Negro electorate. During the 1940s and 1950s, numerous voting studies emphasized the irrationality of the electorate and of the lower income groups in particular. In recent years a critical reevaluation has occurred. The late V. O. Key, in *The Responsible Electorate*, concluded that "voters are not fools." He wrote: "To be sure, many individual voters act in odd ways indeed; yet in the

13 Robert Blauner, "Black Culture: Lower-Class Result or Ethnic Creation?" in Lee Rainwater (ed.), *Soul* (Chicago: Aldine-Atherton, Inc.; Transaction Books, 1970), 163.

large the electorate behaves about as rationally and responsibly as we should expect, *given the clarity of the alternatives presented to it and the character of the information available to it.*"[14]

Analysts of voting behavior sometimes overlook the fact that alternatives frequently are not presented to the voters—that candidates outdo each other in keeping information about public policy from them. The congressional race between Republican George Bush and his Democratic opponent is a case in point. The blacks in the district had only the subtlest clues to go on. They were faced with two avowed racial and economic conservatives. And yet, because the Democrat openly resorted to race baiting and the Republican refused, a third of the Negro voters split their ticket between a Democratic governor and a Republican congressman.

Such elections are commonplace in Houston. Opponents in the Democratic primaries are often indistinguishable in their political views. Even candidates who run on the liberal slate do not always stress their differences with opponents. The very fact that the politics of Texas is still predominantly one-party adds to the blurring of issues. The wealthy, conservative wing of the party has an interest in muting economic issues that, if brought to the surface, would polarize the majority of the electorate against them. Therefore, especially in the races for the most important offices such as senator, governor, lieutenant governor, or attorney general, the conservatives, who have a great deal more money for campaign publicity at their disposal than the liberals, concentrate on personality, "image," "statesmanship," and similar nonissues. At the municipal level, other forces are at work to obscure candidate differences. The elections are nonpartisan and debates on important issues rarely occur.

For this reason, the fact that Negroes, relatively low in education, should perform with such skill in electoral politics, is of especial significance. One is reminded of Myrdal's observation concerning northern Negroes more than two decades ago, that "most Negro voters are more keenly aware of a candidate's attitude toward their

14 V. O. Key, Jr., *The Responsible Electorate: Rationality in Presidential Voting, 1936–1960* (New York: Random House, Inc., 1966), 7. Italics added.

group than are most other Americans." [15] Here again an explanation is required for the oft-voiced belief that southern Negroes are unsophisticated voters. Surely one reason is that many southern whites still cling to a racist stereotype of the Negro as stupid, whether in the realm of politics or in everyday life. But this is not the only reason. Many well-meaning whites probably rationalize the lack of Negro success in getting their share of political rewards. From the pluralist assumption that the vote is an important weapon in assimilation, they conclude that if the Negro is still excluded, he must not have made good use of the vote.

There is no denying the fact that many Negroes (and whites) of voting age in Houston and throughout the South are politically unsophisticated. But, the Houston case suggests that as Negroes become incorporated into the actual electorate, they rapidly acquire the ability to perceive their group's own interests and to choose between candidates accordingly. In examining the Negro electorate, and leaving the nonvoters aside, it becomes obvious that the differences in sophistication between blacks and whites are minimal. Further, southern Negro voting behavior in the few short years since the 1965 Voting Rights Act was passed strongly suggests that this observation is true throughout the South. If it can be shown that Negro gains in Houston during the 1960s were quite limited, the role in political assimilation assigned to the vote by pluralist theory must be seriously doubted.

15 Gunnar Myrdal, *An American Dilemma: The Negro Problem and American Democracy* (1944; 20th anniv. ed.; New York: Harper & Row, Publ., 1962), 497.

V

The Rewards

An adequate description of a group's struggle for political assimilation includes not only an account of its participation, but a tally of the resultant benefits. So far we have seen that Houston blacks, despite tremendous difficulties, have managed to establish numerous politically instrumental organizations, and to take part in the electoral life of the city at about the same rate and certainly with as much sophistication as whites. What, then, have been the results?

There is a strain of pluralist thought that tends to minimize this question. Robert Dahl, for example, in his study of New Haven politics, seldom raises directly the question of who benefits, although he attempts to answer the question of who governs. "What follows," he writes prior to examining the politics of urban redevelopment, ". . . is not an appraisal of the desirability of the program but an attempt to understand the political forces that shaped it. *Whether the program is eventually judged a brilliant effort or a ghastly mistake is irrelevant to the purposes of this book.*"[1]

This simply will not do. The question of who governs—who participates and how—is in part a question of who benefits, as Dahl himself recognizes elsewhere in his book, when he mentions that the material benefits of urban redevelopment accrued to "downtown property owners and construction contractors,"[2] while small businessmen and "several hundred slum dwellers without much

1 Robert A. Dahl, *Who Governs? Democracy and Power in an American City* (New Haven: Yale University Press, 1961), 115n. Italics added.
2 *Ibid.*, 60.

political influence" were hurt by it.[3] Yet these costs and benefits within the New Haven political system are mentioned only in passing and clearly are of minor significance for Dahl. The pluralist school has quite deliberately shifted the study of politics away from the question (as Harold Lasswell put it), of "who gets what, when, and how," to that of who participates.

It would be incorrect to portray the pluralists as having totally ignored the problem of benefits. Rather, in the spirit of the conservative retrenchment of the 1950s, they redefined political benefits (at least those of ordinary people) in an exceedingly narrow manner. This is evident when Dahl describes the position of New Haven Negroes. "In contrast to the situation the Negro faces in the private socioeconomic sphere, in local politics and government the barriers are comparatively slight," he states. In comparison with whites, "Negroes find no greater obstacles to achieving their goals through political action."[4] He mentions as examples of goals or benefits appropriate to political activity, freedom to vote, the right to municipal employment ("they have only to meet the qualifica-

3 *Ibid.*, 244.
4 *Ibid.*, 294. Dahl has since changed his mind about the situation of blacks. In 1967 he wrote:

> There is above all the question that now overshadows all else in American life of how we shall solve the problems presented by race, poverty, inequality, discrimination, and centuries of humiliation. No failure in American society has been as enduring, as profound, as visible, as corrosive, as dangerous, and as tragic as our refusal to enable black Americans to share in equal measure with white Americans the realities of the American dream. Now this problem has become central to the whole future of our cities and indeed to the future of the country. I scarcely need to say that unless and until it is solved neither we nor our children nor our grandchildren nor any future generation can have anything like a decent urban life.

Dahl, "The City and the Future of Democracy," *American Political Science Review*, LXI (1967), 968-69. This was written the same year blacks rioted in New Haven. According to one supplemental study for the so-called "riot reports," New Haven, of six cities hit by Negro riots in 1967 which were studied, had by far the highest percentage of Negro residents who participated in the riot. Of an estimated 3,100 "potential rioters"—Negroes in the riot area in age categories which are most likely to supply participants—an estimated 1,800, or 35 percent, took part. This was far higher than the percentage in Detroit (11) or Newark (15). See Robert M. Fogelson and Robert B. Hill, "Who Riots? A Study of Participation in 1967 Riots," in *Supplemental Studies for the National Advisory Commission on Civil Disorders* (New York: Frederick A. Praeger, Inc., 1968), 231.

tions required of white applicants"), and the right to share in city patronage, city contracts, and "other favors."[5] The implication is that this pretty much exhausts the benefits which Dahl thinks Negroes (or other groups) have a right to expect from politics. If downtown banking and commercial interests profit handsomely from the mayor's urban redevelopment plan and a few hundred slum dwellers and small businessmen pay a rather high price, this is of concern only if one is interested in studying the "private socioeconomic sphere." It is of no moment to the political scientist concerned with the "political" sphere of municipal employment, voting rights, and city patronage.[6]

When politics is defined so narrowly and the nature of the benefits appropriate to political participation so limited, it is easy to judge Negro politics a success, as Dahl does. One of the most significant aspects of the Negro struggle in the 1960s, nevertheless, was an attempt by civil rights leaders to reestablish the older conception of the political sphere that includes a broad range of socioeconomic benefits as appropriate goals—the sort of benefits that the conservative wing of political science prefers to relegate to the "private" sector.

In fact the growing hostility toward the Negro movement exhibited by many erstwhile supporters results from the decidedly more inclusive definition of political goals that even such a moderate civil rights leader as Martin Luther King was advocating by the mid-sixties. In his book *Why We Can't Wait*, written in 1963, King was insistent on this broader conception of politics: "The Negro today is not struggling for some abstract, vague rights, but for the concrete and prompt improvement in his way of life. . . .

5 Dahl, *Who Governs?* 294.
6 Peter Bachrach has pointed out that Dahl defines politics quite broadly in his general treatise on political science, as "any persistent pattern of human relationships that involves, to a significant extent, power, rule, or authority." (See Dahl, *Modern Political Analysis* [Englewood Cliffs: Prentice Hall, Inc., 1963], 6.) Nevertheless, Bachrach argues, when Dahl focuses on political elites, politics is contextually defined much more narrowly to include "either decisions relating to the control of political parties or government decisions on such issues as urban redevelopment, public education, taxation, expenditures, and the like." Bachrach criticizes this narrow conception of politics in his book, *The Theory of Democratic Elitism* (Boston: Little, Brown, and Co., 1967), 72–82.

Negroes must not only have the right to go into any establishment open to the public, but they must also be absorbed into our economic system in such a manner that they can afford to exercise that right."[7]

Lest he be construed as simply demanding the assimilation of the black bourgeoisie into the political system of the white bourgeoisie, King went on to call for a "bill of rights for the disadvantaged," measures to bring about full employment, the radical expansion of work opportunities, and a revision of the welfare laws, for both blacks and whites. He was committed to the struggle for the Negro franchise in the South precisely because he saw this as a means to these socioeconomic ends. "Consciously and creatively developed," he wrote, "political power may well, in the days to come, be the most effective new tool of the Negro's liberation."[8] Nor could this liberation be achieved "by opening some doors to all, or all doors to some."[9]

Bayard Rustin, who with King organized the March on Washington in 1963, was to claim two years later that this goal of fundamental and rapid socioeconomic progress had come to prevail over the more limited, gradualistic approach. "The civil rights movement," Rustin wrote in a widely quoted article in *Commentary*, "is evolving from a protest movement into a full-fledged *social movement*—an evolution calling its very name into question. It is now concerned not merely with removing the barriers to full *opportunity* but with achieving the fact of *equality*. . . . I believe that the Negro's struggle for equality in America is essentially revolutionary."[10] To achieve the revolution, Rustin called for "radical programs for full employment, abolition of slums, the reconstruction of our educational system, new definitions of work and leisure."[11]

7 Martin Luther King, Jr., *Why We Can't Wait* (New York: Harper & Row, Publ., 1964), 148–49.

8 *Ibid.*, 167.

9 *Ibid.*, 141.

10 Bayard Rustin, "From Protest to Politics," in Irving Howe (ed.), *The Radical Papers* (New York: Doubleday & Co., Inc., Anchor Books), 352–53, 355. The italics are in the original. This article first appeared in *Commentary*, XXXIX (February, 1965), 25–31.

11 Rustin, "From Protest to Politics," 355–56.

However sharply Rustin's and King's conception of political benefits may clash with that of some pluralist writers, it is consistent with that of the wealthy, at least when they are considering the legitimate scope of their political benefits. The agribusinessman surely considers his huge annual government income for not growing crops an appropriate political reward. The top managers of any industry that receives government subsidies to stave off bankruptcy and insure them their large salaries no doubt view them as legitimate political benefits. The top 5 percent of the nation's income earners who have succeeded in pushing through tax avoidance laws to increase their earnings by billions of dollars annually count this as a political achievement. Real estate interests, savings and loan companies, and middle- and upper-income homeowners who have successfully pressured the government to direct most of its "public" housing subsidies to middle-income housing no doubt consider this a political triumph.

At the local level, the millions of dollars which flow from public coffers to large contractors, the millions which remain in the pockets of the better-off because of the prevalent regressive tax schedules of municipal, county, and state governments, the huge sums spent annually on highways which in a city like Houston often service the transportation needs of the advantaged at the expense of the disadvantaged—all these are benefits which have been extracted from the political system by the beneficiaries. These benefits are not illegal. They do not, generally speaking, involve corruption. They are not looked upon by their recipients as illegitimate gain. More to the point, these benefits accruing disproportionately to the most affluent are ordinarily viewed by the public at large as within that category of rewards which legitimately come through the exercise of political influence. (The public, nonetheless, may have doubts about the justice of their distribution.)

Yet when the political aspirations of racial and ethnic minorities and the poor are discussed, the claim is made that a guaranteed income, a decent job, a cheap and efficient transportation system, or easy access to good health care, while laudable goals to pursue, should be pursued in the "private socioeconomic sphere," for they are not appropriate political benefits. In plain language the oppressed and the disadvantaged should aspire to different political rewards than the rich.

The injustice of this double standard becomes all the more obvious when it is realized how the decisions made in the "private" sphere affect the life chances of blacks and other oppressed groups. The decision to locate or relocate a large industry in a city will have an immediate impact upon the employment rate, the chance that hundreds or even thousands of workers will have for jobs. The decision of a leading bank to increase the interest rates may preclude the possibility of home ownership for large numbers of families. The decision of physicians to direct their services toward affluent clients is a detriment to the health care of the less affluent.

Obviously if there is a dispute over what constitutes a "political" benefit—that is, over what can legitimately be achieved through political participation—any description of the benefits which accrue to a group such as Houston's Negroes will not be acceptable to everyone. For example, if the median family income of blacks relative to whites is used as one index of Negro political success (or lack thereof), some critics will claim that this statistic is irrelevant, as relative income is not a political reward but a "private" one. So too with occupational achievements, the rate of unemployment, or the level of health care.

The answer to these objections has already been given: most Americans, and especially those in the middle and upper classes, have long striven to improve their life chances through political influence. This was how the laws and institutions favoring the wealthy were put on the books. Therefore, it is only just that we apply the same criterion when judging the political benefits of those on the bottom rungs of the ladder. We can then turn to an account of how blacks in Houston have fared in recent years.

ELECTED OFFICIALS

An assessment of Negro political gains usually begins with an account of the success they have had in electing to office members of their own race or sympathetic whites. In Houston, for example, following legislative redistricting in 1965, ten of the county's nineteen state representatives were "moderate to liberal" and this has been interpreted as evidence that blacks are making progress.

The election of blacks or white liberals is in itself, however, of no significance—or at most, only of minimal import—and should not be confused with substantive political benefits. A politician with a liberal tag, or even a genuinely concerned liberal officeholder, is of no value to his black constituents if he cannot effectively represent their interests on governing bodies. Indeed a legislature composed entirely of liberals or blacks would be useless if it did not effect policies that bring social and economic benefits to the Negro community. Blacks in a legislative body may give Negro voters a twinge of vicarious pride, but their presence is no guarantee that jobs will be created for the black unemployed, that antidiscrimination laws will be enforced, or even that streets will be paved in black neighborhoods.[12] It may be true that at this juncture in American history, blacks are most likely to represent the black community's interests. But just being black is not enough. There are black politicians who are no more competent, honest, or effective than many of their white colleagues, and while they may benefit from the perquisites of office, their constituents do not.[13]

With this caveat in mind, one can tally up the gains in elected and appointed Negro officials very easily. In 1957 there were none. Today Houston's Barbara Jordan is the only black in the state senate, and as a result of redistricting in 1971, she will probably become the state's (and the South's) first black congressional representa-

12 Raymond Wolfinger, writing of ethnic politics in turn-of-the-century New Haven, observes that "the tangible political rewards to the new immigrants from 'bosses' were limited.... But when one Italian was appointed to a public position his success was enjoyed vicariously by other Italians; it was 'recognition' of the worth of Italians. Ethnic solidarity let politicians economize on the indulgences they bestowed." In other words, election to office of "one of their own" was a substitute for actual political rewards. See Wolfinger, "The Development and Persistence of Ethnic Voting," *American Political Science Review*, LIX (1965), 898.

13 Former Congressman Dawson of Chicago was an excellent example of a black politician whose election to office did not benefit the black community.

tive. Houston's Curtis Graves is one of three blacks in the one-hundred-fifty-member house of representatives. Of the seven-member board of trustees for the Houston Independent School District, two are black. One of the eight city councilmen but none of the five-man county commissioners court is Negro. One black has so far been appointed to a part-time municipal court judgeship, another to a domestic relations court, and a third to a hospital district board. These, then, are the Negroes in Harris County who are prominent public officials.

INCOME

For Negroes in the Houston standard metropolitan statistical area (SMSA), income rose between 1949 and 1959. In 1949 the median money income for nonwhite families and unrelated individuals was $1,606. In 1959 it was $2,793. These figures do not represent real income, adjusted for the rise in the cost of living during the decade, and hence the increase would be less when adjusted for price changes. Also the nonwhite income as percentage of the total (white and nonwhite) dropped in this time period from 56.9 percent to 52.6 percent, although the percentage of nonwhite income earners remained constant at about 19 percent of the total. If the 1959 median income of all white persons with income in the SMSA is compared with that of Negroes, the Negro income is only 45.6 percent as great.

These figures, of course, do not include the decade of the 1960s. One could argue that the results of the civil rights movement during that period are only now beginning to be felt and that the 1970 census will tell a different story. Nationally the income of Negroes as a percentage of whites rose a few points in the1960's. It had remained fairly constant between 1950 and 1965. It jumped from 54 percent in 1965 to 60 percent in 1968.[14] But there is reason to doubt

14 United States Department of Labor, *The Social and Economic Status of Negroes in the United States, 1969*, Bureau of Labor Statistics Report No. 375 (Washington, D.C.: United States Government Printing Office), 14.

that this jump, at the time the Vietnam war began to heat up, was a result of civil rights progress and thus permanent.

Evidence suggests that war-induced economic booms may have more impact upon many Negro life chances than civil rights legislation now on the books. World War I and the subsequent boom led to a mass migration of blacks from the farm and into better-paying factory jobs—gains destroyed by the depression a few years later.[15] In the 1940s World War II and the postwar boom once more paid off handsomely for blacks, especially when combined with federal "fair employment" action. A few years later, the median family income of Negroes, which had been 40 percent or less of the white median prior to World War II, rose above 50 percent of the white median at the peak of the Korean war boom. The downturn in Negro relative income and employment in the last half of the fifties has been attributed to the sluggish economy. "It was not until 1966, when the Vietnam buildup and accompanying capital-goods boom brought the economy to full employment," Charles Silberman writes, "that Negroes were able to recapture the relative position they had enjoyed in 1952."[16] Thus in 1968, before the effects of the Vietnam "winding down" began to be felt, black median family income relative to whites had reached its highest peak in the century—60 percent. But by 1970, with the recession under way, it had begun to level off. Blacks (and of course other groups not in as serious trouble) continue to be the victims of an economy that remains insensitive to their needs.

Even if one accepts the questionable assumption that the gain in relative Negro income is permanent, there is a certain wry humor in the exultation many commentators have expressed over the mean annual increase of half a percentage point between 1950 and 1968

15 Charles Silberman, "Negro Economic Gains—Impressive But Precarious," *Fortune*, LXXXI (July, 1970), 77. Silberman does not rule out the influence of political decisions, but he accords importance to the fluctuation of the economy as an independent cause. The link between general economic prosperity among blacks and a tight labor market is argued by James Tobin, "On Improving the Economic Status of the Negro," in Talcott Parsons and Kenneth Clark (eds.), *The Negro American* (Boston: Houghton-Mifflin Co., 1966), 452–57.

16 Silberman, "Negro Economic Gains," 77.

in the Negro family's income relative to whites. At that rate racial parity in incomes is still more than seventy years away. Also it is necessary to remember that the ratio of Negro income to white in the South—where the majority of blacks still live—is smaller than in the nation as a whole. Whereas it was 60 percent for the nation in 1968, it was only 54 percent that of whites in the South, having edged up from 49 percent in 1965.

Finally there is the question of how evenly Negro income gains have been distributed among blacks. Andrew Brimmer has pointed out that the over-all gains deflect attention from some startling backslides. He described as "extremely disturbing" the fact that between 1959 and 1968 the number of nonwhites (largely Negroes) in female-headed families below the poverty line increased by 24 percent. Commenting on the over-all relative gains in income among Negroes during the decade, Dr. Brimmer argued that as blacks had larger families, on the average, than whites, per capita income figures were more meaningful for comparative purposes. On this basis Negro income as a percentage of white income increased from 45 percent in 1959 to 51 in 1967.[17]

In Houston the continuing plight of perhaps half of the Negro population was revealed by a survey of households in 1969 in several central-city poverty areas. The Department of Labor reported that even though Negro workers in these areas had completed more education than their white counterparts, greater proportions of whites held the more desirable jobs. Nearly a third of all full-time workers, white and black, earned less than $65 a week, which is about the equivalent of the $1.60 federal minimum wage for forty hours. The percentage was somewhat higher for blacks, who were overrepresented in the sample; only about 20 percent of the whites were in this extremely depressed wage category. Average weekly earnings for all races in the areas were $83.[18]

17 New York *Times*, March 22, 1970.
18 Houston *Post*, February 17, 1970. Based on a Bureau of Labor Statistics Report on the Houston Urban Employment Survey, in the summer of 1969. The survey was conducted in Houston central-city Concentrated Employment Program target areas.

EMPLOYMENT

Another concern of the Negro movement has been employment, which is closely related to economic well-being and is generally assumed to affect income significantly. A high Negro unemployment rate, for example, is thought to depress Negro income as a percentage of white income. In the Houston SMSA, male nonwhite unemployment increased between 1949 and 1959 (Table 5.1). It also increased as a percentage of the white unemployed. In 1967 total nonwhite unemployment (male and female) averaged 6.3 percent, compared with 2.4 percent for whites, according to the Bureau of Labor Statistics. This continuing high rate of unemployment is partly a reflection of socioeconomic factors pure and simple, and partly a result of intentional discrimination by employers and employment agency officials.[19]

These figures apply only to the labor force. Thus the substantial number of Negroes who neither work nor look for work is excluded. These are people who believe, correctly in many instances, that no jobs exist for them, and they are consequently not counted in the labor force. Some economists suggest that this number nationally is large and may be growing.[20] A recent Department of Labor study concentrating on poverty in Houston's central city found that about one out of four of the men and women not working or looking for work nevertheless wanted a job immediately.[21] Major reasons for not actively seeking employment were poor health and, for women, lack of child care.

In recent years the mayor's office has attempted to help find jobs for one extremely high-unemployment group, Negroes between

19 See *Civil Rights in Texas: A Report of the Texas Advisory Committee to the U.S. Commission on Civil Rights*, February, 1970, p. 23. Blacks hold less than 4 percent of the 2,946 Texas Employment Commission jobs. They hold only 7 of the 527 managerial and supervisory positions.

20 See Eli Ginzberg and Dale L. Hiestand, "Employment Patterns of Negro Men and Women," in John P. Davis (ed.), *The American Negro Reference Book* (Englewood Cliffs: Prentice-Hall, 1966), 236.

21 United States Bureau of Labor Statistics, *Poverty in Houston's Central City*, Regional Report Series No. 6, February, 1970 (Dallas, 1970), 2.

Table 5.1

PERCENTAGE OF CIVILIAN MALE LABOR FORCE UNEMPLOYED
TOTAL AND NONWHITE, HOUSTON SMSA, 1949–1969

Year	Percent of Total Unemployed*	Percent of Nonwhite Unemployed
1949	3.8%	5.4%
1959	4.1	7.3
1969	3.2	6.7

* The nonwhite labor force, as a percentage of the total, was virtually unchanged during this period.

Source: Calculated from United States Bureau of the Census, *U.S. Census of the Population: 1950*, Vol. II, *Characteristics of the Population*, Part 43, *Texas*, Tables 35 and 36; and *U.S. Census of the Population: 1960, General Social and Economic Characteristics, Texas*, Final Report, PC(1)-45C, Tables 73 and 77. Figures for 1969 are from *Negro Employment in the South*, Vol. I: *The Houston Labor Market*, United States Department of Labor, Manpower Administration, Manpower Research Monograph No. 23 (Washington, D.C.: United States Government Printing Office, 1971), 12. Although the Houston SMSA in 1969 was larger than Harris County (unlike 1949 and 1959), the 1969 figures are for the county alone, thus comparable with those in previous decades.

sixteen and twenty-two years old. It first sponsored a "job fair" in 1967, urging businessmen to hire the youngsters. In its first three years, the job fair program provided an estimated 9,200 summer jobs, although a much larger number of applicants were turned away.

JOB OPPORTUNITIES

The percentage of blacks in higher-status, better-paying jobs is also an index of progress. There was an increase in the proportion of nonwhites occupying white-collar jobs between 1940 and 1960. (At the national level, there has been an even sharper increase in the decade of the sixties. Whether this is true in Houston, we do not yet know. Differences between regions and between cities can be great where the job structure is concerned.) Between 1940 and 1960 the percentage of blacks in white-collar jobs rose from 6.2

percent of the employed work force in the Houston SMSA to at least 12.4 percent in 1960 (Tables 5.2 and 5.3).[22]

These gains are small when compared with the proportion of the white work force in white-collar occupations, which figure in the year 1960 was 52.7 percent. Important, too, is the fact that the Negro gain was by no means steady. Most of the progress occurred between 1940 and 1950. Moreover the gains came primarily in the clerical and sales category, which is at the bottom of the white-collar stratum. There was actually a decrease in the proportion of nonwhites in the managers-officials-proprietors category during the 1950s. Even if the overall white-collar gain continues, and if one assumes that the white-collar proportion of the white work force remains constant (which of course it will not: it will rise), nearly one hundred thirty years will be required for blacks to catch up.

Occupational level is tied directly to income—and like income, it cannot presently be directly manipulated through political pressure. If black workers in Houston's "private" sector were distributed in jobs in the same manner as whites, their average earnings in 1969 would have been $6,614 rather than $4,524.[23]

One traditional measure of the influence of an ethnic bloc is its ability to get its members into public jobs. Progress in Houston has been exceedingly slow, although some gains were made in the 1960s. In 1961 a report stated: "Only a few years ago, there were no Negroes with white-collar jobs in Houston city government. While there is only a negligible number now holding such jobs, an effort is being made to increase that amount. . . . This fall, for example, for the first time, two Negro school policemen have been hired."[24]

In 1964 there were 134 Negroes in jobs above the semiskilled level, or about 4 percent of all city employees in such occupations.

22 The relatively high percentage of unreported occupations in 1960 (10 percent of the nonwhites) makes comparisons between years somewhat imprecise.

23 Jerolyn Lyle, *Employment of Minorities and Women in Houston's Private Sector*, A Position Paper, Office of Research and Reports, United States Equal Employment Opportunity Commission (Washington, D.C., 1970; mimeo), 3.

24 Southern Regional Council, *The Negro and Employment Opportunities in the South: Houston* (Atlanta, 1961), 15.

Table 5.2

DISTRIBUTION BY OCCUPATIONS IN THE EMPLOYED WORK FORCE BY COLOR, 1940–1960

Occupation	White			Nonwhite		
	1940	1950	1960	1940	1950	1960
Professional, technical, kindred	8.9%	11.8%	14.3%	2.7%	3.5%	4.8%
Managers, officials, proprietors	11.3	13.0	11.2	1.7	2.9	2.2
Clerical and sales	27.0	27.3	29.2	1.8	4.2	5.4
Craftsmen, foremen, kindred	16.6	19.1	15.7	3.4	4.9	5.4
Operatives and kindred	17.4	13.3	13.4	13.7	18.5	17.6
Private household workers	2.3	4.6	.5	34.8	19.2	16.7
Service	7.3	6.0	5.6	17.8	21.7	22.0
Laborers	4.7	3.2	3.0	20.8	23.2	15.7
Farmers and farm workers	3.1	.6	.5	2.4	.9	.6
OCCUPATIONS NOT REPORTED*	1.4	1.1	6.6	.9	1.0	9.6
	100.0	100.0	100.0	100.0	100.0	100.0

* Most unreported jobs are probably blue-collar ones. Hence the larger proportion of unreported jobs among nonwhites in 1960 would tend to understate the percentage of blacks in blue-collar employ reported in the table.

Sources: The above figures were calculated from the census figures for 1940 through 1960. United States Bureau of the Census: *Sixteenth Census of the United States (1940), Population,* Vol. II, *Characteristics of the Population,* Part 6, Tables 23 and 23a; *U.S. Census of the Population: 1950,* Vol. II, *Characteristics of the Population,* Part 43, *Texas,* Tables 35 and 36; and *United States Census of the Population: 1960, General Social and Economic Characteristics, Texas,* Final Report, PC(1)-45C, Tables 74 and 78.

Table 5.3

SUMMARY OF TABLE 5.2. PERCENTAGE OF WHITES AND NONWHITES
IN WHITE-COLLAR AND OTHER OCCUPATIONS

Type of Occupation	White			Nonwhite		
	1940	1950	1960	1940	1950	1960
White-Collar	47.2%	52.1%	52.7%	6.2%	10.6%	12.4%
Blue-Collar, Farm	51.4	46.8	38.7	92.9	88.4	78.0
NOT REPORTED	1.4	1.1	8.6	.9	1.0	9.6
	100.0	100.0	100.0	100.0	100.0	100.0

By 1970 this figure had risen to 15 percent according to the mayor's office. The city's population is 27 percent black. A Civil Rights Commission report estimated that in 1967 only 3.5 percent of the municipal white-collar work force was black, while 26.5 percent of its blue-collar work force was staffed by Negroes.[25] According to a Department of Labor study published in 1971, two-thirds of the blacks employed by the city (excluding those jobs in public safety) are classified in the laborer category that is excluded from civil service coverage and the job security it affords. By its estimate 93 percent of the blacks municipally employed were blue-collar workers.[26]

Negroes in white-collar occupations in the municipal government are often restricted in their duties. For example, the first Negro attorney was appointed to the city's legal department in 1964. However, it was only in late 1967 that a Negro assistant district attorney was allowed to prosecute a capital case, and then only when both the defendant and the victim were black.[27] (As of this writing, there are no blacks in the city's legal department.) Saul Friedman found that of 174 Negroes in "higher" city positions in 1965 (presumably these are the positions the mayor's office now

25 *Civil Rights in Texas*, p. 26.
26 United States Department of Labor, Manpower Administration, *Negro Employment in the South*, Volume I: *The Houston Labor Market*, Manpower Research Monograph No. 23 (Washington, D.C.: United States Government Printing Office, 1971), 58.
27 Houston *Post*, November 14, 1967.

refers to as "above the semi-skilled level"), only two actually worked at city hall. (As of 1970 the number of blacks there was at least 32.) As for some of the others:

> The one warrant officer seeks only Negro violators; the four dentists care for Negro patients only; the 12 nurses see only Negroes, and the four ward attendants work [in] predominantly Negro clinics. The six library personnel work in libraries which cater mostly to Negroes; the two park patrolmen, the four park helpers, the assistant recreation center supervisor, and the 16 recreation center directors, work in Negro areas. The three Negro water meter readers, the three school safety custodians, and the six general sanitarians are assigned to predominantly Negro areas. Other Negroes [in the "higher" category] are equipment operators, incinerator foremen, sewer repairmen, maintenance men, car attendants, and mechanics. There are no Negro secretaries, cashiers, elevator operators, receptionists, or white collar supervisors.[28]

In the last few years the mayor has hired five Negroes as aides or assistants.

Progress in police force hiring was nil during the 1960s. The first Negro on the force in many years was hired in 1947, through the efforts of the Harris County Council of (Negro) Organizations. By 1960 there were 39 Negroes on a force of more than 1,000. In the spring of 1970, 53 of the department's 1,654 officers were black. The percentage on the force has decreased slightly. Figures obtained in 1970 revealed that the highest position a Negro had attained in the department was detective, or Grade 4 out of eleven grades. Three Negroes occupied this grade. In 1968 one patrol car was integrated. More recently Negroes have been given permission to arrest whites. The mayor and the police chief claim that intensive efforts have been made to recruit qualified Negro officers. Negroes, on the other hand, claim that the black policeman's status in Houston is so degraded that few potential candidates apply.

A delegation from the Harris County Council requested the city council in 1950 to hire Negro firemen, but it was not until five years later that the request was acted on. In 1970 there were 85 Negroes

28 Saul Friedman, "The Negroes in Houston," series of articles assigned in 1965 but not published by the Houston *Chronicle*.

in a department of approximately 1,850. The highest rank attained by a Negro was "junior captain," Grade 5 in a system in which Grade 10 is highest. Five blacks occupied these posts.

No racial breakdown of county employees is available. A tour of the courthouses, where many of the county's white-collar employees work, indicates that Negroes are severely underrepresented in this work force. However, a little progress has been made in recent years. County Judge Bill Elliott, a "moderate-to-liberal" in Harris County politics, appointed Barbara Jordan to his staff after her defeat in a legislative race and before her successful try for the senate.

As late as 1962, there were no Negroes working in the county clerk's office, which today employs about 160 people. Julius Carter, the editor of *Forward Times*, criticized the county clerk in an editorial, claiming that he had promised in his previous election campaign that Negroes would be hired. A Negro Chamber of Commerce pamphlet in 1965 listed ten Negroes as employed in the clerk's office. In 1968 one of the clerk's assistants estimated that "17 to 20" Negroes were then employed. In 1965 the same pamphlet listed 4 Negro employees in the tax assessor-collector's office. In 1967 this number had increased to 9, of a total staff of 220.

Figures on employment of Negroes by the federal government in the Houston metropolitan area (20 percent black) are equally unimpressive. Of 15,799 federal employees in 1967, 22 percent were black, but only 9 percent were in white-collar jobs. Less than 1 percent (.6) of the jobs ranked GS-12 or above were held by blacks. Less than 2 percent of federal jobs paying eight thousand dollars a year or more were occupied by them.[29]

The state of Texas employed 2,834 persons in the Houston metropolitan area in 1967. Only 159 were black and more than half of these were in blue-collar jobs, compared to 25 percent of whites in blue-collar classifications. Less than 1 percent of black state employees were managers and officials.[30]

The nature of the city's segregated school system has required a heavy reliance upon black teachers in the Negro schools, and hence

29 *Civil Rights in Texas*, 26.
30 *Ibid.*

job opportunities are greater in this area than is true of municipal and county employment. Thirty percent of the district's 10,256 teachers in 1968 were Negroes. About 30 percent of the district's pupils were Negroes as well, so this was a fairly equitable situation. Also, in the higher teaching echelons, 30 percent of the district's principals and assistant principals were Negroes, as were 24 percent of the clerks and secretaries in the schools.

The situation was less favorable so far as the central administrative staff is concerned, although this is changing following the accession in 1969 of a liberal majority to the school board. In 1971, 19 percent of the administrative staff was black.

This poor record of minority hiring in government also holds for the city's large private firms and the white labor unions. An investigation by the United States Equal Employment Opportunity Commission in the summer of 1970 revealed that of the 161,913 persons employed by the city's top ten industries, only 13.1 percent were black.[31] Only 4.5 percent of these blacks held white-collar jobs.[32] Most of these leading concerns were major national corporations, such as Humble Oil, Gulf Oil, American Oil, United States Plywood-Champion Paper Company, and International Business Machines. Their employment record was judged to be worse than the city's over-all average and worse than top concerns in other cities. One witness at the hearings, a local Urban League official, told the panel that the Urban League's skills bank had 800 persons available for work, but Houston's businesses refused to hire them.[33]

The commission's staff report said that Houston's equal employment record was "one of the worst, if not the worst" in the country. "For years the Houston economy has been booming," the staff report said. "Yet the industrial expansion and labor shortages that

31 Of the eight Houston labor organizations invited to testify in hearings held in the city by the United States Equal Employment Opportunity Commission in June, 1970, one declined, six never responded to the invitation, and the other did not indicate whether it would testify. Houston *Post*, June 3, 1970. Of the thirty-one companies invited, all responded to the invitation, but eighteen declined to attend.

Neither the city nor the state has a Fair Employment Practices Act or a Human Relations Committee with power to enforce its rulings.

32 New York *Times*, June 8, 1970.

33 *Ibid.*, June 4, 1970.

characterize its economic environment have provided little opportunity for economic advancement to the city's substantial minority
labor force." It went on to say that "while most blacks and Mexican-
Americans are working, the jobs they find are in personal services,
small business enterprises and in declining industries. Where they
have penetrated growth industries, they are overwhelmingly concentrated in the lowest paying occupations."

An investigation by the commission, earlier in the year, that
scrutinized labor-union hiring practices was equally revealing of
discrimination. Indeed the findings led the commission's director
for research to announce that labor's apprenticeship training programs have not resulted in any progress for blacks in the Houston
SMSA. Skilled trade unions included in the study were still lily white,
with no improvement in the situation since 1967. The figures for
the latter year showed that of the 25,000 members of Houston re-
ferral locals (that is, unions with hiring halls), 20.8 percent were
black and 5.5 percent were Mexican-American—proportions not
much different from those of the two groups in the total population.
But almost nine blacks of every ten were in the laborers' union, and
there were virtually no blacks in the mechanical trades unions, according to the report.[34] (The Houston *Post* headlined its article
summarizing the commission's report, "Negroes Big in Area
Unions.") These figures bore out an earlier survey by the Houston
Chronicle which revealed that minority membership in craft unions
in 1969 was almost nil. For example, among 700 members of Bricklayers Local 7, there were four Negro apprentices and no journey-
men. Iron Workers Local 84, consisting of 1,600 members, included
eight blacks. Plumbers Local 68 counted 13 Negroes among its 985
members.[35] Several unions, it should be added, refused to report to
the commission.

White union officials rationalize these statistics by claiming that
Negro high school graduates are unwilling to work and be trained.
On the other hand, the city's most influential black labor leader,
J. E. Middleton, secretary-treasurer of the Laborers International

34 Houston *Chronicle*, February 11, 1970; Houston *Post*, February 4, 1970.
35 Houston *Chronicle*, February 11, 1970.

Union, contends that the white craft unions systematically discriminate against blacks.[36] No matter which explanation is correct, the statistics indicate that politics has not led to significant gains for blacks in organized labor, at least so far as the skilled crafts go. In this respect, the situation is much the same as it is in the country at large.[37]

THE LEGAL SYSTEM

Perhaps the greatest single source of conflict in American society today lies on the interface between the institutions of law enforcement and the black community. Houston is no exception. Indeed the mutual hostility between the almost completely white police department and the black community, by the late 1960s, had come to predominate over the issue of school desegregation as the most emotionally charged symbol of racial unrest and potential mass violence. Any number of serious confrontations between blacks and police from 1966 to the present could be viewed—from one vantage point—as a series of escalating skirmishes in a battle that could lead to major disturbances.

The last serious study of the Negro and law enforcement in Houston was made in 1961 by Henry Allen Bullock, a professor of sociology at Texas Southern University, under the auspices of the Mayor's Negro Law Enforcement Committee. Bullock's observation on the role of the police as perceived by Negroes still seems relevant. "Whenever one hears about the police descending upon a group of Negroes, there is always raised this question: 'How many heads was whupped?' "[38] The charge of "police brutality" is con-

36 *Ibid.*

37 In the highest-paying trades—plumbers, sheet-metal workers, electrical workers, elevator constructors—less than 1 percent of the workers in the United States are black. *Time*, April 6, 1970, p. 92. A report by the Equal Employment Opportunity Commission found that minority membership in the mechanical trades unions was as follows for these southern cities: Houston 0.0%; Birmingham 0.0%; Atlanta 0.1%; New Orleans 0.3%; Memphis 0.9%. New York *Times*, February 8, 1970.

38 Henry Allen Bullock, "The Houston Murder Problem: Its Nature, Apparent Causes and Probable Cures," Report of the Mayor's Negro Law Enforcement Committee (Houston: 1961; mimeo.) 80.

stantly raised by black spokesmen and the black press. Because the mayor has refused to appoint a civilian review board, and Negro leaders have not seen fit to collect and publish evidence systematically from people who claim to have been treated brutally, there are little "hard" data in this area. But as Bullock wrote in 1961: "What gives these reports some degree of validity is that they come from a variety of people who do not know each other, and all of them fit neatly into the above patterns of police brutality."[39]

In the course of my study several blacks of very different political persuasions (some in fact were supporters of the mayor) were interviewed who claimed they had personally been treated roughly by the police. Lawyers of both races asserted that policemen treated poor people, black and white, with a great deal of cruelty. Even one of the mayor's assistants was reported to have admitted "that the mayor's office is unaware of just what is going on in the police department."[40]

The mayor has not denied that policemen sometimes mistreat blacks, but he claims that charges of brutality are exaggerated.[41] He told a reporter that there were only 142 complaints regarding the police in 1970, and he said that only 21 of them were valid.[42]

However, the "credibility gap" continues to widen. The department's attempt at a community relations project, involving policemen and black citizens, failed miserably. A committee formed by Mayor Welch to improve police-community relations and to "publicize progress" disappeared from public view shortly after its founding. The committee's report was not made public, leading the Houston *Chronicle* to editorialize that the committee had "virtually gone underground."[43]

The target of most of the Negro leaders' wrath is Police Chief Herman Short, who has consistently advocated taking a hard line in

39 *Ibid.*, 81.
40 *Forward Times*, May 6, 1967.
41 New York *Times*, November 4, 1971.
42 *Ibid.* Police Chief Herman Short told a reporter that fifty-six charges of brutality had been made against the police in 1971, four of which resulted in suspensions of officers and twenty-one of which led to reprimands. Houston *Post*, December 12, 1971.
43 Houston *Chronicle*, June 6, 1969.

dealing with crime. He is distinctly a conservative on both civil rights and civil liberties. He was recently quoted as telling a reporter that measures to improve the fight against crime "can be accomplished without the violation of the constitutional rights of the individual. And I mean by that the intent of the authors of the Constitution and not the warped interpretation we have seen in recent years."[44] Following the publication of the report of the National Advisory Commission on Civil Disorders, Short said that the commission "and other slobbering groups" offer "an open invitation to engage in riots."[45] Perhaps the best indication of Short's legal philosophy was the statement in 1971 by his personal friend Governor George Wallace of Alabama that Wallace would install someone like Short as FBI director if he became President.[46]

In April, 1970, the entire political spectrum of Houston blacks was incensed over the beating of two black auto theft suspects by police that led to the death of one of the suspects. In the wake of the killing, the mayor's office and the police chief steadfastly refused to admit that this was anything but an isolated incident. The city council was quick to point out that the police department was legally under the mayor's jurisdiction, and therefore not their responsibility. One councilman, however, stated that the incident "awakened some of the supervisory personnel in the Police Department to something they didn't know was going on."[47] The policemen involved were brought to trial in 1971 after obtaining a change of venue. Despite testimony by two fellow officers (both white) that they had observed the defendants beat and stomp the Negro prisoners, the policemen were acquitted of murder charges. Subsequent harrassment of the officers who testified for the prosecution, by fellow officers, led to the resignation of one soon afterwards.[48]

A few months after the beating incident, a confrontation be-

44 Houston *Post*, February 11, 1968.
45 Houston *Post*, March 2, 1968. The commission included Atlanta's chief of police, Herbert Jenkins.
46 Houston *Post*, December 4, 1971.
47 Houston *Post*, April 19, 1970.
48 Houston *Chronicle*, August 15, 1971. The officers who were acquitted still face other charges connected with the case at this writing.

tween the police and black revolutionaries, who were members of a group called People's Party II, led to the fatal shooting by the police of the group's chairman, twenty-one-year-old Carl Hampton.[49] Large numbers of police were dispatched to the area to disperse crowds. Five other persons were wounded by police gunfire in the ensuing melee. Several black organizations and political figures, including Senator Barbara Jordan and Representative Curtis Graves, conducted a brief and unsuccessful boycott of downtown stores to pressure the mayor into firing Chief Short. But the mayor, who in the past had called demands to dismiss Short "incoherent babblings,"[50] refused. He apparently viewed Short as one of his most important political assets, and had decided to stake his administration's popularity on Short's image in the white community.[51]

Another widely voiced complaint is that Negroes do not receive fair treatment in court. Here again no local studies have been made to establish the truth of this allegation, although studies in other areas are suggestive. It is a fact that the legal profession in Houston is desperately short of Negro attorneys. In 1945 it was estimated that only ten Negroes were actively practicing law in the city. In 1967 there were forty, although one of them estimated to the author that only about twenty-nine were "active." According to Kenneth Tollett, dean of the Texas Southern University law school, which produces most of the state's Negro lawyers: "What is alarm-

49 For accounts of the "Dowling Street shootout," as it was referred to, see Houston *Post*, July 27, 28, 1970; *Forward Times*, August 1, 1970; and *Texas Observer*, August 21, 1970. Eyewitness reports differed about who fired the first shots in the incident—the police or the black militants. A grand jury subsequently assigned the blame to the militants. Houston *Post*, September 23, 1970. The report of the grand jury, which contained two blacks, was unanimous. The attorney for People's Party II labeled the report an "expected whitewash." New York *Times*, September 24, 1970.

50 Houston *Chronicle*, July 29, 1970.

51 In the interpretation of reporter Edward Walsh: "Short . . . is considered a political asset for the mayor. According to this view, shared by several councilmen and other observers, the chief's reputation as a tough officer who holds the line against militants has strengthened Welch's position with most Houston voters." Houston *Chronicle*, July 29, 1970. This interpretation was borne out in the 1971 mayoral election campaign, in which Welch made Chief Short the major issue. Houston *Post*, November 2, 1971; Houston *Chronicle*, November 14, 1971. The chief cooperated by implying that he would not serve under Fred Hofheinz, the mayor's chief opponent. Houston *Chronicle*, November 14, 1971.

ing is that even if the wall of discrimination crumbled today [leading to the appointment of Negro judges and officials] we would find some difficulty in massing enough troops to man the legal forts in representative numbers. Even in Houston, in spite of 40 Negro lawyers, we anticipate some difficulty in finding enough experienced and practicing Negro lawyers to fill the many legal positions that our Legal Services War on Poverty Project will create."[52]

Negroes have sat on petit juries in district courts for many years. A Negro first became a jury foreman in 1952. Negroes are appointed by district judges to sit on county grand juries as well. (A few well-known Negroes serve over and over again, however.) A grand jury minority report by four members recently alleged that women, Mexican-Americans, and Negroes were underrepresented on grand juries. The report said in part: "It is to be hoped that the time will come when it will be immaterial whether a grand juror is black, white, pink, green or yellow—man or woman. That time is not yet—there are entirely too many completely irrelevant references, by many appearing before us, to specific ethnic groups."[53]

Apparently a higher percentage of Negroes serve on county grand juries than on federal ones. According to a knowledgeable informant, very few Negroes sit on these latter juries, and it is not uncommon for there to be none at all. In the two grand juries impaneled between January, 1969, and September, 1970, four out of forty-six jurors were black.

It was recently charged by an official of the county sheriff's department that hundreds of "little people" are literally forgotten after arrest and spend months in jail before they are brought to trial. He cited the example of a man in the county jail on a murder charge, who had not yet had a lawyer appointed for him, although he had been there eleven months.[54] A large percentage of the defendants in such cases are blacks.

The county presently has no adequate public defender. The dis-

52 Kenneth S. Tollett, "The Alarming Shortage of Negro Law Students" (speech to the National Bar Association executive board meeting, Houston, April 23, 1966).
53 Houston *Post*, February 1, 1968.
54 Houston *Post*, April 18, 1970.

trict attorney's office serves in a limited capacity in this role, but as the above-mentioned official pointed out: "The DA's office cannot serve two masters. You got to prosecute or you got to be a defender. You can't do both." The Houston Legal Foundation, a poverty organization, provided limited legal services to poor persons before it went bankrupt. It is trying to reorganize, but it would need $10,000 a month to provide minimal public defender services. A good public defender's office, it is estimated, would cost about $700,000 a year, or about half of the district attorney's annual budget.[55]

PUBLIC INTEGRATION

Most public accommodations were integrated without violence between 1960 and 1965, as a result of the sit-in movement and the Civil Rights Act of 1964. However, there is still the institution of the "private club" that remains segregated in large part. These clubs, numerous in Houston, were often established to circumvent the state law which until the summer of 1971 prohibited selling liquor by the drink. Club membership prices range from a nominal fee (or in some cases, particularly hotels, no fee whatever) to thousands of dollars annually. A large proportion of the city's middle-class night life goes on in these clubs which, as private establishments, are able to remain segregated if their owners desire.

School desegregation within the Houston Independent School District—the largest in the county and the one containing most of the county's Negro students—began in 1960, and has gradually increased so that now about 26 percent of the Negro pupils are attending schools with whites (Table 5.4).[56] In September, 1970, at the instigation of a federal court, zoning, pairing, and student transfers were substituted for "freedom of choice" as integration methods, and this probably raised the integration total a few points. Yet

55 *Ibid.*
56 The public school integration figures probably understate the degree of segregation which still exists. It has been estimated by school officials that almost 10 percent of the school-age children in the district attend private schools. A high percentage of these are white. See the Houston *Post*, May 6, 1970.

Table 5.4

RACIAL INTEGRATION IN HOUSTON INDEPENDENT
SCHOOL DISTRICT, 1960–1971

Year	Negroes in Integrated Schools[a]	Number of Negro Pupils In System	Percent of Negroes in Integrated Schools
1960–61	12	No data	No data
1961–62	33	”	”
1962–63	63	”	”
1963–64	255	”	”
1964–65	1,233	”	”
1965–66	No data	”	”
1966–67	3,000[b]	76,000[b]	4[b]
1967–68	12,302	80,000	15
1968–69	No data	81,481	No data
1969–70	13,820	78,126[c]	18
1970–71	22,592	85,965	26

[a] The figures from 1960 through 1965 and 1967–68 apparently are for Negroes in formerly all-white schools. The figures for 1966–67 and 1969–70 are for Negro children attending a school which has a student body at least 10 percent of which is of a different race. This would include, for example, all Negroes in a school which is 90 percent black, but exclude Negroes in a school more than 90 percent white. 1970–71 figures are for Negroes in schools less than 90 percent black. This would include blacks in schools more than 90 percent white. This means that the increase between 1969 and 1970 may be somewhat exaggerated by the figures in the table.

[b] Estimates only. The actual numbers were not released by the school board.

[c] The decrease from the previous year resulted from the elimination of free kindergarten.

whites continue to flee integrated neighborhoods as in other cities, and it is entirely possible that the new methods alone will be unable to prevent resegregation of even those few schools which are now substantially integrated.

Even this modest progress has been achieved at tremendous cost. For example, the school site location plan contained in the school district's sixty-million-dollar building program initiated in 1966 made desegregation more difficult by strengthening the existing patterns of *de facto* segregation. Most "white" schools were built far away from black areas, while the "black" schools were mostly located in the hearts of the ghettos. A lawsuit brought by the parents of black children failed to prevent the plan's implementation.

Until 1969 the school board majority consisted of die-hard segregationists, who used a wide range of tactics to discourage efforts at integration.[57] For a while during the 1960s, according to the liberal members, the board majority made most of its important decisions in informal meetings to which the liberal members were not invited. The liberals also claimed that no verbatim transcripts of official board meetings were kept—instead a summary statement of the proceedings was entered in the records. Statistics that would have enabled investigators to describe the demography of the school district were kept secret even from liberal board members and in some cases were denied to exist.[58]

According to information in a Civil Rights Commission report, based on testimony of a liberal board member, the general budget of some $25,000 for attorney fees a few years ago had risen to $35,000 in the 1964–65 school year, to $44,600 the subsequent year, and to $85,000 the year the board member testified. "A major portion of this," she added, "is used to fight school desegregation."[59] The school attorney became a specialist in fighting school desegre-

57 For a description of some of the tactics employed by the conservatives in the late 1950s and early 1960s, see Harry K. Wright, *Civil Rights U.S.A., Public Schools, Southern States: 1963*, Texas Staff Report Submitted to the United States Commission on Civil Rights (Washington, D.C.: United States Government Printing Office, 1964), 33–85. An informative account of the activities of the school board's chief counsel while the segregationists were in control is found in an article by Art Wiese, "Meet Joe Reynolds, Schools' Counsel in Desegregation Cases," Houston *Post*, September 7, 1969.

58 Interviews with liberal members conducted by the author.

59 *Civil Rights in Texas*, 7. The report included the testimony of a mother who wrote to the Department of Justice and to the FBI in Houston for assistance after failing in her attempt to enroll her child in a white school. She told the committee: ". . . about three days after I wrote the letter I got a call from the F.B.I. in Houston to come to the office and I was questioned for about three hours. Well, he wanted to know just everything, why did I go, who sent me, and what organizations did I belong to, how much money did I have, how much did my car cost, who was paying me to do this and so forth (p. 7)."

gation suits, and at the time his firm's services were dispensed with in 1969, he was handling a large number of cases for districts throughout the South, including more than twenty in Texas alone.

Despite the dogged fight of the segregationists on the board, the percentage of black students in integrated schools had risen from zero in 1960 to more than 20 percent ten years later. Yet there are more Negro children in Houston attending segregated schools today than when the *Brown* decision was handed down in 1954, because of the increase in the black school-age population.

Harris County has twenty colleges and universities, with a total enrollment of more than 40,000. The University of Houston desegregated in 1963, and 800 to 1,000 Negroes were enrolled in 1970, of a total student population of about 24,000. Rice University, a private institution, desegregated in 1965 and had 55 to 60 out of 2,297 undergraduates in 1970. No Negroes were on its faculty.

Housing segregation has increased rapidly in Houston in the last two decades, as was true for much of the South (Table 5.5). No systematic study of the causes of housing segregation has been made in Houston. It has not been a major issue among civil rights groups, and several Negro respondents told the author that there was no barrier to a Negro's buying a house anywhere in town if he had the money for it. Others, however, contradicted this opinion. Some claimed that white neighborhoods exhibited hostility to Negroes, and others—including a real estate salesman—said that loan companies cooperated with white realtors and neighborhood civic clubs

Table 5.5

INDEX OF RESIDENTIAL SEGREGATION
HOUSTON, 1940–1960

Year	1940	1950	1960
Index[a]	84.5	91.5	93.7

[a]An index of "0" indicates no segregation; an index of "100" indicates complete segregation.

Source: Karl E. Taeuber and Alma F. Taeuber, *Negroes In Cities: Residential Segregation and Neighborhood Change* (Chicago: Aldine Publ. Co., 1965), 41.

to prevent Negro loan applications from being approved on houses in white upper middle-class neighborhoods. There has been very little overt violence when Negroes have moved into white neighborhoods, however. Rather there has been, with few exceptions, a mass exodus of whites in a very short period of time.

HOUSING AND NEIGHBORHOOD IMPROVEMENTS

Houston blacks, concentrated either in the central city or in older outlying areas many of which grew out of rural settlements, have long been accustomed to living in run-down neighborhoods lacking such "necessities" as paved streets, drainage systems, sewers, street lights, sidewalks, parks, adequately controlled intersections, or public recreation areas, among other things. In 1965 a newspaper reporter described some of these conditions in Settegast, a poverty area in the northeast section of town: "Only now is the city putting in the main sewer trunk lines. . . . They had to wait until treatment plants were built. Now lateral sewer lines must wait until the trunks are finished, and paving must wait until the sewer lines are in. It will take perhaps five years, city officials say. Settegast was annexed by the city in 1949."[60] A supervisor of the city's street repair division told the reporter that most of the four hundred miles of unpaved streets in Houston were in Negro areas.

The city is perhaps the only large metropolis in the country without residential zoning laws, with the consequence that federal assistance for urban redevelopment has been extremely difficult to obtain.[61] Slum clearance laws were passed in the early fifties but have gone unenforced. Low-rent public housing is scarce and compares unfavorably with that in many southern cities. In 1966 Houston needed at least fifteen thousand units of good housing for low-income families, according to the commissioner of the Public

60 Friedman, "The Negroes in Houston."
61 After numerous delays and a good deal of subterranean political infighting, Houston qualified for a thirteen-million-dollar Model Cities grant from the Department of Housing and Urban Development. How the Model Cities program will benefit blacks in comparison with whites is not known.

Housing Administration, who visited Houston that year.[62] No federally subsidized housing units have been built in Houston for two decades.[63]

In the mid-sixties Mayor Welch began to make some improvements in Negro neighborhoods and has made headway in honoring residents' requests for streetlights, paving, and the like. Table 5.6 compares the expenditures on public works made in Negro areas by Welch's recent predecessors with those made during his administration, beginning in 1964.

Table 5.6
MONEY SPENT ON PUBLIC WORKS PROJECTS
IN NEGRO NEIGHBORHOODS

Type of Project, Time Period	Amount of Money
Topping Projects	
1953–63	$6,600,000
1964–67	7,100,000
Structures[a]	
1961–64	540,000
1964–67	7,200,000
Paving and Sanitary Sewers	
1961–64	2,400,000
1964–67	4,700,000
Storm Sewers	
1961–64	1,300,000
1964–67	1,700,000
Water Lines and Mains	
1961–64	Figures not available
1964–67	5,900,000

[a] Includes fire stations, health centers, parks, miscellaneous buildings, and so forth.

Source: Louie Welch, "Dear Citizen . . . ," *A Report on Minority Group Problems and Progress*, (Houston, 1967), 13.

62 Houston *Post*, January 19, 1966.
63 Houston *Chronicle*, June 27, 1971. The housing authority recently announced that it is planning to build two thousand new public housing units. At this writing, it is not certain that these will benefit the poor primarily.

THE CLIMATE OF OPINION

Most of the Negro informants interviewed who were adults in Houston before the end of the white primaries agreed that the city's social atmosphere had changed greatly. In fact the most clear-cut progress was seen by them to have occurred in this respect. Today the mass media are generally moderate in their attitudes on race. Neither the Houston *Post* nor the Houston *Chronicle* contains the vitriolic racism on their editorial pages which is a stock in trade of many papers in the Deep South. The *Post* has carried a weekly society column in its Sunday supplement written by a Negro, as well as a column by the nationally syndicated black journalist Carl Rowan and a column on "Negroes in Houston." Occasionally the picture of a black bride appears in the society pages. Both dailies sometimes give support to Negro goals that have minimal impact upon the white community, and they criticize such arch-segregationists as George Wallace. However, both papers fail to give the black community adequate coverage and often do not report significant facts that the editors judge would not be in the best interest of the public to know.[64]

The white religious and civic organizations have yet to undertake any major steps toward changing the Negro's position. A few individual white clergymen have been outspoken, and a few courageous pastors have integrated churches. Organizations of clergymen have occasionally issued statements asking for greater racial tolerance, but more concrete actions are seldom taken.

THE BENEFITS OF BLACKS' PARTICIPATION: AN INTERPRETATION

The array of information so far presented points to two important facts. First, the progress that has been made by Houston's blacks has been exceedingly slow. This fact is often lost on whites

64 See Ben H. Bagdikian, "Houston's Shackled Press," *Atlantic Monthly*, CCXVIII (August, 1966), 87–93.

whose contact with the black experience is infrequent. One reads the newspaper headline, "Negro Income Up," and this is taken as ample evidence that blacks are rapidly attaining equality with whites. The grinding day-to-day struggle behind what are often quite meager gains is beyond the imagination of many white newspaper readers. Those who are slightly more sophisticated take comfort in these gains, even when they are aware of the price paid for them, on the grounds that they will eventually lead to racial equality.

But what is the force of "eventually" here? Decades? Generations? A century or longer? As pointed out above, at the present rate of progress, Houston Negroes would not achieve income parity for seventy years or more, and they would not achieve job parity for at least one hundred thirty years. It is easy to take comfort in "long run" progress if the brutal reality of the present is ignored. It is easy to counsel moderation on the grounds that long-term trends are generally favorable, so long as the implication of this position is not clearly spelled out—namely, that while things are working themselves out, the present generation of blacks is being asked to sacrifice its legitimate claim to justice now. Americans are quick to condemn the Stalinist strategy of sacrificing present generations for future ones. Yet many of them subscribe to a similar morality so far as blacks in this country are concerned. The Negro child who, because of his race, is denied a chance for a good education between 1970 and 1982 will in all likelihood still be suffering the consequences in the year 2034, long after we are dead.

The second conclusion to be drawn from the above data is that many gains are counterbalanced with losses. It is a gross distortion of the facts to argue that blacks are making progress—or even holding their own—relative to whites in most important respects. The most unambiguous progress has concerned Negro social status: the ability to use public accommodations, to obtain somewhat more civil treatment by officials, merchants, and opinion makers, and to occupy a few positions in politics and business that were once the sole preserve of whites. On the other hand, changes relative to whites in job opportunities, income, education, and neighborhood improvements have been small. The percentage of black males in some of Houston's higher-paying jobs dropped in the 1950s, even though the tempo of black political participation quickened. So, too, black unemployment increased during the same decade. Nonwhite income, for families and individuals, dropped as a percentage of white income between 1949 and 1959. Housing segregation—a reflection of Negro central-city influx—increased steadily between 1940 and 1960. And changes in these areas, as pointed out earlier, have become more and more important in the eyes of blacks during the decade of the 1960s. Kenneth Clark has observed that "successful litigation, strong legislation, free access to public accommodations, state open housing laws, strong pronouncements on the part of the President, governors or mayors, and even the right to vote or to hold office [are] not relevant to the overriding fact that the masses of Negroes [are] still confined to poverty and to the dehumanizing conditions of the ghetto." [65]

If we examine national statistics, we see a similar pattern: moderate progress in some areas, regress in others. Income increased in the 1960s, yet housing segregation—the main cause of school segregation today—was still almost complete in the large cities. School desegregation is increasing in the South (at least temporarily while the vestiges of de jure segregation are eradicated by judicial decree), but in the North, segregation is on the increase. Black unemployment as compared to white unemployment has remained relatively constant. But in absolute numbers, it has almost doubled between 1966 and 1971.

To put the matter differently, there does not seem to be any clear-cut connection between the political pressure exerted by Negro interest groups, Negro politicians, and the Negro electorate on the one hand, and progress in obtaining benefits on the other. [66] The tre-

---

[65] Kenneth B. Clark, "The Present Dilemma of the Negro" (address before the annual meeting of the Southern Regional Council, Atlanta, November, 1967).

[66] Compare the view expressed by Roy Reed in the New York Times, February 8, 1970: "It appears that economic necessity will finally open more jobs for blacks in the South than political power will. Several industries, particularly textile and furniture manufacturers, are losing white workers to higher-paying industries and are turning to blacks to replace them." It is also true, however, than an eco-

mendous gains of blacks in the twenties were devoured by an economy gone berserk ten years later. The war-boom decade of the forties restored and augmented their previous gains. Yet, after another sharp ascent in the early fifties, there was stagnation and decline later in the decade and during the first years of the sixties. Then, once more there was moderate progress, which is now being hailed as a "major breakthrough." These fluctuations have been accompanied by a fairly steady groundswell of black political participation from the turn of the century onward.

Thus, the future of blacks remains precarious and uncertain. In the opinion of Charles Silberman, Negroes will not be able to catch up with whites unless the economy returns to a steady rapid growth rate over many years. "Indeed," he writes, "a rate of growth fast enough to keep the economy at full employment [N.B.] for an extended period of time is a prerequisite for any Negro progress at all. Full employment is the most effective solvent of discrimination in the labor market, because the alchemy of labor shortage turns people previously classified as unemployable into highly desirable employees."[67] Sar Levitan, of George Washington University's Center for Manpower Policy Studies, expressed a similar view in his analysis of gains made by Negro blue-collar males since 1960. While predicting that the gains would continue if the national economy avoids a prolonged recession, he said that if it does not, "Then we'll have real problems and the gains could be, I suspect, eliminated."[68]

A recession, increased unemployment, or even an insufficient demand for unskilled labor will pose especially serious problems for southern Negroes. James G. Maddox and his associates write in their book on the southern economy:

> In and of themselves, the factors that are tending to break down racial discrimination are unlikely to result in really significant improvements in the Negro job situation. In other words, it will not be enough for artificial barriers to employment of Negro

---

nomic slump will close jobs down for southern blacks, equally independent of their political efforts.

67 Silberman, "Negro Economic Gains," 124.
68 New York *Times*, June 21, 1970.

workers to be broken, as important as this is. Negro youth entering the labor force during the next decade will face manpower problems increasingly different from those of a few years past. Technology has significantly decreased the demand for unskilled labor and has increased the demand for manpower of high quality. The occupational and educational structure of the Negro work force does not lend itself to ready adaptation to such changes. *Indeed, unless the demand for unskilled labor increases, many poorly educated Negroes may face even greater difficulties in finding jobs in the future than in the past.*[69]

In other words economic decisions which vitally affect blacks are beyond their control. Given the marginality of most blacks to the socioeconomic structure, they are far more vulnerable than the average white to any malfunctioning of the labor market. "Last hired, first fired" is the truth firmly embedded in the collective consciousness of blacks. In order for blacks to achieve economic parity with whites, therefore, the decisions that shape the character of the economy must become accessible to their influence. It is not, as the conservative political scientists argue, that job security is in the nonpolitical realm. On the contrary, it is a goal that can be achieved only through politics. If and only if marginal groups can punish economic decision makers for putting some of their number out of work will job security become a reality. This is true both on the national level and the local one.

The same argument applies to other rewards besides income. Housing is a good example. The decisions of the local real estate industry involving the type of housing to be built and the social class of the customer it is to be built for must be made subject to the influence of numerous publics and interest groups. The same can be said for the health care system's decision makers.

Insofar as these types of decisions remain beyond the influence of average citizens, the central aims of the black struggle for socioeconomic justice will remain unfulfilled. This is not to deny that some gains will continue to be made (just as setbacks will continue to oc-

---

69 James G. Maddox, E. E. Liebhafsky, Vivian W. Henderson, and Herbert M. Hamlin, *The Advancing South: Manpower Prospects and Problems* (New York: Twentieth Century Fund, 1967), 153. Italics added.

cur). But the basic economic justice that has so far eluded blacks will continue to elude them so long as they do not have a say in what are now called "private" decisions by those who make them.

In this sense Negro political participation in Houston has yet to realize a significant breakthrough. It has, however, been responsible for a changed climate in the city, as well as a sharpened awareness among blacks and some of their white allies of what has to be done. Given the growing political consciousness of the repressed minorities in the city and the nation, there is reason to hope, as will be argued in the remainder of the book, that at least the groundwork for Negro progress has been laid by the efforts of blacks during the past two decades.

VI

In Search of White Allies

Once it is admitted that Houston's blacks are still very far from achieving their legitimate goals, despite the gains of previous decades, a practical question confronts us. How can the process of political assimilation be accelerated? The difficulties faced by blacks are a function both of discrimination and the fact that they constitute a minority. To achieve a working majority in Houston, they usually must garner the support of about a third of the white electorate, assuming that blacks are strongly unified. Sometimes they have succeeded in obtaining this support and sometimes they have not. Under what conditions is this support forthcoming? Which whites are more likely to enter into alliances with blacks? Assuming such alliances are possible, what must be done to transform the politics of the poor and the unassimilated from the relatively ineffective weapon it is today into one that is truly workable? These are the problems that remain to be considered.

The question of likely white allies has usually been posed in class terms: Which class tends to cooperate with blacks in achieving racial justice? Will "upper class" or "lower class" whites be more receptive to Negro overtures? One traditional view sees less affluent, or "working-class" whites as the logical friends of blacks, because of the similarity of their economic interests. Bayard Rustin, for example, has called for a shift from "protest" to "politics" based upon the coalition of progressive forces which staged the march on Washington in 1963: Negroes, trade unionists, liberals, and religious groups. The same coalition formed the backbone of the national Democratic victory in 1964—a victory, Rustin claims, which "proved

. . . that economic interests are more fundamental than prejudice."[1]

Such a coalition would form around the interests common to people of all races and ethnicities who belong to the less affluent class. The labor unions are viewed as one of the organizational instruments for awakening this class consciousness. Ralph Bunche, as a young scholar engaged in the Myrdal study during the depression years, described the theory clearly:

> This conception [that of class consciousness and class unity] . . . postulates the identity of interests of the working masses of the two races, and that these interests can be protected only by the unity of action by both groups, against the employers and the capitalistic structure which dictates their exploitations. . . . The strength of the working class is in its unity and its ability to present a unified front to the bosses. Therefore, white and Negro workers must cast aside their traditional prejudices, in their own welfare; they must lock arms and march shoulder to shoulder in the struggle for the liberation of the oppressed working masses. The overwhelming majority of Negroes are working class, and most of these are unskilled. Thus, practically the entire Negro race would be included in the scope of this ideology. The black and white masses, once united, could employ the terrifying power of their numbers to wring concessions from the employers and from the government itself.[2]

1 Bayard Rustin, "From Protest to Politics," *Commentary*, XXXIX (February, 1965), 29–30.

2 Quoted in Gunnar Myrdal, *An American Dilemma: The Negro Problem and American Democracy* (1944; 20th anniv. ed.; New York: Harper & Row, Publ., 1962), 789. This interpretation has been popular since the nineteenth century. For example, the Negro journalist, T. Thomas Fortune, writing in 1884, divided the South into four classes: the poor whites, "a careless, ignorant, lazy, but withal, arrogant set, who add nothing to the productive wealth of the community because they are too lazy to work, and who take nothing from that wealth because they are too poor to purchase"; the blacks "the great labor force of the South . . . the bone and sinew of the South, the great producers and partial consumers of her wealth"; the small white farmers; and the "hereditary landlords,"—"the gentlemen with flowing locks, gentle blood and irascible tempers, who appeal to the code of honor . . . to settle small differences with their equals and shoot down their inferiors without premeditation or compunction, and who drown their sorrows, as well as their joviality in rye or Bourbon whiskey." The latter are also those "who constantly declare that 'this is a white man's government,' and that 'the Negro must be made to keep his place.' They are the gentlemen who have their grip upon the throat of Southern labor." Fortune believed that the "moneyed class" was "hastening the conflict of labor and capital in the South. And, when the black laborer and

It was only with the coming of the New Deal, and the new-found strength of the labor movement, wrote Myrdal, that labor solidarity became "a realistic basis for Negro policy."[3]

Although variations of the labor solidarity thesis are still current, it does not rest on a firm empirical foundation. Few studies have appeared that explore the potential for class-based alliances. In the absence of electoral studies, other kinds of evidence, obtained primarily from attitude and opinion surveys, have been examined. As a result many social scientists have come to accept the belief that class-based biracial coalitions are the *least* likely to occur, and that the white middle and upper classes are the probable allies of blacks. As Myrdal demonstrated, the theory that "the best people among the whites," that is, the upper classes, are the true friends of the Negro is as venerable as that of labor solidarity. It was first popularized by Booker T. Washington as a short-range strategy prior to World War I when labor unions hardly existed in the South and were still extremely weak in the North.[4] But by 1940 Myrdal could write that "the trends of change in American society have made this optimistic, gradualistic philosophy increasingly unrealistic even as a short-range strategy." The federal government was severing its ties with the upper classes, as Myrdal saw it, depending more for its power and direction upon the general electorate and "in labor issues, increasingly upon organized labor."[5] Myrdal's revisionism was itself revised in the 1950s, and the findings of numerous attitude studies, not to mention the implications of some influential theories in the

---

the white laborer come to their senses, join issues with the common enemy and pitch the tent of battle, then will come the tug of war." Fortune, *Black and White: Land, Labor and Politics in the South* (1884; New York: Arno Press and the New York *Times*, 1968), 199–210.

3 Myrdal, *An American Dilemma*, 788.

4 The theory of upper-class beneficence toward blacks has its roots in the putative paternalism of the slaveholding class. However, Forrest G. Wood has written: "Some scholars have suggested that southern paternalism did not really begin until the reconstruction era was almost over, and that there were often economic kinships between blacks and poor whites that overcame the color difference....In the final analysis, the planters had been just as prejudiced as the poor whites, only in a different way." Wood, *Black Scare: The Racist Response to Emancipation and Reconstruction* (Berkeley: University of California Press, 1968), 3.

5 Myrdal, *An American Dilemma*, 788.

field of social psychology, were cited as evidence for a relatively greater hostility toward blacks among lower-class whites.[6] This has led to skepticism about the labor solidarity thesis among academic social scientists, journalists, and political commentators.

WORKING-CLASS WHITES: ATTITUDES

Perhaps the most widely quoted article on this subject is Seymour Martin Lipset's "Working-Class Authoritarianism," which attempts to explain the allegedly greater anti-Negro hostility of the working class by utilizing the general theory of authoritarianism formulated by T. W. Adorno and his colleagues in their book *The Authoritarian Personality*.[7] Lipset's thesis is that conditions of lower-class life tend to give rise to the personality syndrome of "authoritarianism," and that persons with this syndrome are more likely than nonauthoritarians to support undemocratic movements, including those which would deny civil rights to minorities like Negroes. Lipset cites almost no evidence for a correlation between class and racial tolerance.[8] Actually his argument for a correlation rests primarily

6 Myrdal has now deferred to the "new revisionists." In an interview in 1968, he said: "When I was here studying the Negro problem back more than a quarter of a century ago, it was supposed by people—and not only by radicals—that it would be natural for the poor to get together. Of course, the fact is just the opposite. It is the poor who are in conflict with each other, who are in competition with each other, who hate each other. The worst enemy the Negro has is the poor white; the only superiority the poor white has is the fact that he is not Negro, and this is the basis for your backlash." (Boston *Globe*, May 26, 1968.)

7 Seymour Martin Lipset, *Political Man* (Garden City: Doubleday & Co., Inc., Anchor Books, 1963), 87–126; T. W. Adorno, Else Frenkel-Brunswik, Daniel J. Levinson, and R. Nevitt Sanford, *The Authoritarian Personality* (New York: Harper and Bros., 1950).

8 One of the main studies cited to support the contention that there is "clear and consistent" evidence that "the lower strata are the least tolerant" is Arnold W. Rose, *Studies in Reduction of Prejudice* (Chicago: American Council on Race Relations, 1948.)

Actually Rose cites (pp. 40–41) only six studies bearing on socioeconomic class differences in attitudes toward outgroups. Three of the studies found *no* class differences in attitudes toward minority groups. Two of the remaining studies dealt with anti-Semitism only, and these showed an increase in anti-Semitism as social class increased. The final study, dealing with children's attitudes toward several minority groups, found the middle-class children most tolerant and rich

upon his more general assertion that people with one "undemo-cratic" attitude tend to have several which are manifested as an identifiable syndrome (and of course upon his further assertion that these people are concentrated in the lower classes).

The theory is open to question on several grounds. First, it relies in part upon research making use of the so-called F-scale, a pencil and paper instrument devised by the Adorno group to measure authoritarianism. Yet the F-scale, which has been widely employed in attitude surveys for twenty years, has never been validated. It remains to be shown that a person who scores high on the F-scale has the personality traits which define authoritarianism. Herbert H. Hyman and Paul B. Sheatsley have demonstrated that Adorno's attempt to establish a correlation between high scores on the F-scale and a generalized hostility toward outgroups, including blacks, has failed to comply with accepted research procedures. In concluding

---

children least tolerant "toward a whole group of nationalities." There was a "slight tendency" for the poor children to be less tolerant toward the Negro.

Elsewhere, in summarizing polling data prior to 1948, Rose mentions (p. 66) one study which showed "the upper classes" as more prejudiced against Negroes, and two others which support Lipset's position (pp. 67–68), so far as Negroes are concerned. Another study (p. 72) involving anti-discrimination laws found manual workers most favorable to such laws.

It is interesting to note that Lipset is not alone in citing as evidence of lower-class prejudice works which do not support this thesis. Peter Blau and Otis Dudley Duncan, in their important work on the American occupational structure, cite the work of Samuel Stouffer, *Communism, Conformity, and Civil Liberties*, (Garden City: Doubleday & Co., Inc., 1955) as arguing that "educated persons are generally considered to be more enlightened and, specifically, to be less prejudiced against Negroes and other minorities than less educated ones." Stouffer's study did not deal with racial attitudes, however, but with attitudes towards civil liberties. See Blau and Duncan, *The American Occupational Structure* (New York: John Wiley & Sons, Inc., 1967), 239n.

Donald Matthews and James Prothro write: "After all, racial prejudice and discrimination are most pronounced among people with little formal education." Matthews and Prothro, *Negroes and the New Southern Politics* (New York: Harcourt, Brace and World, 1966), 126. None of the works cited to support this claim measured the discrimination against blacks by whites of different social classes. All of the works relied solely on verbal responses to questionnaires. The works in question were: Bruno Bettelheim and Morris Janowitz, *The Dynamics of Prejudice: A Psychological and Sociological Study of Veterans* (New York: Harper and Bros., 1950); Herbert H. Hyman and Paul B. Sheatsley, "Attitudes Toward Desegregation," *Scientific American*, CXCV (December, 1956), 35–39; and Melvin Tumin, *Desegregation: Resistance and Readiness* (Princeton: Princeton University Press), 1958.

their analysis of the methodology of *The Authoritarian Personality*, they claim that "the authors' theory has not been proved by the data they cite ... the mistakes and limitations—no one of them perhaps crucial—uniformly operate *in favor* of the authors' assumptions, and cumulatively they build up a confirmation of a theory which, upon examination, proves to be spurious."[9] S. M. Miller and Frank Riessman claim that while there does seem to be some connection in the middle classes between high F-scale scores and independently assessed authoritarian qualities, no such connection was discovered in the working class.[10] Angus Campbell and his colleagues, utilizing University of Michigan National Survey Research Center data, demonstrated that the usefulness of measures involving the F-scale has been seriously reduced by the tendency of lower-class respondents to agree to any plausible statement which is presented positively in a questionnaire.[11] More recently John P. Kirscht and Ronald C. Dillehay reviewed a decade's research on authoritarianism and concluded that the syndrome has so far proved too elusive for measurement, if indeed it is a genuine clinical "entity."[12] (A significant yet little-noted fact is that authoritarianism, as an

9 Herbert H. Hyman and Paul B. Sheatsley, " 'The Authoritarian Personality'— A Methodological Critique," in Richard Christie and Marie Jahoda (eds.), *Studies in the Scope and Method of 'The Authoritarian Personality'* (Glencoe: The Free Press, 1954), 119, and 121.

10 S. M. Miller and Frank Riessman, "Working Class Authoritarianism: A Critique of Lipset," *British Journal of Sociology*, XII (1961), 273.

11 Angus Campbell, Philip E. Converse, Warren E. Miller, and Donald E. Stokes, *The American Voter* (New York: John Wiley & Sons, Inc., 1960), 512–15. For a recent summary of the discussion of the "response set" debate as it applies to the F-scale, see John P. Kirscht and Ronald C. Dillehay, *Dimensions of Authoritarianism: A Review of Research and Theory* (Lexington: University of Kentucky Press, 1967), 13–29.

12 Kirscht and Dillehay, *Dimensions of Authoritarianism*. They write (pp. 130–31): "We suffer from the apparent ease with which authoritarian behavior can be identified in real-life examples ... [but] our confidence in a diagnosis of authoritarianism is not matched by our skill in objective measurement.... The conception and execution of research in this area has suffered from the fact that authoritarianism, as it is currently formulated, is a relatively poor explanatory variable. It suggests so many connotations which have been inadequately verified. As specified in *The Authoritarian Personality*, the various components, such as rigidity and stereotypy, have not stood up as a coherent and unified set of dispositions.... In fact, the concept has so many different aspects that investigators lack a common core of established meaning, and often assume connections among various dispositions that have never been examined satisfactorily."

abnormal personality syndrome, has not in the past two decades found its way into the vocabulary of practicing psychiatrists.) One is forced to conclude that as the F-scale, which purports to measure authoritarianism, has not been validated, the finding that lower-class respondents often score higher than upper-class ones is problematic.

There are other difficulties that beset Lipset's theory. For example, it systematically ignores the positive aspects of the personalities of poor people. Herbert Gans has recently restored some balance to the prevalent view of "lower-class" people by reviewing works which have described these positive traits.[13] There is also the question of the source of the lower-class pathology that does exist. Lipset claims that it is the conditions of lower-class life itself. However, data examined by Joseph Greenblum and Leonard I. Pearlin, obtained from the Elmira study, suggest that vertical social mobility may play an important role in the disproportionately biased responses among the working class. When upward and downward mobile persons are separated from the "stationary" members of manual and nonmanual occupations, the stationary working class responses appear more tolerant in some dimensions than the nonmanuals.[14] In a secondary analysis of data obtained from three national sample surveys, Lewis Lipsitz found that with education controlled, most of the differences in "authoritarian" responses between the working class and middle class disappeared. He concluded that "the greater authoritarianism of the working class, as opposed to the middle class, appears to be largely a product of lower education," and not, as Lipset hypothesized, a product of the concomitant conditions of lower class life.[15] These studies support the fact that the working class gives more authoritarian responses to

13 Herbert Gans, "Poverty and Culture: Some Basic Questions About Methods of Studying Life-Styles of the Poor," in Peter Townsend (ed.), *The Concept of Poverty* (London: Heinemann Educational Books, 1970), 147.

14 Joseph Greenblum and Leonard I. Pearlin, "Vertical Mobility and Prejudice: A Socio-Psychological Analysis," in Reinhard Bendix and Seymour Lipset (eds.), *Class, Status and Power: A Reader in Social Stratification* (1st ed.; New York: The Free Press, 1953), 486.

15 Lewis Lipsitz, "Working-Class Authoritarianism: A Re-Evaluation," *American Sociological Review*, XXX (1965), 103–109.

F-scale type questions. But they strongly suggest that the reasons for this difference are other than Lipset suspected.

Some authors who cite Lipset's thesis as a reason why biracial working-class coalitions will not work have overlooked a very important qualification which Lipset attaches to his theory—it applies only when "other things are equal." He stipulates at least four conditions under which they are not equal. Lipset claims that authoritarianism and, hence, undemocratic attitudes, will not, in themselves, lead to a decision to support an undemocratic movement, candidate, party, and so forth, when: (1) loyalty to moderate or democratic groups overrides the appeal of extremist politics; (2) nonpolitical extremist movements—especially religious ones—serve as substitutes for political extremism; (3) an extremist political party represents a more complex alternative than a moderate one; (4) there is not a crisis situation. Thus, for example, the fact that the national Democratic Party since the New Deal has generally been more racially enlightened than the Republican Party and has at the same time drawn its support disproportionately from the American working class presents no difficulty for the theory. This is simply one of those situations where other things are not equal— in this case, the workers' loyalty to an economically liberal party overrides their allegedly greater racism.

However, there is a problem in Lipset's stipulation of these four conditions under which other things are not equal. For although it may salvage his theory by accommodating data which would otherwise seriously weaken it, there is also the possibility that it limits so severely the occasions under which the theory is operable as to render it, for practical purposes, useless. For example, one might argue that the fourth condition that must obtain in order for the theory to apply, that is, a crisis situation, has existed very rarely in twentieth century America. On the other hand, one could argue that a crisis has existed throughout the twentieth century. Unfortunately, the matter cannot be settled with ease, as Lipset mentions no criteria for determining whether a crisis exists or not. At any rate, what is of crucial importance is Lipset's recognition that attitudes, for example, hostility toward minority groups, are often tempered by one's commitment to a party which nevertheless supports civil rights for minorities. Therefore, even if Lipset's theory of working-class authoritarianism is well founded (and there is reasonable doubt that it is), it does not follow that the white working class is not a potential ally of blacks.

A study of white Southerners' attitudes toward school desegregation, carried out by Melvin Tumin, appeared at about the same time as Lipset's article and led to similar conclusions, so far as class differences in anti-Negro hostility are concerned. Tumin argued that people with more formal education, higher occupational status, and greater exposure to the mass media were more ready for desegregation.[16] Yet although Tumin's findings have been mentioned in support of the position that lower-class whites are not suitable allies of blacks, Tumin makes no claims of this sort.[17] His study is concerned solely with the feasibility of school desegregation. Even on this score, Tumin admits that attitudinal data such as he collected are not by themselves very trustworthy predictors of action in the face of school desegregation. "What men are prepared to do by way of acceptance or rejection of desegregation depends as much if not more upon the conditions under which they live and what actions are possible," he writes, "as upon the feelings regarding Negroes and desegregation."[18] The truth of this observation is dramatically borne out by James W. Vander Zanden's analysis of the results of a 1956 segregationist referendum in Greensboro, the major urban center of Guilford County, North Carolina. Tumin's study was carried out at approximately the same time in the same county. Vander Zanden found no evidence that lower-class precincts were appreciably more segregationist than upper-class ones.[19]

16 Tumin, *Desegregation*, 195–96.
17 Tumin's work is cited, for example, by Harry Holloway in support of such a position in "Negro Political Strategy: Coalition or Independent Power Politics?" *Social Science Quarterly*, XLIX (1968), 539n.
18 *Ibid.*, 22.
19 James W. Vander Zanden, "Voting on Segregationist Referenda," in Vander Zanden, *Race Relations in Transition* (New York: Random House, Inc., 1965), 108–109. This chapter originally appeared in *Public Opinion Quarterly*, XXV (1961), 92–105.

Several studies concerned with the attitudes of different social classes toward ethnic minorities have revealed a far more complex situation than the Lipset thesis suggests. For example, Bruno Bettelheim and Morris Janowitz in their study of prejudice among Chicago war veterans shortly after World War II found no correlation at all between class and anti-Semitism. They did find a significant inverse correlation between occupational status and anti-Negro hostility.[20] However, when income rather than occupation was used as an index of class, the proportion of tolerant individuals was the same in the two income categories. Moreover the lower category had a markedly lower percentage of veterans who were "most intolerant."[21]

Herbert H. Hyman and Paul B. Sheatsley, analyzing National Opinion Research Center survey data, reported in 1956 that the proportion of whites both nationally and in the subregions of the North and South who said they favored desegregation of schools and public transportation increased with education, which is a correlate of class.[22] But, contrary to expectations, they found no important difference from one educational level to the next with regard to the desirability of having Negroes as neighbors. Inasmuch as the barriers to school integration in many large cities consist primarily of *de facto* residential segregation, one could argue that it is the whites' attitudes toward neighborhood desegregation rather than school desegregation per se which is of most significance in determining their readiness for desegregation.[23]

20 Bettelheim and Janowitz, *Dynamics of Prejudice*, 57, 151. A positive correlation was also discovered between ethnic prejudice of both kinds and rapid upward and downward mobility. As is true of Tumin's study, that of Bettelheim and Janowitz depended upon a rather limited sample—one hundred fifty persons—in which certain categories were underrepresented or excluded. As the authors point out (p. 57n), the exclusion of veterans who were officers led to a sharp underrepresentation of higher socioeconomic levels, and thus the sample "permits no generalizations about the top social strata."

21 *Ibid.*, 224.

22 Hyman and Sheatsley, "Attitudes Toward Desegregation," 35–39.

23 More recently, Paul B. Sheatsley constructed a scale of "pro-integration sentiments" based on response to eight questions asked a national sample of whites in 1963. He concluded that an individual's socioeconomic status, as measured by occupation, educational level, and family income, is positively related to his score on the Pro-Integration Scale. See Sheatsley, "White Attitudes Toward the Negro,"

Bruno Bettelheim and Morris Janowitz, writing in 1964, summarized attitude and opinion survey data and reached this cautious conclusion: "National surveys reveal that for the population as a whole and for very broad socioeconomic groupings a limited association with very general forms of ethnic prejudice does emerge. *The upper social groups are at least more inhibited in their expression of ethnic intolerance.*"[24] The last sentence suggests that the authors are not sure whether to take at face value verbal responses in matters concerning prejudice.[25] But further, they point to the fact that the data they cite from the 1957 Detroit Area Study do not reveal a linear correlation between socioeconomic status, as measured by the respondent's occupation, and Negro prejudice.[26] There was almost no variation in the proportion of "tolerants" (the most tolerant classification) from one category to the next. As for the "strongly intolerants," the highest occupational category did have the lowest percentage, and the lowest category the highest percentage. But the middle-class occupations of "clerical, sales, and kindred" had a markedly higher percentage of "strongly intolerants" than did the craftsmen and foremen category in the working class.[27]

A study of white attitudes toward desegregation in Norfolk, Virginia, in 1959 by Richard Lamanna revealed a higher degree of desegregationist sentiment among respondents of low social rank (18.5 percent) than among either those of medium rank (11.7 percent) or high (13.2 percent). There was no appreciable difference in the degree of strong segregationist sentiment at any social level.[28]

---

in Talcott Parsons and Kenneth B. Clark (eds.), *The Negro American* (Boston: Houghton-Mifflin Co., 1966), 310.

24 Bruno Bettelheim and Morris Janowitz, "Trends in Prejudice," in Bernard Berelson and Morris Janowitz (eds.), *Reader in Public Opinion and Communication* (2nd ed.; New York: The Free Press, 1966), 106. Italics added.

25 They differ in this respect from Hyman and Sheatsley who, without adducing any evidence aside from the "liveliness of interest" in racial questions shown by respondents, state that "there can be little doubt that on racial segregation people honestly expressed their deeply felt opinions." See Hyman and Sheatsley, "Attitudes Toward Desegregation," 37.

26 Bettelheim and Janowitz, "Trends in Prejudice," 106.

27 *Ibid.*, 106–107.

28 Richard Lamanna, "Ecological Correlates of Attitude Toward School Desegregation," *American Catholic Sociological Review*, XXII (1961), 245.

Richard Hamilton, in a secondary analysis of numerous national opinion surveys, found only partial evidence for the lower-class bigotry hypothesis. After examining the difference in verbally expressed racial tolerance between manual and nonmanual groups, he concluded:

> On the whole, the evidence presented here yields only very restricted support for the "working-class authoritarianism" claim. In six of the eight comparisons of the non-South groups there is basically no support for the claim. In the remaining two comparisons, the maximum difference amounts to eight percentage points. In the South, there is again no support in six of the eight comparisons. In the Southern responses to the school integration questions, those of 1964 and 1965, there is some support for the received claim, here the maximum difference being one of 17 percentage points.[29]

Further analysis revealed, moreover, that among the nonmanuals, the lower-middle class was not markedly less tolerant than the upper-middle class.

Donald Matthews and James Prothro interviewed a South-wide sample of 694 voting-age whites in the early 1960s, and found that "the proportion of whites who are strict segregationists decreases with every increase in formal education."[30] In addition to their attitude survey, the authors analyzed almost a thousand southern counties in an attempt to discover demographic correlates of Negro registration rates. There was a strong inverse correlation between median school years completed by whites and the registration rates of blacks. The correlation remained even when the influence of several other variables was controlled.[31] Significantly this ecological analysis took into account actual behavioral data—the extent of Negro voter registration—rather than only attitudes. The authors interpreted their findings as follows: "Short of the highest levels, the higher the average education in a county, the more actively and effectively they seem to enforce the traditional mores of the region

29 Hamilton, *Class and Politics in the United States*, chapter 11, in press.
30 Donald R. Matthews and James W. Prothro, *Negroes and the New Southern Politics* (New York: Harcourt, Brace and World, 1966), 343.
31 *Ibid.*, 126–29.

against Negro participation in elections. An increase in average schooling for whites in the South seems to give them more of the skills they need to express effectively their anti-Negro sentiment."[32]

A similar type of inconsistency in findings occurs in Thomas Pettigrew's study of school desegregation in Texas in the 1960s. Opinion surveys conducted on a statewide basis between 1954 and 1961 showed that upper socioeconomic groups were somewhat less likely than lower groups to advocate defiance of the law in order to resist school desegregation.[33] The pattern was less clear when education rather than socioeconomic status was examined as a determinant of expressed segregationist sentiment. Respondents with grade school education were more favorable to desegregation than those with high school education, although those with college education were the most tolerant of the three groupings.[34] However, when education was controlled for age and city size, this pattern was even less consistent. For example, among the middle-aged respondents in medium-sized cities, those with grade school education were more likely than those with high school or college degrees to support school desegregation. The same was true among the youngest category of respondents in rural areas. In nine comparisons of this sort, the college-educated gave the most tolerant replies in seven, but the least educated—those with less than a high school education—gave the least tolerant replies only once.[35] Thus, even the survey data alone did not reveal the expected pattern in an unambiguous fashion.

When ecological data involving actual behavior were examined, the evidence did not support the lower-class bigotry thesis at all—paralleling the Matthews-Prothro study in this respect. Using counties as the unit of analysis, Pettigrew found no significant correlation between socioeconomic status (as measured by median house value) and either the earliness of initiation of desegregation or the extent of desegregation, when other variables were controlled. This held

32 *Ibid.*, 128.
33 Thomas F. Pettigrew, *A Study of School Integration*, Cooperative Research Project No. 6–1774, United States Department of Health, Education, and Welfare, (Washington, D.C.; August, 1970; mimeo.), 53.
34 *Ibid.*, 121.
35 *Ibid.*, 124.

both for the state at large and for the state's three principal sub-regions.[36] Pettigrew's analysis of northern white voting patterns led him to emphasize the sense of relative deprivation rather than social class per se as a crucial variable influencing support for antiblack electoral candidates.[37]

Other polls of the white southern population have been cited by scholars as showing greater bigotry among lower-class whites. Alfred O. Hero adduces National Opinion Research Center and American Institute of Public Opinion data to support the "working class bigotry" thesis.[38] Even so, Hero is careful not to depict the upper-class Southerners as racially progressive. He characterizes the upper- and middle-class whites who were more moderate in their attitudes toward blacks prior to 1954 as "paternalistic segregationists." They were against violence, and somewhat more tolerant toward "faithful" Negroes, at least, than other whites. Yet he estimates that "the total number of truly paternalistic whites might be liberally estimated at 2 percent of the white population in areas with considerable proportions of Negroes."[39]

Even these whites were not really sympathetic to emerging Negro aspirations. They "hold many of the same racial views as the white majority—that Negroes were unreliable, hedonistic, shiftless, loose in morals, lacking in 'character,' childlike, and innately inferior to whites."[40] After the school desegregation decision of 1954, Hero claims that much of the paternalist "moderation" of the southern gentry quickly evaporated.

> According to interviews in 1959–62 and impressions from other experiences with this group, a considerable fraction of former paternalists—apparently a majority in some traditionalist settings— have developed more uncompromising opposition to racial change as the quickening tempo of desegregation or the threat of it seemed to menace their secure, traditionally related, genteel hierarchical

36 Pettigrew, "A Study of School Integration," 37, 43.
37 Ibid., chapters 6, 7, and 8.
38 Alfred O. Hero, The Southerner and World Affairs (Baton Rouge: Louisiana State University Press, 1965), 391.
39 Ibid., 387.
40 Ibid.

system. . . . Some . . . have become leaders in . . . groups designed to prevent racial change. Others have supported these organizations. . . . Still others have agreed with the objectives of these groups, but have resisted participating in sections where the leadership and active membership have been made up largely of "uncouth" people from the lower orders.[41]

From the foregoing it can be seen that the findings of attitude and opinion surveys hardly support Lipset's claim of "clear and consistent" evidence that "the lower strata are the least tolerant."[42] The difficulty of establishing hard and fast generalizations regarding class and prejudice was made especially clear in Charles Stember's review of nationwide surveys during the fifteen-year period preceding 1959. He found that there was no clear-cut relationship between level of schooling (one important index of class) and prejudice. In three respects the better educated did seem to be less prejudiced, at least in verbal responses to interviewers. They were not as apt to hold traditional anti-Negro and anti-Semitic stereotypes, to favor discriminatory policies, and to reject casual association with members of minority groups. Yet the better educated were more likely to have highly emotional and derogatory stereotypes, to favor informal discrimination in some areas of behavior, and to reject intimate (as opposed to casual) contacts with minorities.[43] Undoubtedly Gordon Allport's observation about the results of attitude surveys linking demographic variables to prejudice still holds today. "A large number of studies bear on this matter," he wrote in 1954, "but they tend to contradict each other. . . . It seems safest at the present time to conclude that while claims of this order may hold for single studies, they do not form a firm basis for generalization."[44]

41 *Ibid.*, 404.

42 Lipset, *Political Man*, 94.

43 Charles H. Stember, *Education and Attitude Change* (New York: Institute of Human Relations Press, 1961), 168.

44 Gordon W. Allport, *The Nature of Prejudice* (1954; Garden City: Doubleday & Co., Inc., Anchor Books, 1958), 77–78. Allport did go on to list three generalizations: "Regarding education, it generally but not always appears from researches that people with college education are less intolerant than people with grade school or high school education (at least they answer questions in a more tolerant way [N.B.])." With regard to region, the South is more anti-Negro than the North or West, while anti-Semitism seems greatest in the Northeast. Regarding socioeco-

Why this is true ought to be obvious upon reflection. There are several reasons why the type of evidence so far considered has limitations. Respondents may be dishonest. This is all the more likely to be true when questions deal with emotionally charged issues and when certain answers may evoke strong approval or disapproval. Stember, in his above-mentioned work, suggests that the more tolerant responses of better educated groups are due not so much to greater tolerance, but to their reluctance to express attitudes which run counter to "acceptable" opinions.[45]

On the other hand, responses may not reflect dishonesty so much as ideal values—those to which people more or less sincerely pay lip service, while honoring them primarily in the breach. Another difficulty in basing predictions of behavior on verbal responses is that people have trouble envisaging an actual situation in all its complexity, and even when they more or less succeed, they are not very good at predicting their own behavior in such circumstances. "If an order to desegregate came, I would . . ." often means no more than "in such a situation, other things being equal, I think that I should . . . ."

V. O. Key was aware of this problem when he interpreted class differentials in expressed attitudes toward civil rights. Summarizing his review of national survey data on the relation of class and occupation to attitudes toward civil liberties and civil rights, he wrote:

> That differentials in opinion on specific issues exist and that they can be of disturbing practical importance there can be no doubt, but the odds are that their explanation must be sought pragmatically issue by issue rather than in some pervading quality of personality or outlook especially common among workers. Thus, regarding views on school segregation in the North the odds are simply that the families of unskilled workers would more frequently be affected by integration than would those of the professional classes.[46]

---

nomic status, white people at lower levels are "more bitterly anti-Negro" than whites at higher levels, while the reverse holds for anti-Semitism. Allport (p. 78) stresses, however, that these generalizations are nothing more than "tentative assertions."

45 Stember, *Education and Attitude Change*, 11.

46 V. O. Key, Jr., *Public Opinion and American Democracy* (New York: Alfred A. Knopf, Inc., 1961), 137–38.

A quite different problem is that people who genuinely have anti-Negro attitudes may express them only in certain ways and not in others.[47] Allport divided the mode of expression of prejudice into three broad gradations: verbal rejection or "antilocution"; actual discrimination, including segregation; and physical attack, in varying degrees of intensity.[48] His point was that antilocutionary expressions of prejudice are not necessarily linked to discrimination or violence. He cited the classic experiment of La Piere as an example of the disjunction between antilocutionary and other expressions of prejudice. La Piere, an American, traveled extensively in this country with a Chinese couple, stopping at 66 sleeping places and 184 eating places. They were refused service only once. After the trip the proprietors were sent questionnaires asking whether they would take "members of the Chinese race as guests in your establishment." More than 90 percent of both restaurants and hotels said they would refuse service to Chinese. A control group of establishments which had not been visited gave similar responses to questionnaires. Allport commented: "To raise the question which of these two sets of behavior was an expression of their 'true' attitude is, of course, foolish. The outstanding contribution of La Piere's study design consists in showing that both are 'true' attitudes, fitted to two different situations. The 'verbal' situation aroused more hostility than the actual situation. People who threaten to discriminate may not do so."[49] Allport also observed that epithets such as "nigger" may mean much less when used by lower-class whites than when used by upper-class people, "whose vocabulary is flexible enough to avoid them—if they

47 Charles Tittle and Richard Hill have recently reviewed numerous studies which have attempted to discern the relationship (if any) between attitudes expressed in survey research and actual behavior of the respondents. Certain kinds of attitude measurements seem to be somewhat more reliable predictors of behavior than others; but as the authors point out, it is not clear whether this is because of a greater reliability inherent in some of the measuring instruments, or merely the result of chance. But even the most successfully applied instruments yield only very modest results in predicting behavior. See Tittle and Hill, "Attitude Measurement and Prediction of Behavior: An Evaluation of Conditions and Measurement Techniques," *Sociometry*, XXX (1967), 199–213.

48 Allport, *The Nature of Prejudice*, 48.

49 *Ibid.*, 55. La Piere's findings have been confirmed by other studies.

wish to do so."[50] This same point is made by Pat Watters. "What kind of answer," he asks, "would an 'opinion survey' have received from the white lady quoted as follows in an article about Atlanta housing?": "Sure . . . we got niggers all around. Niggers on this side, niggers on that side, niggers across the street and over yonder, niggers around the corner both ways. They taken over the place." How was it working out? "Jes' *fine*! You couldn't ask for nicer neighbors. We don't have no trouble. They all nice people."[51] The point is also implicitly made by Malcolm X in his autobiography: "Some of the white kids at school, I found, were even friendlier than some of those in Lansing had been. Though some, including the teachers, called me 'nigger,' it was easy to see that they didn't mean any more harm by it than the Swerlins [his foster parents]."[52]

The value of a questionnaire designed to elicit the respondent's specific attitudes is that it separates these attitudes from the complex tangle of concomitant ones, many of which act in concert to bring about an individual's behavior. Where politics is concerned, the polls, as David Riesman has written, "pull asunder what the parties have joined together." Attitude survey data, therefore, if they are to be of use in political analysis, must be interpreted judiciously. Most important, they should whenever possible be supplemented by behavioral observations. Consequently any systematic assessment of the feasibility of a class-based biracial coalition must take into account any evidence, however fragmentary, of the ways different classes of whites behave toward blacks.

WORKING-CLASS WHITES VS THEIR "BETTERS": BEHAVIOR

Much is made in sociology texts as well as the popular press of the competition between black workers and white ones, and the

50 *Ibid.*, 49.
51 Pat Watters, *The South and the Nation* (New York: Pantheon Books, 1969), 24.
52 *The Autobiography of Malcolm X* (New York: Grove Press, 1964), 28.

difficulties this leads to so far as alliances are concerned. Widespread segregation in labor unions, the participation of "ordinary" whites in mobs and lynchings, the dependence of the Ku Klux Klan upon people of low status are often mentioned as evidence for the greater intolerance of working-class whites. But there is also a large body of evidence to suggest that upper-class whites have contributed in important and often decisive ways to racial discrimination and anti-Negro violence. A recent analysis of the American occupational structure by Peter M. Blau and Otis Dudley Duncan revealed that Negro-white occupational differentials increased at each educational level.[53] That is, the gap between occupational levels for the two races increased as education increased. A college-trained black was farther behind a college-educated white, in terms of occupational prestige and income, than was a grade-school-educated black relative to a grade-school-educated white. The authors interpret this as follows:

> . . . whereas educated persons are generally considered to be more enlightened and, specifically, to be less prejudiced against Negroes and other minorities than less educated ones, the data show that *in actuality there is more discrimination against Negroes in highly than in less educated groups.* It can hardly be a pattern of prejudice unique to the uneducated laborers and operatives that forces enlightened employers to discriminate against hiring Negroes on these levels, as is sometimes alleged, for there is even more discrimination on higher levels.[54]

An explanation of the mechanisms by which businessman bigotry becomes operative has been given by Louis Ferman, based on his study of racial discrimination in a national sample of business firms:

> There is clear evidence in this study that a set of values exists in the business community that has implications for the more effective utilization of Negro workers. These values emphasize efficiency of operation and the priority of work standards over equal employment goals, resistance to modifying employment standards to hire

53 Peter M. Blau and Otis Dudley Duncan, *The American Occupational Structure* (New York: John Wiley & Sons, Inc., 1967), 208.
54 *Ibid.*, 239–40. Italics added.

Negroes, resistance to increasing Negro job mobility through special quotas for Negroes, and resistance to special employment programs that are not integrally a part of the present employment structure of the company. There is a pronounced tendency to blame the "inferior" or "different" educational and social background of the Negro for his job difficulties. The Negro job problem is also seen as a community rather than company responsibility. In other words, it is community rather than company resources which must be primarily brought into play to equalize the Negro's job opportunities. . . . There is repeated emphasis on the belief that whatever management does must be primarily within "normal" employment standards and practices and must not jeopardize work efficiency or production standards. The point was repeatedly made in interviews with local plant officials that an equal employment program must be set within the cost and employment structure of the company and not be an activity in itself.[55]

The insight of Matthews and Prothro mentioned above is especially plausible here. Middle- and upper-class people can actually use their education to accomplish a more sophisticated sort of discrimination (which includes denying that it occurs) than is possible for the poorly educated whites. Allen Rosenzweig's account of the ingenious maneuvering of a New Orleans voter registrar—an old-family Bourbon—in keeping Negroes and poor whites from registering to vote in the early 1960s is illustrative of this point.[56] Another example is found in Harry Holloway's account of Birmingham business leaders' double dealings in the face of the 1963 crisis. "A settlement of sorts was achieved that did stop the demonstrations," he writes, "but not much came of the supposed agreement. . . . Negro leaders felt they had been deceived and misled, especially in the matter of jobs promised Negroes in downtown stores."[57] Robert Crain concludes from his study of the New Orleans school desegregation crisis that the upper-class power structure "is committed to traditional values and is oblivious to the social costs of trying to maintain these

55 Louis Ferman, *The Negro and Equal Employment Opportunities* (New York: Frederick A. Praeger, Inc., 1968), v–vi.

56 Allen Rosenzweig, "The Influence of Class and Race on Political Behavior in New Orleans: 1960–1967" (M.A. thesis, University of Oklahoma, 1967), 134–48.

57 Harry Holloway, *The Politics of the Southern Negro* (New York: Random House, Inc., 1969), 166.

values."[58] This is consistent with Warren Breed's earlier account of the refusal of New Orleans businessmen to support open public schools in the 1950s.[59]

Although Lipset, in his above-mentioned article, alludes to the blue-collar support for White Citizens Councils in the South as evidence for his theory of "working class authoritarianism," James Vander Zanden's account of the councils reveals that they recruited members from the "most prominent, well-educated, and conservative businessmen in each community."[60] He quotes the council leader in Jackson, Mississippi, who was also the editor of the movement's national newspaper: "If you take the Farm Bureau, Rotary, Kiwanis and Lions Clubs out of the Citizens Council movement, you wouldn't have much left."[61] Watters refers to the councils as "the 'nice' people's organizational mode of expressing racism and resistance to desegregation."[62] For this reason, Watters argues, the council movement was far more effective than the latter-day Klan. James Silver's evaluation of the councils is less charitable still. While asserting that they maintained a façade of respectability and nonviolence, Silver prefers Hodding Carter's description of them as an "uptown Klan." He documents cases in which the councils resorted to intimidation and threat in order to force moderates to leave Mississippi.[63] Numan Bartley has documented the upper-class leadership of the councils in Texas, Tennessee, Alabama, South Carolina, and North Carolina.[64]

58 Robert L. Crain, *The Politics of School Desegregation* (Garden City: Doubleday & Co., Inc., Anchor Books, 1969), 380.

59 Warren Breed, "Institutionalization, Group Structure and Resistance to Desegregation in the Deep South" (revised version of paper read before the American Sociological Association, August 30, 1960; dittoed.

60 Vander Zanden, "Voting on Segregationist Referenda," 26.

61 *Ibid.*

62 Watters, *The South and the Nation*, 30.

63 James Silver, *Mississippi: The Closed Society* (New York: Harcourt, Brace and World, 1964), 36.

64 Numan V. Bartley, *The Rise of Massive Resistance: Race and Politics in the South During the 1950's* (Baton Rouge: Louisiana State University Press, 1969), 89–104. According to Bartley (pp. 99–100), some councils in Tennessee had lower-class bases. But "in Nashville, where the organization was most vigorous, the federation represented a Snopesean perversion of the aristocratic agrarian tradition. Donald Davidson, a professor of English at Vanderbilt University, served as president, and a number of people associated with the cultural and artistic community in Nashville, filled other offices. Since some of these individuals were men of sub-

Speaking of the council movement South-wide, Bartley cites numerous sources to substantiate his conclusion that "the Councils were the instruments of the middle class," even though they enlisted workers in southern cities.[65]

The Klan is a better example of the blue-collar extremist organization which Lipset had in mind. But even in this case, there is evidence that it has received financial support and encouragement from better-off whites. This was clearly the case during the Klan revival of the 1920s. For example, many of Texas' leading politicians and businessmen were openly identified with the Invisible Empire (if that is not a contradiction) until it was no longer expedient to do so. Floyd Hunter, in his study of Atlanta in the late 1940s, discovered links between the city's "top leaders and the mobile understructure of violent force," including the Klan.[66] W. J. Cash had perceived a similar pattern a few years earlier. He wrote of the Klan: "Its body was made up of the common whites . . . but its blood . . . came from the upper orders. And its bony framework and nervous system, the people who held it together and coordinated and directed it, were very near to being coextensive with the established leadership of the South."[67] Watters, too, sees the "nice people" who composed the membership of the Citizens Councils as having quietly encouraged the Klan to violence, while openly claiming to eschew such methods.[68]

Arthur Raper's study of mob lynching a generation earlier revealed the same pattern of cooperation: action by ordinary whites, complicity and encouragement from their social betters, including the law enforcement officers, the municipal officials, and the city fathers.[69] Lillian Smith, whose novels reveal an uncommon percep-

---

stantial means, the organization was relatively well-financed, retaining its own legal staff to do battle for such causes as an attack on the validity of the Fourteenth Amendment."

65 *Ibid.,* 104.

66 Floyd Hunter, *Community Power Structure* (1953; Garden City: Doubleday & Co., Inc., Anchor Books, 1963), 144.

67 W. J. Cash, *The Mind of the South* (New York: Random House, Inc., 1941 [Vintage edition]), 344.

68 Watters, *The South and the Nation*, 30.

69 Arthur F. Raper, *The Tragedy of Lynching*, (1933; New York: Negro Uni-

tion of southern social realities, speaks of the region's genteel racists as "Mob No. 2."

> Not all our business and professional men belong to it, by any means. But many do. It is a quiet well-bred mob. Its members speak in cultivated voices, have courteous manners; some have university degrees, and a few wear Brooks Brothers suits. But they are a mob nevertheless. For they not only protect the rabble, and tolerate its violence, *they think in the same primitive mode*, they share the same irrational anxieties, they are *just as lawless in their own quiet way*, and they are dominated by the same "holy idea" of white supremacy.[70]

Robert Sherrill's report on "gothic politics" in the South is filled with examples of the cooperation between the rich whites and the

---

versities Press, 1969). Raper's analysis of known lynchers in 1930, that is, those positively identified as taking active part in a lynch mob—revealed that they consisted mostly of younger, poorer, "unattached," propertyless white males (although in many cases well-to-do males, as well as females and even children, were part of the mob). But Raper argues (p. 12) that "those sympathizers who stood by shared in the lawlessness, and curious onlookers who rushed in merely because something unusual was happening were not without guilt. This last named element, made up of the 'better people,' provided the active mobbers with a semblance of decency and no small measure of immunity from official interference." The law enforcement officers and "courthouse crowd" were also indicted by Raper, who wrote that "most of the sheriffs along with their deputies and the municipal officials not only failed to resist the mob effectively but later reported under oath to the grand jury that they did not recognize a single member of the mob." See pp. 10–14.

Leonard L. Richards has recently done an excellent job of destroying the myth that the typical antiabolitionist mobs of the 1830s were lower class in composition. After a meticulous examination of historical records of such mobs in Utica and Cincinnati, he concludes that "the typical anti-abolitionist mob consisted largely of 'gentlemen of property and standing'—lawyers, politicians, merchants, shopkeepers, and bankers whose careers were identified not only with the mercantile economy of preindustrial America, but also with the local political establishment." Richards, *'Gentlemen of Property and Standing': Anti-Abolition Mobs in Jacksonian America* (New York: Oxford University Press, 1970), 149.

70 Lillian Smith, "No Easy Way, Now," *New Republic*, December 16, 1957, p. 12. Quoted in Watters, *The South and the Nation*, 25. Watters adds (p. 26): "Racism has been common at all levels of the society and, as in all other things, is expressed most successfully at the top." And further (p. 28): "It is merely the difference in style, the difference between 'nice' people and the 'common' sort which gives rise to the fallacy that only the most ignorant are racist. 'Common' people have, of course, only expressed their racism more vehemently, crude in their expressions of it, and in the Klan has been found the most vehement and crude expression of all."

poor in racist enterprises. The rich, he points out, are not simply the southern rich, either. Sherrill refers to Donald Leslie, Sr., board chairman of Hammermill Paper Company of Erie, Pennsylvania, who gave George Wallace moral support during the Selma crisis by announcing his decision to build a twenty-five-million-dollar plant in that town.[71] He quotes a large industrialist in Alabama as saying: "It is common knowledge that big business like U.S. Steel and Goodrich have been subsidizing the White Citizens Council and the Ku Kluxers and the John Birch Society for years."[72]

Sherrill's illustrations of upper-class collusion in and encouragement of violence are surely not isolated ones. The late Richard Hofstadter argued—contrary to the dominant assumptions of the "working class authoritarianism" school—that "most" American violence in the nation's history "has been initiated with a 'conservative' bias"—perpetrated by "the top dogs or the middle dogs" against ethnic or religious or ideological minorities.[73]

Tom Hayden, who was a civil rights worker in Georgia in 1961–1962, took strong issue with "the conventional notion that the southern racial crisis is caused and prolonged by 'white trash'—an isolated and declining remnant in our society."[74] And indeed, the racist policies for which the South is notorious have been conceived and implemented on school boards, city councils, in statehouses, and in Washington by politicians who are recruited overwhelmingly from the middle and upper classes—a fact which is reflected in the economically conservative legislation which these Bourbons also sponsor.[75] Men whose names are synonymous with intransigent southern

71 Robert Sherrill, *Gothic Politics in the South* (New York: Grossman Publ., Inc., 1968), 130. Harry Holloway's observation on northern absentee owners in Birmingham probably applies far more widely than publicists of "the New South" are willing to admit: "Whether . . . [they] sympathized with Birmingham's racial customs or not, they were not inclined to interfere with them." Holloway, *The Politics of the Southern Negro*, 153.

72 *Ibid.*, 120.

73 Richard Hofstadter and Michael Wallace (eds.), *American Violence: A Documentary History* (New York: Alfred A. Knopf, Inc., 1970), 11.

74 Tom Hayden, "The Politics of 'The Movement,'" in Irving Howe (ed.), *The Radical Papers* (Garden City: Doubleday & Co., Anchor Books, 1966), 362.

75 A survey by William Mitchell, for example, revealed that 76 percent of school board members in a national sample were businessmen or professionals,

opposition to integration in Congress are recruits from the upper reaches of southern society. In Texas two of the state's most conservative governors in recent years, Allan Shivers and John Connally, were supported by the wealthy, the near wealthy, and the very wealthy who vote for conservative Democrats in Texas primaries and for Republicans in November. Shivers' actions in 1956 during the school desegregation crisis in Mansfield, Texas, were a dress rehearsal for Orval Faubus' performance in Little Rock the following year.[76] Connally openly fought John F. Kennedy's 1963 civil rights bill in the summer preceding the latter's assassination in Dallas.

The entire massive-resistance movement of the 1950s, it must not be forgotten, was conceived and led by Bourbon politicians. Alan Meyer's study of several major segregationist referenda in southern states reveals they were engineered by a fairly united front of state politicians and officials.[77] Silver makes the point forcefully: "Some people may still wonder why eighteen-year-old freshmen charged

although these occupational categories constituted only 15 percent of the work force at that time. Mitchell, *The American Polity: A Social and Cultural Interpretation* (Glencoe: The Free Press, 1962), 162.

V. O. Key has shown that southern congressmen in Washington are far more conservative in economic matters than the total adult population they represent. We shall return to this point in chapter 8. See Key, *Public Opinion and American Democracy* (New York: Alfred A. Knopf, Inc., 1961), 103–104.

76 For an account of the Mansfield incident, see Sherrill, *Gothic Politics*, 87–89. Shivers, a man of strong opinion, made headlines in Texas during the McCarthy era by suggesting the death penalty for "convicted Communists."

77 Alan Samuel Meyer, "The Not-So-Solid South: A Study in Variability in Southern Sentiment in School Desegregation" (Ph.D. dissertation, Columbia University, 1962). In Virginia, "the top political leaders and education officials of the state were solidly in support" of an amendment to the state constitution which would permit use of public funds as tuition grants to children attending private schools (p. 24). Meyer wrote (p. 25) that in Texas "the fact . . . that the major candidates for Governor—liberal and conservative alike—all advocated segregation may have helped to create a stronger-than-usual segregationist climate." The segregationist "Pearsall Plan" in North Carolina was "supported wholeheartedly" by Governor Hodges and his administration, as well as by the Patriots of North Carolina, the State Junior Chamber of Commerce, the Junior Order of American Mechanics, the North Carolina Education Association, Exchange Clubs, and state associations representing school superintendents, school boards, county commissioners and firemen (p. 27). Most of the state's leadership, including Terry Sanford, head of the liberal Democrats, backed it—although it was speculated that some backed it to forestall more extreme measures (p. 28).

through tear gas at United States marshals and later compared themselves to Hungarian Freedom Fighters [referring to the riot at 'Old Miss' when James Meredith, a Negro, was enrolled]. The answer is that they had been listening to Mississippi politicians from the time they were ten years old."[78]

The same point is made by Carey McWilliams, who points out that the Southern Manifesto was the work of Virginia's Senator Byrd, and that it was signed by a hundred southern members of Congress. The document was issued on March 12, 1956, the day Autherine Lucy, a black, was expelled from the University of Alabama. Drawn up and signed by southern leaders at a time when white southern public opinion had not yet reacted forcefully and massively to the *Brown* v *Board of Education* decision, the manifesto was interpreted by many observers as catalyzing white opposition. The ensuing attacks upon the Supreme Court, writes McWilliams, "were not voiced by 'red-necks,' by ignorant and impoverished 'poor whites'; they were voiced by the patricians, by the tidewater aristocrats. An open incitation to nullification, the manifesto silenced the Southern moderates and gave a green light to every demagogue in the South."[79]

A more recent, dramatic demonstration of the attitude of Bourbon officialdom is Florida Governor Claude Kirk's seizure of the Manatee County school system to prevent a court-ordered integration plan from being carried out. In the course of the dispute, Kirk threatened force and violence. According to the New York *Times*: "One of the Governor's aides, Lloyd Hagaman called to testify . . . in the proceedings against Governor Kirk, said that he and others who barricaded themselves in the Manatee County school building behind armed guards yesterday had been instructed by the Governor to resist arrest by force if necessary. 'My instructions were to stand

78 Silver, *Mississippi*, 45. He mentions the State Sovereignty Commission, "the watchdog of segregation," created by the Mississippi legislature in 1956. Among its activities were witch hunts for "subversives" and periodic financial contributions to the Citizens' Councils (p. 8n).

79 Carey McWilliams, *Brothers Under the Skin* (rev. ed.; Boston: Little, Brown and Co., 1964), vii.

pat and stay right there.' Hagaman said. 'If I had to meet force with force, so be it.' "[80] The previous day's *Times* reported that a United States attorney in Tampa said one of Kirk's men had warned him that any federal marshals attempting to enter the school headquarters and arrest anyone "will be fired upon."[81]

Despite these rather common acts of defiance and threatened violence by wealthy businessmen-politicians, political cartoonists almost invariably depict the southern opponents of school desegregation as lower class. A typical cartoon in this genre appeared in the Los Angeles *Times* early in 1970. Drawn by the gifted cartoonist Conrad, it portrays a Neanderthal-like character in overalls and clodhoppers, with a bowl haircut, buttons missing from his suspenders, and a polka-dotted handkerchief hanging out of his rear pocket. He is standing in front of a blackboard on which is written in large letters, "Never." With one hand he covers his eyes, and with the other he takes a swipe through the word with an eraser. The message seems clear: it is the poor and unlettered who are holding up school desegregation.

Yet such a stereotype utterly fails to do justice to the truth that intransigence and even violence are encouraged at the highest levels of southern officialdom. It fails to explain the suppression of a biracial antipoverty effort in Georgia by upper-class whites, including a college president, a county official, and local newspaper officials.[82] It fails to account for the governor of a southern state vetoing some five million dollars in Head Start funds for four of his state's counties,[83] or the ongoing vendetta some southern senators have waged against Head Start.[84]

The effects of the bigotry of one wealthy and powerful politician

80 April 11, 1970.
81 Like his fellow governors in Texas, Kirk has done well for himself in the business world. Between 1956 and 1962 he made $500,000 by exercising stock options for the American Heritage Insurance Company of Jacksonville, which he helped form. New York *Times*, April 7, 1970.
82 New York *Times*, January 14, 1968.
83 Betsy Fancher, "Mississippi Replay," *South Today*, April, 1970.
84 Nick Kotz, *Let Them Eat Promises* (Englewood Cliffs: Prentice-Hall, Inc., 1969), 16.

outweigh those of a large number of "little people." Leon Panetta, a civil rights official ousted by the Nixon administration for being too enthusiastic in his support of racial justice, subsequently charged that a southern senator had singlehandedly pressured the administration to request a delay in Mississippi school desegregation in 1969 by threatening to withdraw his support of the President's embattled Safeguard Antiballistic Missile system.[85] Numan Bartley, summarizing the influence of politicians on the "massive resistance" movement, concludes that:

> The Klan's willingness to resort to violence, the Council's use of economic and other sanctions, and the chilling winds of social ostracism visited upon dissenters by southern white society—all these promoted conformity. The primary responsibility for enforcing orthodoxy, however, rested with governmental officials. The Councils demanded protection of white supremacy by "legal" means, and many southern officeholders responded promptly, showing considerable ingenuity in finding "legal" methods to discourage dissent.[86]

The source of large financial contributions to segregationist politicians should not be overlooked. As most southern politicians are racial conservatives and their largest contributors are, almost by definition, affluent, the working-class community is all but excluded from this particular form of support for racism. George Wallace is undoubtedly the most racially conservative of today's southern politicians, and contributions to his 1968 campaign reportedly came in small sums. Nevertheless, the larger individual contributions to the American Party coffers that year—those of five hundred dollars or more—came almost entirely from the middle and upper classes, including politicians, judges, heads of corporations, professionals, and businessmen of various sorts.[87] The money of the wealthy is more effective and its allocation more socially significant than that

85 New York *Times*, March 1, 1970.
86 Bartley, *The Rise of Massive Resistance*, 211. See his chapter 12 for accounts of government officials in the South impeding desegregation.
87 This information was obtained from data analyzed by the author and Professor William Martin at Rice University, and supplied by Herbert Alexander, Citizens' Research Foundation, Princeton, New Jersey.

of the poor. This is as true in the realm of electoral politics as it is elsewhere. And the same classes that have been so generous in their support of segregationist candidates for office have been quite parsimonious in investing their capital in ways which would benefit the larger community. "Southern money has continued to contribute stingily to answering the most basic, uncontroversial needs of southerners," one observer of the New South writes, "and in their last days of waning power, in the mid-1960's, the old dinosaur leadership, pea-brained and still bellowing, and a newer, more cunning, more cynical leadership were either allowing or abetting the building of ghettos, the white flight to the suburbs, and a whole new structure for the continuation of racism on the Northern *de facto* model."[88]

Wealth and a more sophisticated bigotry also come together in the institution of the private club, the affluent classes' refuge from leisure-time integration. In cities like Houston, Dallas, or Atlanta, the same members of the "power structure" who receive the applause of the national press for their occasional statesmenlike gestures on the civil rights front barricade themselves within the exclusive confines of the private club to partake of the social life available to those who are wealthy enough to join. These segregated preserves are seldom noticed until an untoward incident brings them into the light of publicity. In Houston, for example, the Negro comedian Godfrey Cambridge invited some of his black friends to a performance he was giving at a well-known club atop a downtown office building. His friends were refused admittance. Quite recently an official of one of the city's largest industries first denied but later acknowledged to an Equal Employment Opportunity Commission panel that his company maintained segregated social clubs and deducted club dues from the paychecks of blacks.[89] The public scrutiny of Supreme Court nominee Harold Carswell's past revealed his role in a common scheme of Bourbons: incorporating a private club to keep blacks off their golf links and tennis courts.[90] Such plots,

88 Watters, *The South and the Nation*, 49.
89 New York *Times*, June 5, 1970.
90 *Ibid.*, March 25, 1970.

of course, are not confined to the South. In 1968 a minor scandal occurred when it was discovered that the exclusive Chevy Chase Club in the Maryland suburbs of Washington refused to play tennis with teams that had Negro members.[91] Ferdinand Lundberg, writing of the exclusionary policies of the clubs of the very wealthy, writes: "It is doubtful if any Negro has ever been so much as proposed for membership. It would be erroneous to say Negroes are barred. They are simply not noticed."[92]

Private schools for upper- and middle-class children serve essentially the same function as private clubs. In Houston, Kinkaid School, which caters to the socially prominent, was barred to blacks until the late 1960s.[93] A teacher reported in 1968 that the children had started a Negro scholarship fund, kept in escrow against the day the school would integrate.[94] In 1970 two blacks were enrolled in a student body of 1,031. Watters describes an elite Episcopal school in Atlanta that held out against integration long after the public schools gave in.[95] During the Little Rock school crisis of 1957, lower-middle-class and working-class mothers were in the forefront of the segregationist movement. National television gave extensive coverage to the screaming, spitting mobs of women surrounding Central High School. A few years later, however, when the school board, briefly guided by a liberal majority, proposed a busing plan which would lead to integration of schools in the affluent area of town, the successful fight against the proposal was led by businessmen and professionals from the area which was to be affected. As one reporter described it: "The old segregationist followers of Gov. Orval E. Faubus are silent now. The opponents are from middle and upper class neighborhoods. Some of these opponents helped in the fight to open the city's high schools in 1959 after Mr. Faubus had closed them to avert desegregation."[96]

91 Ibid., August 23, 1968.
92 Ferdinand Lundberg, The Rich and the Super-Rich (New York: Bantam Books, Inc., 1968), 354.
93 Information supplied by the administration office at Kinkaid School.
94 Interview with teacher at Kinkaid School, 1968.
95 Watters, The South and the Nation, 150.
96 New York Times, July 17, 1967.

A similar response from better-off whites occurred in Atlanta, "the city too busy to hate," when these whites discovered that their schools, rather than the schools of lower-income whites, were "threatened" with desegregation in 1970.[97] In Houston, too, whites in the fashionable Westheimer area of the city (which includes the River Oaks subdivision) created a movement to "secede" from the school district in 1971 when their children for the first time were thought likely to be involved in school busing.[98] Suggestive here is a finding reported by John and Lois Scott. In a study of Louise Day Hicks's political support in Boston, it was discovered that those most likely to express support for integration are least likely to expose their own families to it.[99]

Perhaps the most enlightening case to date concerns the integration of Raleigh, North Carolina, schools. In the fall of 1970, a desegregation plan was implemented by the board that, as in many other cities, placed the greatest "burden" of integration on lower- and middle-income whites. The latter, in turn, joined with blacks in adjacent neighborhoods to demand racially balanced schools throughout the city, thus affecting affluent whites as well. A spokesman for the less affluent whites told a reporter: "We understand the black man's problems for the first time. A lot of the whites now have a better appreciation of what confronts the blacks."

Opposing this fairer integration plan were the Raleigh school board "and the city's white power structure, which is regarded as the influence behind the board."[100]

The mentality of genteel racism is captured in a recent article on the "plantation aristocracy" of Natchez, Mississippi. A woman known as "the first lady of Natchez" expressed pride in the peaceful

97 New York *Times*, February 23, 1970.

98 Houston *Chronicle*, December 12, 1971. The "secessionists" deny that racial motives are involved. Rather, it is a matter of "quality education," they say. The interpretation of a school board trustee, Mrs. James Tinsley, contradicts this: "whatever they say on the surface, I think that their real motive is escape from an integrated school district." *Ibid.*

99 John Finley Scott and Lois Heyman Scott, "They Are Not So Much Anti-Negro as Pro-Middle Class," New York *Times* Magazine, March 24, 1968, p. 117.

100 New York *Times*, August 24, 1970.

way the city had accepted public school integration that year. The year was 1970. The woman herself was childless. It was then pointed out that most of the children of the "old families" attended an all-white Episcopal elementary and high school.[101] Another article reporting on the political preferences among the old and new rich of Macon, Georgia, during the 1968 elections revealed much the same situation. Several wealthy Maconites expressed a preference for the racial policies of Wallace, but they ultimately rejected him for Nixon because of his coarse personal style. According to Nan Robertson, a reporter, "the doyennes of the Old South and the country-club set of the new South are incensed about the same things this year. They send their grandchildren and children to private schools and resent the integration of the public schools as being 'rammed down their throats.' "[102] Miss Robertson writes further:

> Like some other women in the North, Macon's society women express, however veiled, the belief that the Negro is congenitally lazy, that he does not work as hard as the whites, that he is being given special privileges he does not deserve and that he is ruining the public school systems. One aristocratic and imperious grandmother spoke of how integration in the schools meant her grandchildren would face intermarriage. "I could just die over it," she said. She thinks Mr. Wallace is "an ignorant man—a rabble-rouser"; but goes right down the line with all of his views about "the Negro situation." She will vote, however, for Mr. Nixon.[103]

The segregation academy movement of the early 1970s is led by and largely recruited from the people in the South who can best afford private schools—the affluent. Kitty Terjen, a reporter, describes Hillyer Rudisill III, the headmaster of three segregation academies in Charleston, as having "once sat in the open driver's seat of an antique Rolls Royce during a hard rain in order to convey his mother in style to the St. Cecilia Ball."[104] He belongs to the Hugenot Society, Preservation Society, Classic Car Club, and St. Cecilia Society.

101 *Ibid.*, March 29, 1970.
102 *Ibid.*, October 31, 1968.
103 *Ibid.*
104 "Private Schools, Charleston Style," *South Today*, January–February, 1971.

Mr. Rudisill, who is also a member of the South Carolina association's accrediting team and one of the leading spokesmen for that organization, is wary of publishing a statement of non-discrimination in the newspaper and then claiming that no qualified Negro has applied. Even that would be "capitulation" to the Union forces, in his view. "If you said there were no qualified Negro applicants, some Yankee psychologist would come down and say the tests are culturally biased," he said. "If you took one (Negro student), it would become unmanageable. You couldn't flunk it or expel it." [105]

In Jackson, Mississippi, it was discovered in 1970 that two banks had made extensive loans to five segregation academies in the area. The banks were headed by local gentry who were members of a committee set up by the Nixon administration to promote support for public schools in Mississippi. [106]

The evidence presented so far obviously raises questions about the vaunted racial enlightenment of southern gentility. Even so, one might be inclined to argue that the racism among Southerners of lower status still overshadows that of the wealthy. It is true, for example, that the discrimination against blacks in white labor unions is blatant. However, any balanced account of trade unionism and the black man must include the positive aspects of this relationship as well as the shameful ones. Studies reveal that significant cooperation has developed between black and white workers once integration has occurred. In general the findings indicate that blacks and whites get along well on the job, but there is little leisure-time fraternizing. [107] This indicates that even white workers who cooperate with blacks on the job have not been purged completely of their racism. (It reflects as well, perhaps, the lack of desire among blacks for integrated social life.) But what is important is that one need not be totally unprejudiced in order to enter into cooperation with

105 *Ibid.*
106 New York *Times*, August 27, 1970.
107 Thomas F. Pettigrew, in summarizing the effects of integration on white attitudes, writes that "white steelworkers learn to work easily with Negroes as co-workers and vote for them as union officers; but this acceptance does not carry over to attitudes and action concerning interracial housing." Pettigrew, "Racially Separate or Together?" *Journal of Social Issues*, XXV (1969), 43–69. See also D. C. Reitzes, "The Role of Organizational Structures: Union Versus Neighborhood in a Tension Situation," *Journal of Social Issues*, IX (1953), 37–44.

blacks in political and economic endeavors. There are degrees of racism, and contrary to the sentiment of some black separatists, who profess to admire outspoken and unqualified racists because of their "honesty," the white who can work well with a black of equal or superior position is a more likely candidate for political cooperation than the thoroughgoing Negrophobe.[108]

Ray Marshall's account of the Negro and southern unions brings to light not only instances of antagonism between white workers and blacks—the latter have often been used as scabs—but examples of cooperation as well.[109] He points to the well-known efforts of many Populists during the 1890s to bring Negroes into the alliance and their espousal of political and economic equality across racial lines. The Knights of Labor adopted a similar policy, as did the American Federation of Labor until the reaction of the 1890s set in. In the building trades, which are generally conceded to be strongly anti-Negro, Marshall mentions the alliance of Negro and white bricklayers in New Orleans, "one of the most successful histories of racial harmony on an integrated basis of any union in the south." He cites the United Mine Workers' racial policies as being relatively enlightened in the Deep South.[110] According to George Brown Tindall, the AFL craft unions were the worst regarding Negro exclusion:

> The CIO, however, exhibited a different spirit from its birth in 1935. Unlike the craft unions, whose strength depended upon strategic skills, the industrial unions sought power in numbers, by organizing all the workers in an industry. Moreover, some of the

108 During the 1968 presidential campaign, it was common to read of militant blacks who preferred Wallace and his "honesty" to the "double-dealing" white liberals. In the same vein, Leroi Jones has said of Tony Imperiale, the organizer of anti-Negro paramilitary groups in Newark, "At least Tony Imperiale is an authentic spokesman for his people." Paul Goldberger, "Tony Imperiale Stands Vigilant for Law and Order," New York *Times* Magazine, September 29, 1968, p. 117.

109 Ray Marshall, "The Negro in Southern Unions," in Julius Jacobson (ed.), *The Negro and the American Labor Movement* (Garden City: Doubleday & Co., Inc., Anchor Books, 1968), 128–54.

110 *Ibid.*, 134, 138. Paul B. Worthman has recently described remarkable instances of black-white cooperation in the Birmingham labor movement at the turn of the century. Worthman, "Black Workers and Labor Unions in Birmingham, Alabama, 1897–1904," *Labor History*, X (1969), 375–407.

leading unions in the new group, like the United Mine Workers, brought to the CIO long records of interracial amity. Among miners the interracial character of employment in the pits compelled interracial solidarity in the union. In Alabama, where Negroes constituted 53.2 per cent of the miners, the UMW developed a standard pattern of mixed locals in which the two races shared the offices. The president was usually white and Negro members usually sat apart. But they participated in the meetings and experienced friendly if sometimes awkward relations with their white brethren. . . . The CIO and its affiliates gave more than lip service to the policy of universality. No CIO national excluded Negroes and none shunted them into Jim-Crow locals. The single exception to this rule apparently was the Textile Workers' Union of America, which sometimes accepted the expedient of separate locals in the South where the numbers were large. Other CIO unions, moreover, hesitated to demand equalitarian practices in promotions.[111]

Other examples of moderately progressive unions are the United Packinghouse Workers, the Auto Workers, the Rubber Workers, and the International Union of Electrical Workers, who have been involved since World War II in challenging job segregation.[112] Harry Holloway mentions that in the midst of the Birmingham crisis in 1963, national labor unions raised large sums of bail money for blacks.[113] The all-black Drug and Hospital Workers' successful 1969 strike in Charleston received badly needed funds from the AFL-CIO (George Meany led a campaign which raised $100,000), while the rival Alliance for Labor Action, led by Walter Reuther, contributed $35,000. According to one report, the threat to shut down the city's port by Thomas Gleason, head of the International Longshoreman's Association, was the most helpful contribution of all.[114] Most noteworthy, Marshall points to the growth of labor-Negro alliances in non-Deep-South states such as Texas, Tennessee, and Kentucky. He might have added North Carolina and Florida as well. "The political influence of both the unions and Negroes is in-

111 George Brown Tindall, *The Emergence of the New South, 1913–1945* (Baton Rouge: Louisiana State University Press, 1967), 572–73.

112 *Ibid.*, 144.

113 Holloway, *The Politics of the Southern Negro*, 167.

114 A. H. Raskin, "A Union with 'Soul,' " New York *Times* Magazine, March 22, 1970, p. 39.

creasing in the South," he writes, "making Negro-liberal-labor coalitions important determinants of the region's political future."[115]

But what about the ordinary whites, the blue-collar workers, the people who are not even part of the union movement: those who are often referred to contemptuously by journalists and academics as "rednecks"? Is not their racism deep-going and ineradicable? The truth is that social science knows very little about how these people might act if the middle and upper classes did not encourage bigotry among them for obvious political ends.

Reese Cleghorn's report on integration of a textile mill in North Carolina indicates that the blue-collar workers in the mill were less averse to job desegregation than the town's businessmen. And what was especially perplexing to Cleghorn, himself a Southerner and a perceptive observer of the racial front, was that a prototypical poor white whom he interviewed, an impoverished, uneducated white who still refers to blacks as "niggers," could almost casually accept mill integration where he works. He recounts this conversation with "Cross," the mill hand:

> "My boy has a nigger teacher this year," Cross said slowly, hunching over and looking at the floor. There is a waiting now for an eruption of the kind expected of a poor white Southerner who finished only the eighth grade and who works in a cotton mill. He finally goes on: "He says he likes her all right." Another silence. But what about *that*, he is asked. "It's all right with me," he says. "I went back to Bainbridge [his home town] a while back, and every nigger I saw down there would speak to me."[116]

Watters' description of a black's perception of some poor whites provides a complement to this anecdote:

> A Negro teacher . . . the only black on a white faculty, is invited by white parents to attend a picnic for teachers, apparently an annual affair in the spring. It is far out in the country; the old fears (rational and irrational—it might be a trap) consume her, but she forces herself to go. "It was so good. These are poor people, mostly.

115 Marshall, "The Negro in Southern Unions," 141.
116 Reese Cleghorn, "The Mill: A Giant Step for the Southern Negro," New York *Times* Magazine, November 9, 1969, p. 147.

And they were just so genuinely gracious and kind. I learned so much that day—including that you can't keep on holding things against them."[117]

Much of the literature concerning the controversy over lower-class prejudice against blacks fails to do justice to the complexity of their racial attitudes. In-depth studies of lower-class whites reveal an ambivalence toward blacks growing out of what Myrdal called the "American dilemma": racial hostility coupled with traditional American egalitarian beliefs. Todd Gitlin and Nanci Hollander discovered, through the use of lengthy open-ended interviews, that many of the poor whites of southern provenance in Chicago have mixed feelings about blacks. The intensity of their hostility seems to be, in many cases, "situation specific." Thus, some respondents admit that they have developed a different attitude toward blacks in Chicago now that they have left the South. Others seem to vary in their response to blacks from time to time, now exhibiting a fairly tolerant and egalitarian view (especially when through force of circumstance, they come to work with blacks as political allies), now lapsing into a strongly expressed bigotry in moments of frustration, particularly when the Negro scapegoat is handy.[118] The words of "Dawson," a white of southern background who found himself allied with blacks in a grassroots antipoverty effort, illustrate this.

> You know, after I left home I used to hate the niggers—colored people; I called em niggers. But I don't call em niggers any more and I'm not prejudiced against em. That's been the trouble in this country for a long time, is settin the whites against the niggers and sech as that. You know I'm from North Georgia and they hate the Nigras, but my granddaddy taught me, and he's dead now, but he's workin in me. I was raised up hard. If I was ever heard to say anything against the Nigras, my granddaddy would whup me with

117 Watters, *The South and the Nation*, 285.
118 Todd Gitlin and Nanci Hollander, *Uptown: Poor Whites in Chicago* (New York: Harper & Row, Publ., 1970) is a rich source of data collected by social activists. While not obtained in a systematic way, many of the interviews are extremely suggestive of the ambivalence of poor whites toward blacks.

this old leather belt. I was taught not to low-rate any nationality, any race of people.[119]

Or consider the words of a twenty-eight-year-old white woman, now living in Chicago but born and raised in Rome, Georgia. She is a recent arrival in the city.

> They never did say too much about the colored people when we went to school, they wasn't havin this thing about colored folks then. Our teachers just said it wasn't right for them to go to school with the whites is all. Which now there in Rome, from the first grade through the sixth they're goin together, goin to school together now. My kids have to go to school with em up here. I don't see when it makes any difference. I think it's all right, but the people that live there, they don't like it. Well, some people thinks if you don't like the colored, you know, somewhere back in your generations they may be colored in your family.[120]

This vacillation may not be so different from the inconstancy of middle- and upper-class attitudes toward blacks noted by Stember. How many college professors or "establishment" liberals, one wonders, would maintain an attitude of racial tolerance if their livelihood were thought to be threatened by blacks with similar qualifications? It seems likely, in other words, that much racial hostility evaporates with a change in cultural climate or political circumstance and is not anchored in the personality by psychodynamic forces. By the same token, someone who is not personally prejudiced may be indirectly contributing to discrimination within his business firm, his church and clubs, and his private education system. To put it in current terms, the argument so prevalent in the 1950s and 1960s that disparaged the possibilities of biracial cooperation among the less affluent failed to make the distinction between "individual racism" and "institutional racism." Once the distinction is made, it is no longer surprising to find that a poor white who moves from a small southern town to a large northern city can suddenly, under certain circumstances, become relatively tolerant. Nor is it difficult to un-

119 *Ibid.*, 181.
120 *Ibid.*, 70.

derstand how someone of racially moderate views may nonetheless find himself supporting an extremely racist organization such as the present lily-white Republican Party in the South.

To sum up, it should be evident that the simple dichotomy of upper-class racial moderation *vs.* lower-class prejudice is misleading, not only when it is based upon attitude survey data, but more especially when behavior is considered as well. Any objective reading of recent southern history must include the pattern of collusion among businessmen, politicians, the social elite, and the mass media in encouraging discrimination and even violence. This is not to deny that many of the region's "ordinary people" are bigoted. Nor is it to overlook the genuine instances of courageous, enlightened leadership among the more affluent whites (leadership all the more dramatic because of its rarity). But one's membership in a social class is only one of many factors that influence, in a complex manner, his attitude and behavior towards ethnic groups. The truth of this will become even clearer in the chapters that follow.

VII

The Structure of
Coalition Politics

The evidence reviewed in the preceding chapter strongly suggests that there is no intrinsic association between class and verbally expressed racial tolerance. It has also raised the question of whether the verbal expression of such tolerance by whites to interviewers is directly related to behavior toward blacks in actual situations. Is it not likely, therefore, that historical and social circumstances may play an important if not a dominant role in determining how whites respond to blacks? To explore this question, it is useful to examine in a systematic fashion the voting behavior of whites when racial issues are salient. By doing so one can exceed the limitations inherent in both attitude studies and the necessarily unsystematic accounts of race-related behavior culled from the literature of southern politics.

In the area of voting behavior, as in that of attitude studies, opinion is sharply divided on the question of which class of whites is the most likely to cooperate with blacks in the South. A recurring theme in V. O. Key's classic work *Southern Politics*, published in the late 1940s, is the role that the race issue has played, since the days of Populism and before, in obscuring the antagonism between poor whites and the wealthy Bourbons.[1] The one-party system, Key wrote,

1 Later writers on the subject of southern politics all too often ritualistically cite Key's *Southern Politics* in an introductory paragraph, quote an apposite sentence or two from it, and go on to ignore the major themes of that work. The interpretation of the region's politics as a class struggle, muted by a racial antagonism often encouraged by upper-class whites, is not widely shared by writers on the South today. It is significant, nevertheless, that the "revisionists" who claim to see evidence for a Bourbon-Negro voting alliance have seldom taken issue with Key's arguments or the data with which he supported them. Instead, they simply ignore them.

builds on fundamental elements of class structure and attitude that depress political interest. Among these social characteristics is an impressive solidarity of the upper economic classes that disciplines without mercy, where it can, those who would arouse and rise to power with the votes of the lower third. Those who cannot be disciplined are bought without hesitation and without remorse. Further, the presence of the black provides a ready instrument for the destruction of tendencies toward class division among the whites.[2]

Southern politics, his argument runs, is not simply a struggle of black against white, but also of class against class. The Bourbons have erected many of the electoral barriers to political participation in order to disfranchise Negroes and poor whites alike. Moreover they have skillfully manipulated the race issue in order to destroy the possibility of political coalitions between the lower classes of both races. The implication of Key's work is clear: there is a potential for cooperation between the white laboring man and the black. Yet the southern Bourbon, whether planter aristocrat or antiunion businessman, is dead set against it. This interpretation, Key observed, is contrary to the folklore of the South, perpetuated by wealthy Southerners, attributing all the racial ills of the region to the poorer whites. He claimed that it is precisely the latter who have supported candidates who were both racially moderate and economically liberal. "The line is by no means, of course, sharply drawn between rich and poor," he wrote, "but the economic conservatives are by interest thrown on the side of those who wish to maintain discrimination, to keep alive racial antagonisms."[3] For this reason Key believed that in the cities the growth of urban labor would provide a fertile breeding ground for liberal biracial coalitions which would in time change the South beyond recognition. He pointed to the role that labor unions had played in the movement to abolish the poll tax and other voting restrictions. While he did not foresee a radical movement developing, he claimed to perceive on the horizon a gradually increasing class awareness and political consciousness among the

2 V. O. Key, Jr., *Southern Politics in State and Nation* (New York: Alfred A. Knopf, Inc., 1949), 655.
3 *Ibid.*, 671.

workers of both races, which would ultimately be sufficient to wring major concessions from the upper classes.[4]

A similar account of southern politics is developed in Alexander Heard's *A Two-Party South?*: "The southerners who have capped the economic and social matrix of southern society since the Civil War have, in instance after instance, opposed the organization of lower-income groups into unions of employees. And they have appealed unconsciously to race prejudice to divide groups that possessed a common interest in liberal government policies."[5] Heard, writing in the early 1950s, also detected the emergence of a politics in which race was less salient and economic issues were more so.[6]

This interpretation of southern politics has often been ignored in the past two decades, and the formulations of writers like James Q. Wilson are now being given attention. Wilson, who believes that the middle and upper classes exemplify the virtues he and Edward Banfield have lumped together as "public regardingness," argues that the white working class in the North as well as in the South is unfit for an alliance with blacks, who should therefore enter a *mariage de convenance* with the business and professional strata.[7] Citing the case of Atlanta, Wilson has written that "whatever the limitations or difficulties . . . there can be little doubt that the natural ally of the Southern Negro, for the foreseeable future, is the cosmopolitan white bourgeoisie."[8] The Atlanta coalition, formed in the 1950s, was "a tacit alliance between upper-middle-class whites and Negroes against lower-middle-class whites. In even blunter terms, the Bourbons and the Negroes have voted together to exclude the rednecks from power in the city."[9] In his conclusion

4 *Ibid.*, 673–75.
5 Alexander Heard, *A Two-Party South?* (Chapel Hill: University of North Carolina Press, 1952), 167.
6 *Ibid.*, 248.
7 The concept of the "public regarding" upper classes is elaborated in James Q. Wilson and Edward Banfield, *City Politics* (Cambridge, Mass.: Harvard University Press, 1963), 46. For a damaging critique of the public-regarding ethos theory, see Raymond E. Wolfinger and John Osgood Field, "Political Ethos and the Structure of City Government," *American Political Science Review*, LX (1966), 306–26.
8 James Q. Wilson, "The Negro in Politics" in Talcott Parsons and Kenneth Clark (eds.), *The Negro American* (Boston: Houghton Mifflin Co., 1966), 427–28.
9 *Ibid.*, 427.

Wilson argues that "the possibility for an effective radical Negro political strategy seems remote and the effort to achieve it costly. In the South, the potential supporters of at least current Negro objectives are the members of the commercial and industrial elite. Although they are everywhere slow to emerge and in some places wholly absent, there is at present no reasonable alternative. Atlanta is an example of both the strengths and weaknesses of such an alliance."[10]

Despite the generality of Wilson's claim, it rests on the single case of Atlanta. But many electoral studies of southern constituencies do not support the thesis. William Ogburn and Charles Grigg found that white family income correlated inversely with the segregationist vote (−.45 for counties; no figure was given for cities) in the 1956 Virginia school segregation referendum. Yet they found only a small negative correlation between the segregationist vote and education (−.17 for counties and −.04 for cities).[11] James Vander Zanden analyzed voting on segregationist referenda in fifteen southern cities. The results, in his words, were "inconsistent and even contradictory."[12] In only three of the cities was there a clear inverse relationship between the socioeconomic status of the sampled white precincts and the segregationist vote. In Birmingham he found a direct relationship. In the other cities no clear pattern of differential class voting was discernible.

After analyzing the vote on segregationist referenda in five southern states, Alan Meyer was hesitant to place much importance upon the class variable in explaining the moderate vote. He concluded that "the present findings . . . reinforce . . . [Vander Zanden's] conclusion that the relationship between county socioeconomic status and moderate voting is not necessarily simple or crucial."[13]

10 *Ibid.*, 442.

11 William F. Ogburn and Charles M. Grigg, "Factors Related to the Virginia Vote on Segregation," *Social Forces*, XXXIV (1956), 301–308.

12 James W. Vander Zanden, "Voting on Segregationist Referenda," *Public Opinion Quarterly*, XXV (1961), 105.

13 Alan Samuel Meyer, "The Not-So-Solid South: A Study of Variability in Southern Sentiment in School Desegregation" (Ph.D. dissertation, Columbia University, 1962), 139–40.

Samuel Lubell's analysis of Dixiecrat Strom Thurmond's support in the Outer South in 1948 revealed his greatest strength to lie in the extremely wealthy suburban residential areas that were Eisenhower strongholds four years later.[14] As Kevin Phillips has written: "These areas are *not* in any way poor, uneducated or uncultured, as detractors are often wont to say about locales of Dixiecrat support. On the contrary, [they] are among the richest and best educated in the South—and in the nation."[15]

Ernest Campbell and Thomas Pettigrew discovered a changing basis of support for Governor Orval Faubus during the 1950s.[16] In the Democratic primaries of 1954 and 1956, Faubus, who was identified as a racial and economic moderate, received a disproportionately large percentage of votes from the counties in the Ozarks—the area with the lowest Negro ratio, lowest white median family income, and least degree of industrialization. However, in 1958, following the Little Rock school desegregation crisis, his pattern of support changed drastically. In the primary that year, his regional support was directly reversed from that in his previous races, with the mountain region giving him the least support (it actually decreased from its previous levels) and the Delta area, with the highest white median family income and Negro ratio, giving him the most support.

Norman Parks's study of Davidson County (Nashville), Tennessee, in 1964 revealed strong working-class support for Ross Bass, an economic and racial liberal, in both his primary and general contests against conservatives. Blacks supported Bass overwhelmingly, and there was a strong inverse correlation between income and Bass support in the white precincts.[17]

Allen Rosenzweig's analysis of voting in New Orleans revealed a negative correlation between the socioeconomic status of white

14 Samuel Lubell, *The Future of American Politics* (New York: Harper and Bros., 1952), 114.

15 Kevin B. Phillips, *The Emerging Republican Majority* (Garden City: Doubleday & Co., Inc., 1970), 263n.

16 Thomas F. Pettigrew and Ernest Q. Campbell, "Faubus and Segregation: An Analysis of Arkansas Voting," *Public Opinion Quarterly*, XXIV (1960), 436–47.

17 Norman L. Parks, "Tennessee Politics Since Kefauver and Reece: A 'Generalist' View," *Journal of Politics*, XXVIII (1966), 159.

precincts and liberal or moderate support in six out of the nine elections that involved a liberal-conservative split on the race issue.[18] In three of the eleven such elections examined by Kent Jennings and Harmon Zeigler in Atlanta, there was a negative partial correlation between socioeconomic status and racially moderate support with race and partisanship controlled.[19] Bernard Cosman's study of the Republican vote in fourteen southern cities in the years 1960 and 1964 is of special interest. In 1960 support among white precincts for the racially more liberal John F. Kennedy was greater among the lowest socioeconomic category than among the highest in every city analyzed, including eight that were in the Deep South. In 1964 class polarization decreased, yet the same statement that held for 1960 held for 1964, with the single exception of Birmingham, where 86 percent of the lowest economic group supported the Republicans and 82 percent of the highest-ranked group did. In other words, in twenty-seven out of twenty-eight cases analyzed by Cosman, the less affluent whites gave more support to the racial liberal than did the Bourbons.[20]

CLASS AND RACE IN HOUSTON

To make sense of the disparate results of these studies, it is helpful to turn to the Houston case for a closer examination of the dynamics of race and class in electoral politics. There are three broad categories of elections in Houston around which the political life of the city and county revolves. There are the party primaries that until the 1960s had been virtually synonymous with the Democratic primaries.[21] Both the liberal and conservative factions of the

18 Allen Rosenzweig, "The Influence of Class and Race on Political Behavior in New Orleans: 1960–1967" (M.A. thesis, University of Oklahoma, 1967), 243.

19 M. Kent Jennings and Harmon Zeigler, "Class, Party, and Race in Four Types of Elections: The Case of Atlanta," *Journal of Politics*, XXVIII (1966) 391–407.

20 Bernard Cosman, *Five States for Goldwater* (University, Alabama: University of Alabama Press, 1966), 87, 106.

21 The creation in 1966 of a new congressional district in the western section of the county—including a part of the most affluent area of the city—and the election to office of a popular Republican in the district, have gone a long way toward

party field candidates and work in an organized fashion to elect them to office and to capture the majority of the county's delegation to the state convention. Liberal-conservative battles are hardfought, economic and racial issues are never far from the surface of campaign rhetoric, and almost all of the candidates for the more important offices identify with—and actively seek the support of—one camp or the other.

Then there are the general elections. Until the 1960s these were seldom more than formal ratifications of the results of the Democratic primaries, so far as state and county offices were concerned. In presidential elections the state has seesawed between Democratic and Republican standard-bearers since 1948. As crossover voting is permitted, a large number of conservative Democrats cast their ballot for Republican presidential nominees in November. Conversely, many liberal Democrats in recent years have backed Republican candidates like Senator John Tower or gubernatorial candidate Paul Eggers, when they opposed equally or more conservative Democrats. As liberal Democrats running for statewide office seldom made it as far as the general elections during the decade of the sixties, the races involving these offices were usually between conservative Republicans and conservative Democrats, and hence there was little substantive difference between them on economic and racial issues. The notable exception was liberal Senator Ralph Yarborough's contest with conservative Republican George Bush in 1964. In both 1960 and 1964, there was a perceptible difference on the race question in the presidential campaign.

Nonpartisan elections and referenda constitute the third category. Both the school board and municipal contests fall into this class. The Houston Independent School District, which covers most of the city, holds elections every two years, generating widespread interest and public comment because of the salience of the school integration question. In fact school board politics in Houston throughout the past decade was, practically speaking, single-issue

---

establishing a tradition of sizable Republican turnout in their primaries as well, but as our voting analysis does not cover the latter years of the 1960s, we shall be concerned only with the Democratic primaries.

politics. Most candidates were known as integrationists or segregationists, even if they tried to shy away from such labels, and it was
where they stood on "the issue" which seemed to make the most
difference to the electorate. By contrast the municipal elections were
with few exceptions devoid of any well-defined public issues.

Our purpose is to determine the class basis for support of the
racially more liberal candidates, in the white precincts alone. To
do this a group of twenty contests held between 1960 and 1966 was
chosen, representing all three types of elections. The analysis involved selecting a sample of all-white voting precincts whose
boundaries did not change during the period under study, and that
could be ranked according to median family income, an index of
class.[22] Then the correlation (Pearson r) was established between
income and the percentage of votes for the racially liberal candidate or issue.[23] There were three criteria for the choice of elections.
First, they had to involve a contest between distinguishable liberal
and conservative positions on the race question. Second, the liberal
had to be a serious candidate, that is, one who was fairly well known,
did some systematic campaigning, and received at least 20 percent
of the white vote. Third, only those elections were included in

[22] The product-moment correlation between the precinct median family income as an index of social class, and the precinct composite socio-economic index—
income, education, and occupational status—was .73.

[23] For a description of the procedures for selecting the sample of white precincts, see Appendix C.

The use of census tracts or, as in the present case, areal subsets of such tracts,
in social and political analysis involves several problems, which have been discussed
by Donald L. Foley, "Census Tracts and Urban Research," *Journal of the American Statistical Association*, XLVIII (1953), 733–42. One difficulty is that tracts are
not homogeneous in their social characteristics. Thus, if such tracts are used as
ecological units of analysis, it is dangerous to generalize from correlations between
characteristics of these units to correlations between characteristics of the individuals (in this case, voters) within the units. It has been demonstrated that
ecological correlations are generally larger than individual ones, and that the
larger the unit, the larger the correlation. See W. S. Robinson, "Ecological Correlations and the Behavior of Individuals," *American Sociological Review*, XV
(1950), 351–57. Frederick Stephan's opinion, appearing in the 1930s, is still valid
today: "Census tract research will probably be most effective when considered
not as a method of study complete in itself but as one step in a sequence of investigations." See Stephan, "Sampling Errors and Interpretations of Social Data Ordered
in Time and Space," *Journal of the American Statistical Association*, XXIX (1934),
165–66.

which the range of support for the liberal (among the sampled precincts) exceeded a few percentage points, so as to give substance to the correlation coefficients obtained. For example, if the votes for a liberal only ranged between 20 and 24 percent, even a statistically significant correlation between income and liberal support would not have much importance. Therefore elections were excluded in which the range of liberal support was less than 18 percentage points. The average range was 42 points. Below is a brief description and classification of the twenty contests.

Identifying Numeral	Description	Year	Electoral Unit
	REFERENDA		
1	School Desegregation	1960	School District
9	Abolition of Poll Tax	1963	County
	STATE AND COUNTY ELECTIONS		
2	Eckhardt, white liberal, for state house of representatives, first Democratic primary	1960	County
3	Kilgarlin, white liberal, for state house of representatives, first Democratic primary	1960	County
5	Jordan, black liberal, for state house of representatives, first Democratic primary	1962	County
6	D. Yarborough, white liberal, for governor, first Democratic primary	1962	County
7	D. Yarborough, white liberal, for governor, second Democratic primary	1962	County
10	Jordan, black liberal, for state house of representatives, first Democratic primary	1964	County
11	R. Yarborough, white liberal, for U.S. Senate, first Democratic primary	1964	County
12	D. Yarborough, white liberal, for governor, first Democratic primary	1964	County
18	Spears, white liberal, for state attorney general, first Democratic primary	1966	County
19	Spears, white liberal, for state attorney general, second Democratic primary	1966	County

Identifying Numeral	Description	Year	Electoral Unit
20	Woods, white liberal, for governor, first Democratic primary	1966	County
	SCHOOL BOARD ELECTIONS		
8	White, black liberal, for trustee	1962	School District
13	Butler, black liberal, for trustee	1964	School District
14	Barnstone, white liberal, for trustee	1964	School District
15	Novarro, Mexican-American liberal, for trustee	1964	School District
	GENERAL (PARTISAN) ELECTIONS		
4	Kennedy, for President	1960	County
16	R. Yarborough, for U.S. Senate	1964	County
17	Johnson, for President	1964	County

Let us begin with the two referenda. The first, held in 1960, was in compliance with a recently passed state law of dubious validity requiring local option elections before a dual school system could be abolished. It was put on the ballot after the school district was already under federal court order to begin desegregation. The second referendum, in 1963, was part of a special statewide balloting for the purpose of considering an amendment to the Texas constitution, repealing the poll tax as a voting requirement. Table 7.1 indicates the product-moment correlation between income and liberal support. The correlation (expressed in the "r" column of the tables which follow) between income and liberal support is represented on a scale ranging from 1.0 (perfect correlation) to −1.0 (perfect inverse correlation). An r of zero indicates no correlation.

In the first referendum, there was a positive correlation. This fact has been pointed to by some observers as proof that the white middle class in the city is the most reliable ally of blacks. Yet, on the question of poll tax repeal, the direction of the correlation was reversed. On the face of it, one could argue that the desegregation

Table 7.1

SUPPORT FOR LIBERAL POSITION IN TWO REFERENDA, SAMPLED HOUSTON WHITE PRECINCTS, BY MEDIAN FAMILY INCOME*

Number	Referendum	Year	Precinct Income Categories				r	p	% Negro Support	% White Support[a]	Outcome
			$5117– 6904	$6940– 7433	$7478– 8601	$10,486– 21,102					
1	School de-segregation	1960	17%(6)	20%(6)	21%(6)	27%(6)	.42	<.05	93%	23%	Defeated
9	Poll tax repeal	1963	42%(8)	46%(7)	46%(8)	39%(7)	–.36	<.05	87%	45%	Passed (In Harris County)

[a] All white precincts in county or school district

* Correlations calculated on the basis of individual precincts in the sample, rather than on the four categories of grouped data in the table. Figures in parentheses represent the number of sampled precincts in the income category for the year in question. Percentages in the income categories are averages of the liberal support in the precincts.

referendum offered sharply defined alternatives: to vote for or against school integration in one's own district. Matters were not so simple, however. The president of the school board, who opposed desegregation, announced before the election that the real purpose of the vote was to decide which areas would be integrated first.[24] Those with the highest prointegration vote, he implied, would be immediately integrated. At that time it was widely (and correctly) believed that when integration came, it would be in the lower-income white and mixed areas bordering the Negro ones. The residents of the outlying, relatively affluent areas may not have considered integration as a possibility in their neighborhood schools. They were probably confident that *de facto* barriers would protect them when *de jure* ones collapsed. The lower-income groups, closer to the central city, undoubtedly believed integration in their neighborhoods to be more likely and took the board president's threat at face value. For them the issue was not abstract. Their children would be the ones going to school with blacks.

Why, then, did the support for the poll tax repeal reflect a different pattern? A fact often overlooked in discussions of the poll tax is that, as is true of any unprogressive tax, it discriminates against lower-income people regardless of race. The poll tax in Texas was intended to disfranchise poor whites along with blacks, as a hedge against the recrudescence of Populism; and it seems to have had that effect throughout most of the present century. Thus, although many less affluent whites may have had some hesitation to repeal the tax (as did the more affluent ones) because of the anticipated effect on black turnout, many of them were probably more anxious to repeal it out of regard for their own self-interest. Forty-five percent of the county's white vote, coming disproportionately from precincts with incomes under nine thousand dollars, combined with 87 percent of the black vote to carry the county by a margin of almost six thousand votes out of more than eighty-six thousand cast. Repeal was defeated statewide, however.

Table 7.2 indicates the results of four nonpartisan school board contests.

24 Houston *Post*, May 10, 30, 1960.

Table 7.2

Support for Racial Liberal in Four School Board Races, Sampled Houston White Precincts, by Median Family Income*

Number	Candidate, Position	Year	Precinct Income Categories				r	p	% Negro Support	% White Support[c]	Outcome
			$5117–6904	$6940–7433	$7478–8601	$10,486–21,102					
8	White,[a] Trustee	1962	27%(6)	35%(6)	31%(6)	30%(6)	-.14	n.s.	93%	34%	Won
13	Butler,[a] Trustee	1964	37%(6)	32%(6)	30%(6)	20%(6)	-.79	<.001	87%	31%	Won
14	Barnstone, Trustee	1964	39%(6)	40%(6)	33%(6)	40%(6)	-.05	n.s.	75%	42%	Won
15	Novarro,[b] Trustee	1964	26%(6)	33%(6)	24%(6)	20%(6)	-.35	n.s.	66%	27%	Lost

a Negro candidate
b Mexican-American candidate
c All white precincts in school district

* Correlations calculated on the basis of individual precincts in the sample, rather than on the four categories of grouped data in the table. Figures in parentheses represent the number of sampled precincts in the income category for the year in question. Percentages in the income categories are averages of the liberal support in the precincts.

Again the pattern of white support for the liberal candidates is inconsistent. For although there is a negative correlation between income and liberal support in all four races, it is statistically significant at the .05 level in only one. This finding is important, for it is precisely in nonpartisan elections that lower-income whites are asserted to be most likely to vote their alleged racism.

Banfield and Wilson, for example, suggest that urban voters who are normally Democratic in partisan elections will "favor candidates [in nonpartisan elections] who are ideologically closer to the Republicans," presumably both on racial and economic issues. As evidence, they cite David Greenstone's observations on politics in Detroit: "Many white union members, particularly Poles and native Southerners, are loyal Democrats who support the party's domestic programs. But these same voters are also homeowners laboring under Detroit's heavy property taxes who are concerned about maintaining the economic level and white racial character of their neighborhoods. They are not friends of the Negroes. If city elections were partisan, they would probably vote Democratic and therefore for liberal candidates. But in non-partisan elections, they are free to desert the liberal alliance to support conservative, pro-white candidates like Mayor Cobo, without repudiating the Democratic Party."[25]

Yet, in Houston the contest with the strongest negative correlation involved a liberal Negro opposing white conservatives. In the other three elections, the lower-income precincts did not give less support to the liberals than did the more affluent ones. Thus, in none of the four races was a Bourbon-Negro pattern operative.

The reason lower-income white precincts contributed disproportionate liberal support in one race but not the others is unclear. Mrs. White, a Negro, first ran for the school board in 1958, winning election by a plurality in a race against several white segregationists. The black precincts backed her strongly; she received about a third of the white vote as well. Many observers felt that her victory was

25 David Greenstone, *A Report on the Politics of Detroit* (Cambridge, Mass.: Joint Center for Urban Studies, 1961: mimeo.), pp. II-7, II-8; cited in Wilson and Banfield, *City Politics*, 160.

the result of ignorance among whites that she was a Negro. Upon assuming office she became an outspoken advocate of school integration, and by 1962, when she was up for reelection, the continuous coverage she had received on television and in the newspapers during her first term insured that both blacks and whites were under no illusion as to the color of her skin or of her political views. As the first Negro elected to office in Houston since Reconstruction and as the only elected black official in the county in 1962, her name had become a local household word both for her supporters and for her enemies. She ran that year on a platform of school integration, academic freedom for high school teachers, and the banning from the high school curriculum of canned right-wing propaganda. She was reelected by a plurality of 47 percent. In 1964 Mrs. Barnstone, new to the electorate, ran on a "good government" platform, demanding more expenditures for pupils in less affluent areas and lashing out at the influence of the John Birch Society and the lack of academic freedom in the schools. Like Mrs. White she campaigned in all areas of the city. Both women were identified in the press as racial liberals. Both were the wives of professionals. Mrs. Barnstone also won a plurality, combining three quarters of the black vote with about 42 percent of the whites'.

The two men, on the other hand, did not campaign as vigorously as did the women. Butler in fact made an effort to stay out of the white neighborhoods and admitted after the election that he had banked on a confusion between his last name and that of Joe Kelley Butler, an incumbent segregationist running for reelection in another position on the ballot. Elsewhere it is argued that Butler's election may have been due to such a confusion.[26] Subsequent research casts doubt on this. There was a high negative correlation (−.61) between the vote for the two Butlers on the ballot. If there had been genuine confusion, it is likely that the unsure voters would have displayed a tendency to vote for both Butlers, as they were in different races, just to make sure that Joe Kelley Butler was elected. But this was not so. An analysis of the newspaper accounts of the

26 Chandler Davidson, "Negro Politics and the Rise of the Civil Rights Movement in Houston, Texas" (Ph.D. dissertation, Princeton University, 1969), 165–66.

Table 7.3

SUPPORT FOR RACIAL LIBERAL IN ELEVEN DEMOCRATIC PRIMARY RACES SAMPLED HOUSTON WHITE PRECINCTS, BY MEDIAN FAMILY INCOME*

Number	Candidate, Position	Year	Precinct Income Categories				r	p	% Negro Support	% White Support[d]	Outcome[e]
			$5117–6904	$6940–7433	$7478–8601	$10,486–21,102					
2	Eckhardt, Texas House	1960	64%(8)	65%(7)	51%(8)	29%(7)	-.82	<.001	87%	57%	Won
3	Kilgarlin, Texas House	1960	45%(8)	53%(7)	34%(8)	16%(7)	-.77	<.001	80%	39%	Lost
5	Jordan,[a] Texas House	1962	22%(8)	24%(7)	18%(8)	14%(7)	-.51	<.01	96%	23%	Lost
6	D. Yarborough, Governor	1962[b]	35%(8)	35%(7)	22%(8)	9%(7)	-.72	<.001	68%	30%	Lost
7	D. Yarborough, Governor	1962[c]	62%(8)	61%(7)	46%(8)	23%(7)	-.81	<.001	65%	53%	Won

10	Jordan,[a] Texas House	1964	30%(8)	29%(7)	23%(8)	18%(7)	-.62	<.001	98%	32%	Lost
11	R. Yarborough, U.S. Senate	1964	57%(8)	57%(7)	46%(8)	29%(7)	-.83	<.001	90%	52%	Won
12	D. Yarborough, Governor	1964	37%(8)	36%(7)	25%(8)	13%(7)	-.75	<.001	61%	32%	Lost
18	Spears, Attorney General	1966[b]	47%(8)	47%(7)	40%(8)	26%(7)	-.78	<.001	77%	43%	Won
19	Spears, Attorney General	1966[e]	46%(8)	53%(7)	40%(8)	19%(7)	-.73	<.001	88%	44%	Won
20	Woods, Governor	1966	31%(8)	32%(7)	21%(8)	9%(7)	-.71	<.001	54%	27%	Lost

[a] Negro candidate.
[b] First primary.
[c] Runoff primary.
[d] All white precincts in county.
[e] Applies to Harris County only.

* Correlations calculated on the basis of individual precincts in the sample, rather than on the four categories of grouped data in the table. Figures in parentheses represent the number of sampled precincts in the income category for the year in question. Percentages in the income categories are averages of the liberal support in the precincts.

election reveals that Asberry Butler's picture appeared several times, clearly indicating that he was a Negro. The Houston electorate seems to be well informed on the racial identity of candidates. There is no reason to believe this was not true in 1964. Most certainly the voters were aware of the ethnicity of Novarro, simply by virtue of his Spanish surname.

Butler spoke out several times on the need to salvage high school dropouts and on the importance of increasing the quality and accessibility of vocational education in the high schools. He was quoted in one newspaper article as saying: "I am interested in eradicating some of the economic problems that also cause these dropouts." Nonetheless this hint of economic liberalism was not significantly different from the position of Mrs. Barnstone, who spoke of the higher quality of education available to the students in the affluent southwest area of town. In short the two candidates Butler and Novarro, who got relatively more support from lower-income whites, were males; they did not campaign extensively in the white areas of the district; and they were not as knowledgeable about educational policy as were their opponents. Why the lower-income whites gave them greater backing is not clear.

Even so, the picture of nonpartisan elections and referenda in Houston does not fit the expectations engendered by the theory of relatively greater working-class racism. Of the six elections considered, only one gave evidence of a Bourbon-Negro pattern. Three did not involve a significant class differential among whites. In two cooperation between lower-income whites and blacks was in evidence. In four of the six contests, the liberal candidate or position won, at least in Houston. It should be noted that Harris County Democrats, the formal liberal coalition, did not take an official stand in any of the six races, as their constitution at that time limited them to Democratic primary and partisan election activity.

We come now to the primaries. All of the races in Table 7.3 below were chosen for analysis because they involved clear-cut contests between liberals (racial and economic) and conservatives. In none of the races were the liberal's opponents to the left of him either economically or on the question of civil rights. All of the liberal candidates had the endorsement of the liberal coalition, and they were identified in the mass media as racial and economic liberals. All received a majority of the Negro vote in Harris County and usually the Negro precincts were highly unified. The average black support in these eleven contests was 78 percent.

The results are striking. In every single race there was a high inverse correlation between income and liberal support. The lower-income white, who is supposed to be adamantly opposed to civil rights candidates, gave disproportionate support to every liberal. Some of these races are remarkable. Barbara Jordan, a candidate for the legislature in 1962 and 1964 (and later a state senator), is a black. She ran countywide in these two races, campaigning for civil rights, a state minimum wage, and industrial safety laws, among other goals. As a lawyer she had handled labor and civil rights cases. She campaigned in the white and black communities, making no effort to play down the fact that she was black. The mass media so identified her. In both elections her opponent was an incumbent white conservative. Miss Jordan lost these two contests. However, her support among whites increased between 1962 and 1964, from 23 percent to 32 percent. In the latter year she came within 6 per-centage points of winning. In both races she received least support, of the sampled precincts, from a wealthy River Oaks precinct (5 and 10 percent, respectively), while her greatest strength (35 and 40 percent) lay in precincts which fell below the median income level.

Ralph Yarborough, United States Senator from Texas from 1957 to 1971, was by far the most liberal national political figure the state had produced in the twentieth century up to that point. He is an anomaly. He comes from a small town in East Texas, an area where traditions of racism, lynching, voter intimidation, and support for third-party candidates such as Strom Thurmond and George Wallace are very similar to those of the Deep South. And yet East Texas was also a base for the Populist revolt in the state during the 1890s. Yarborough, as a supporter of the New Deal, denounced racism and advocated a liberal economic philosophy as a young man. Following his hard-won election to the Senate in 1957, he voted for every civil rights measure brought before that body. He backed measures designed to benefit organized labor, the small businessman and the small farmer, veterans, and the ordinary working man. He came out strongly against big business both on the national level and in state politics, and he provoked the fulsome wrath of the Bourbon Democrats who control state government. (The monumental feud between Yarborough and then Governor John Connally, a conservative, brought John F. Kennedy to Dallas on November 22, 1963.) [27] Yarborough carried the state and Harris County as well. But as Table 7.3 indicates, his support increased in the lower-income precincts. Statewide he received strong support from many of the East Texas counties that had given heavy backing to the Dixiecrats in 1948 and would give George Wallace strong support in 1968.

The performance of Bob Eckhardt, now a congressman from Houston, is another example of the success which is possible by uniting racial and economic liberalism. Eckhardt, while in the state legislature, was well known for his sympathies for civil rights, labor unions, and conservation of natural resources. He had also acquired notoriety among the Austin lobbyists for his efforts to shift the state's tax burden onto the shoulders of the out-of-state oil and gas industries that exploit Texas' raw materials. He was at one time the chairman of the Houston liberal coalition. In Eckhardt's successful 1960 primary race, his lowest degree of support in the white precincts sampled—20 percent—also came from River Oaks. His highest support—77 percent—came from a distinctly working class precinct.

Before interpreting these results, let us briefly consider the general (partisan) elections. Here, as in the primaries, contests were chosen in which a racial and economic liberal Democrat was confronted by a Republican who was less liberal on both counts.

27 Yarborough was defeated in the 1970 Democratic primary by Lloyd Bentsen, Benson a conservative who made the race issue, patriotism, prayer in the schools, and law and order his major campaign themes.

Table 7.4

Support for Racial Liberal in Three Partisan Elections,[a] Sampled White Houston Precincts, by Median Family Income*

Number	Candidate, Position	Year	Precinct Income Categories				r	p	% Negro Support	% White Support[b]	Outcome[c]
			$5117–6904	$6940–7433	$7478–8601	$10,486–21,102					
4	J. F. Kennedy, President	1960	46%(7)	43%(7)	32%(8)	17%(7)	−.77	<.001	88%	42%	Lost
16	R. Yarborough, U.S. Senate	1964	52%(8)	47%(6)	37%(8)	19%(7)	−.84	<.001	99%	42%	Won
17	L. B. Johnson, President	1964	57%(8)	56%(7)	48%(8)	32%(7)	−.83	<.001	99%	53%	Won

[a] Two-party vote.
[b] All white precincts in county.
[c] Applies to Harris County only.

* Correlations calculated on the basis of individual precincts in the sample, rather than on the four categories of grouped data in the table. Figures in parentheses represent the number of sampled precincts in the income category for the year in question. Percentages in the income categories are averages of the liberal support in the precincts.

The pattern of liberal support is quite similar to that seen in the primary data. The difference between candidates, from both a racial and an economic point of view, was greatest in the 1964 senatorial contest when the incumbent, Yarborough, opposed Goldwater Republican George Bush, a wealthy Houston oil man with an Ivy League background (his father was former Senator Prescott Bush of Connecticut). Bush tried to make Yarborough's recent vote for the civil rights bill a central issue. Yarborough had been the only southern senator to support the bill, a fact which was widely publicized in Texas. The inverse correlation is similar in the Kennedy-Nixon contest, as well as in the Johnson-Goldwater one. Thus, in all three partisan elections there is an inverse correlation between income and support for the racial liberal, who in the cases analyzed was a Democrat. This relation between class and Republican support is a phenomenon of long standing in Houston. Samuel Lubell has traced it back at least to 1936.[28]

If the results of these twenty contests are now viewed in the aggregate, an important fact emerges, which is rendered especially dramatic if voting precincts at the top and bottom of the income ladder are singled out for inspection, as is done in Table 7.6. At the top of the income ladder, Precincts 227 and 135 are both located in River Oaks, a residential enclave a few miles west of the downtown area, bordered on the north by meandering Buffalo Bayou. It was developed in the 1920s by a group of businessmen who wished to establish a golfing club, complete with a new course and an area surrounding it for members' homes.[29] Since then it has been the most exclusive sanctuary for the city's elite and may well be the most affluent residential area in the South (or the nation) today.[30] It is here that the social life of Houston comes to full froth; River

28 Samuel Lubell, *Revolt of the Moderates* (New York: Harper & Row, Publ., 1956), 186.

29 I owe this information to a study of River Oaks by Edward Polk Douglas, a student at Rice University.

30 An analysis of a 1967 edition of the city's unofficial "blue book" (Houston is not affiliated with the nationwide social register) revealed that the city's socialites were heavily concentrated in River Oaks. Harry Rhodes III and Sheila Reifle, Rice University students, constructed a map indicating the residences of the city's social elite.

Oaks is the recruiting ground for the Junior League, the debutante societies such as L'Allegro and Assembly, the clubs such as the Bayou, the River Oaks, and the Houston Country Club.

River Oaks is not the exclusive domain of "old family" status groups. Many of the city's captains of finance and corporate wealth have located there. (The city's social elite—among whom "old family" seems to connote more than two generations of wealth—is not clearly distinguishable from its economic elite.) A study of the club memberships of twenty-one men judged to occupy positions at the pinnacle of corporate power in the city in 1969 revealed that thirteen belonged to River Oaks Country Club.[31] When Governor Connally retired from office that year and moved to Houston to become a senior partner in one of the most powerful law firms in Texas, it was considered quite natural and proper that he should choose a River Oaks residence. Here, if anywhere in Houston, one should expect to discover the "cosmopolitan" (and racially tolerant) business class of which James Q. Wilson speaks.

Precincts 75 and 57, the two least affluent in the sample, are both located on Houston's North Side, which is in large part inhabited by the city's working class, white and black. It has a reputation for being a "rough" area of town. Houston Heights, a North Side subdivision, claims Clyde Barrow among its native sons. Old timers say that the Klan in the 1920s was especially strong north of the bayou. The two precincts were located adjacent to sizable black ghettos. A tour through Precincts 75 and 57 reveals numerous old frame houses dating from the 1920s and before in various stages of dilapidation, great quantities of unsightly commercial property encroaching upon residential areas, and many other indications of central-city blight. As Table 7.5 reveals, these two precincts are below the city average, for blacks and whites combined, in terms of every socioeconomic indicator listed. The occupations of employed males are about two-thirds blue collar. The median family income is only about a fourth that in River Oaks. It would be difficult to find a more dramatic contrast in the socioeconomic status

---

31 This study was carried out by Barbara Byrd, a student at Rice University.

Table 7.5

SELECTED SOCIOECONOMIC CHARACTERISTICS OF
FOUR HOUSTON CENSUS TRACTS

	River Oaks*		North Side		City of Houston Black and White Tracts
	Tract 29	Tract 66C	Tract 2	Tract 4	Combined
Median no. school yrs. completed (25 yrs. old or older)	14.6	15.2	9.0	10.3	11.3
Median no. of rooms in house	7.2	6.1	4.7	4.6	4.8
Median value of owner-occupied housing	$25,000+	$25,000+	$7,800	$8,300	$10,900
Median family income, 1959	$21,102	$18,586	$5,173	$5,117	$ 5,902
% Nonmanual (of employed males reporting occupation)	91.6%	91.6%	29.5%	39.9%	44.5%
% Professional, technical, and managerial (of employed males reporting occupation)	74.8%	78.3%	11.5%	26.6%	27.4%

* Tract 29 is totally within River Oaks. Tract 66C includes other wealthy residential areas, as well as part of River Oaks. Precinct 227 is within Tract 29; Precinct 135 is in 66C; Precinct 75 is in Tract 2; Precinct 57 is in Tract 4.

Source: United States Bureau of the Census, *U.S. Censuses of Population and Housing: 1960. Census Tracts, Houston, Texas,* Final Report PHC(1)-63 (Washington, D.C.: United States Government Printing Office, 1962).

of whites than between the two River Oaks precincts and the two on the North Side.

The figures in Table 7.6 indicate a sharply contrasting voting pattern as well. Of the twenty races analyzed, the wealthy precincts gave more support to the racially liberal position in only one—the 1960 desegregation referendum (No. 1). In four other races (Nos. 5, 8, 9, there was relatively little difference in support between the two sets of precincts. In the remaining fifteen races, the two least affluent precincts gave greater support to the racially liberal candidate or position. In addition, in thirteen of the elections, the River Oaks precincts were not simply less liberal than the two North Side ones: they were among the four least liberal precincts in the entire sample.[32] On the other hand, in nine elections both North Side precincts were either in the first or sceond quartile of liberal support.

The Bourbon-Negro combination, we may conclude, is not often found in Houston. In only two races of twenty was there a positive correlation between income and support for racial liberalism. One of these two was statistically insignificant. Of the remaining eighteen negative correlations, fifteen were significant at the .05 level, and twelve were significant at the .001 level, indicating cooperation between a disproportionate number of lower-income whites and blacks.

By classifying the contests into three main categories: nonpartisan (school board races and referenda), Democratic primaries, and partisan races, one can discern different patterns of electoral support. Nonpartisan elections entail the least likelihood of a working-class-based coalition, while partisan elections and primaries entail the greatest. The data suggest the hypothesis that a candidate who is clearly more liberal than his opponent on both racial and economic issues will, *ceteris paribus*, receive a disproportionate vote from lower-income whites as well as blacks. The primary contests analyzed provide such a liberal-conservative clash in every instance, and a working-class alliance across racial lines consistently came into being to support the liberal, even if he (or she) was black. The same dynamics were operative in the partisan elections. Accord-

---

32 River Oaks does not qualify as especially enlightened in matters of civil liberties any more than it does in civil rights. The area served as a base for far-right-wing organizations like the Minute Women in the 1950s and early 1960s. George Norris Green, "Some Aspects of the Far Right Wing in Texas Politics," in Harold M. Hollingsworth (ed.) *Essays on Recent Southern Politics* (Austin: The University of Texas Press, 1970), 74–75.

Table 7.6
Support for Racial Liberals in High- and Low-Income White Precincts
RACES (By Type and Identifying Numerals)

Percentage Support for Liberal

PRECINCTS	Referenda		Democratic Primaries											Partisan			School Board			
	1	9	2	3	5	6	7	10	11	12	18	19	20	4	16	17	8	13	14	15
River Oaks																				
227	23%	37%	23%	14%	12%	9%	19%	15%	27%	12%	24%	15%	8%	23%	12%	32%	28%	18%	40%	18%
135	23	29	20	9	17	5	15	13	17	7	17	15	4	10	15	25	26	17	34	13
North Side																				
75	9	34	66	45	21	43	72	29	65	42	45	49	35	51	58	61	25	40	38	25
57	14	38	61	45	18	31	58	25	57	33	45	34	29	a	54	61	28	40	39	24

Pro-Liberal Ranking[b]

("1" represents most liberal support)

PRECINCTS	Referenda		Democratic Primaries											Partisan			School Board			
	1	9	2	3	5	6	7	10	11	12	18	19	20	4	16	17	8	13	14	15
River Oaks																				
227	7	27	29	29	29	27	28	27	27	28	28	28	27	24	28	26	16	22	9	22
135	8	29.5	30	30	22.5	29	30	29	30	30	29	29	30	29	27.5	29	20	23	21	23
North Side																				
75	24	23	6	13	8	5	5	9	2	6	11	9	6	5	3	5	21	3	16	11
57	22	24	13	12	16.5	10	10.5	15	10	11	9	21	12	a	5	7	17	4	14	15

a Data not available.

b Data for elections 1, 8, 13, 14, and 15 are based on an analysis of 24 precincts, which are thus ranked from 1 to 24. Data for elections 4 and 16 involve 29 precincts, the lowest rank being 29. The data in the remaining elections are based on an analysis of 30 precincts. Scores denoting pro-liberal rankings, in the bottom half of the table, are usually integers, but ties of two or more precincts are given a value of one-half the sum of the combined scores, had a tie not existed. The percentages in the top half of the table were rounded off after pro-liberal rankings were computed.

ingly, if the hypothesis is correct, given the assumption (to be considered in the following chapter) that economic liberals are a potential majority of the electorate, it will be in the interests of the Bourbons to obscure class cleavages by introducing such issues as race, communism, religion, the morality of liquor-by-the-drink, the radicalism of college students, and intrastate and interstate sectionalism, to mention but a few items from the repertoire of Texas conservatism. This is precisely what happens, often with splendid benefits for the conservative candidate.

CLASS AND RACE IN ATLANTA
AND NEW ORLEANS

Is the Houston example one from which we can generalize or is it an exceptional case? An examination of voting patterns in Atlanta and New Orleans reveals some interesting parallels and differences among all three southern cities. Jennings and Zeigler, in their study of voting in Atlanta, included eleven elections in which one candidate was perceptibly more liberal (or "moderate") than his opponents.[33] They found, consistent with previous studies of Atlanta, that in nonpartisan mayoral races there was a positive correlation between socioeconomic status and liberal support (Table 7.7).

Unlike the Houston case, social class was directly related to the liberal vote in all primaries as well. The pattern shifted, however, in the general elections, in which three out of five races involved a negative relation between class and liberal support, and the other correlations were negligible.

How explain the differences between Atlanta and Houston voting behavior? Probably the single most important factor is the lack of any sharp, salient, and consistent disagreement among contending candidates on economic matters. Relatively speaking, the presidential elections constitute an exception to this generalization, and in two of the three analyzed, class and Democratic vote are negatively correlated.

33 Jennings and Zeigler, "Class, Party, and Race," 395-96.

Table 7.7

PARTIAL CORRELATIONS BETWEEN SOCIOECONOMIC STATUS AND
SUPPORT FOR RACIAL LIBERALS IN ATLANTA PRECINCTS,
WITH "% NEGRO" HELD CONSTANT

Contest	Year	r	Racial Liberal	Economic Liberal
General Elections				
President	1956	−.65	Yes	Yes
President	1960	−.50	Yes	Yes
President	1964	.14	Yes	Yes
Congress	1962	−.57	Yes	Yes
Congress	1964	.06	Yes	Yes
Democratic Primaries				
Congress	1954	.27	Yes	Yes
Congress	1962	.59	Yes	Yes
Congress	1964	.38	Yes	Yes
Governor	1962	.76	Yes	?
Municipal Elections (nonpartisan)				
Mayor	1957	.70	Yes	No
Mayor	1961	.67	Yes	No

Source: Figures in this table were obtained from data supplied the author by M. Kent Jennings and Harmon Zeigler. The partial correlation coefficients differ in some respects from those reported in Jennings' and Zeigler's article, "Class, Party and Race in Four Types of Elections: The Case of Atlanta," *Journal of Politics*, XXVIII (1966), 395–96. These authors made use of a third independent variable—partisanship—in addition to race and class. However, partisanship was measured in part in terms of the precincts' Democratic vote in the elections being analyzed. This constitutes contamination (of a rather minor sort) of the dependent variable by the independent variable. In the above table, therefore, the correlation of class and race with liberal support has not been controlled for partisanship.

Two contests reported in the table published by Jennings and Zeigler have been dropped from this analysis, because they did not involve a racial liberal or moderate opposing a conservative. These were the 1956 general congressional contest, and the 1958 primary governor's race.

The clearest difference in electoral "ethos" between the two cities is seen in the Democratic primaries. In Texas the liberal and conservative factions represent a microcosm of the partisan struggle at the national level: racial and economic liberals aligned against racial and economic conservatives. In Georgia, as in the other states of the Deep South (and quite unlike Texas, Tennessee, or North Carolina), no such cleavage has developed. The few racial liberals or "moderates" who have emerged have not taken a strong or visible stand for economic liberalism. Indeed the economic issues are usually played down by all the candidates, so that their economic views are difficult to distinguish.

Given this vacuum in the area of economics at campaign time, it has been relatively easy for a racial demagogue to pass himself off, however spuriously, as a "populist"—a friend of the "little man" —without being seriously challenged.

In an important sense, therefore, the candidates in Table 7.7 who are listed as "economic liberals" are such by default. Charles Weltner, for example, who was able to obtain significant lower-income white support in his 1962 congressional race, had the backing of organized labor and a sizable proportion of blacks, which increased in 1964, but his economic liberalism would have been considered anemic alongside that of Texas liberals such as Ralph Yarborough or Bob Eckhardt. The same could be said for racial moderate Morris Abrams in 1954 or Carl Sanders in 1962. For practical purposes, then, economics—the substance of the electoral class struggle—was simply not an issue in Atlanta primary politics.

The same is true (as in Houston) for municipal politics. Many articles describing the strategy of Mayors Hartsfield and Allen speak of them as "progressive," "liberal," "forward looking." And in terms of the civil rights issues of the 1950s and early 1960s, they were undoubtedly less backward than their opponents. Yet they embraced an economic philosophy that was consonant with the interests of big business in Atlanta.[34] Ironically these interests were in direct conflict with the economic needs of most of the city's

34 According to Edward Banfield, ". . . the principal politician [in Atlanta] is a big businessman, the white middle class takes its cues from the business community (as do many of the Negroes), and the city government's policies for the most part are business-serving." Banfield, *Big City Politics* (New York: Random House, Inc., 1965), 18. Banfield points out (p. 36) that Allen's accomplishments regarding blacks had been the usual "civil rights" ones: employing Negro firemen

blacks. But in those days when the civil rights movement was still rising toward its crest and legal rights such as open public accommodations were the primary goal of blacks, this conflict was not so apparent. It remained for a new breed of black leaders, symbolized by Julian Bond, to point out the discrepancy between the token racial moderation of Atlanta's mayors and their conservative economic policies, which were disastrous for most blacks and lower-income whites as well. Thus the nonpartisan election effectively separated class issues from race issues and facilitated a Bourbon-Negro pattern.

New Orleans evidence supports this view. Rosenzweig examined eleven separate races in that city, nine of which involved differences between the candidates on the race question.[35] The results are shown in Table 7.8.

---

and policemen, desegregating municipal swimming pools "in response to a court order", trying to persuade proprietors of hotels and restaurants to desegregate, endorsing a pending civil rights bill, and appointing "several Negroes" to important jobs. "His Negro appointees are all 'doves', wealthy, middle-aged or older, and in a position to deliver votes."

Harry Holloway, too, claims that the leaders of the Atlanta coalition largely ignored the problems of the poor, both black and white: ". . . city leaders tended to think of city improvements in terms of buildings, highways, and appearances but not in terms of improving people." Holloway, *The Politics of the Southern Negro* (New York: Random House, Inc., 1969), 224.

Accounts of the "forward looking" business community in Atlanta seldom mention that downtown Atlanta merchants were adamant in refusing to negotiate with blacks during the days of the sit-ins. In the autumn of 1960, the mayor was unable to get the downtown merchants together even to discuss the issue. Desegregation of public accommodations in Atlanta came, not as a result of business community moderation, but in order to put an end to a Negro boycott of downtown stores between November, 1960, and March, 1961. It is important to note, as well, that the sit-in movement and the boycotts of the early 1960s were not directed against poor whites, but against the business community. See Jack L. Walker, "Protest and Negotiation: A Case Study of Negro Leadership in Atlanta, Georgia," *Midwest Journal of Political Science*, VII (1963), 103.

Charles Weltner, an Atlanta Congressman who went on record supporting the voting rights section of the 1963 civil rights bill, but rejected the public accommodations section that year, later wrote that "at home, most organizations which memorialized upon the subject took an opposition stance. This was true initially of both Atlanta daily newspapers. The Chamber of Commerce resolved against the section, but at the same time urged its member businesses to lower racial barriers. Substantially the same action was taken by the hotel and restaurant associations." Weltner, *Southerner* (Philadelphia: J. B. Lippincott Co., 1966), 62.

35 Rosenzweig, "The Influence of Class and Race," 243.

Table 7.8
CORRELATIONS BETWEEN SOCIOECONOMIC STATUS AND SUPPORT FOR
RACIAL LIBERALS IN WHITE NEW ORLEANS PRECINCTS

Contest	Year	r	Racial Liberal	Economic Liberal
General Elections				
President	1960	–.817	Yes	Yes
President	1964	–.754	Yes	Yes
Congress	1964	–.770	Yes	Yes
Congress	1966	–.839	Yes	Yes
Council	1967	–.830	Yes	Yes
Democratic Primaries				
Governor	1960	.860	Yes	No
Governor	1964	.871	Yes	No
Nonpartisan Elections				
Mayor[a]	1962	.831	Yes	No
Council[a]	1967	–.436	Yes	No

[a] The inclusion of these two races under this heading is somewhat arbitrary. Although the municipal primaries are nominally Democratic primaries, they have been described as "functionally nonpartisan." In the 1967 council general election, a Republican opposed a Democrat, along party lines.

Source: Allen Rosenzweig, "The Influence of Class and Race on Political Behavior in New Orleans: 1960–67" (M.A. Thesis, University of Oklahoma, 1967), 243.

The municipal elections in New Orleans are, according to Rosenzweig, formally partisan but functionally nonpartisan, as no Republicans have run in the general elections until recently. The mayoral elections, as in Houston and Atlanta, usually do not involve any clearly delineated class issues. Indeed it is not obvious which candidate is for what, except that all of them seem to have the backing of at least one element of the business community, and the winning candidate is sure to perpetuate what has for many years been a businessman's government. In the 1962 mayoral contest, Adrian Duplantier, "a polished French Catholic who was moderate-to-liberal on the race issue and sufficiently aristocratic to appeal to the upper and upper-middle classes," opposed Victor Schiro, the incumbent mayor appointed by his predecessor, Delesseps Morrison, after President Kennedy had chosen Morrison as United States Ambassador to the Organization of American States.[36] Both men were involved in a scramble for the various elements of Morrison's "carefully pieced together coalition of classes and races."[37] Schiro won after injecting the race issue into the campaign, defeating the efforts of an essentially Bourbon coalition.[38]

Yet it would be unwise to attribute Schiro's victory to the "natural" bigotry of the lower classes. The election came on the heels of the school desegregation crisis in New Orleans, and as was often the case elsewhere, the white schools that were desegregated were predominantly lower-middle and working class. It is plausible that once Schiro raised the race issue in his campaign, those people rallied to it who had been most affected by desegregation. If so, there may be a parallel between what happened in New Orleans and in the Houston school desegregation referendum of 1960, discussed earlier. In the latter instance, the positive correlation between support for desegregation and income of white precincts may have been due to desegregation's greater impact which lower-income voters anticipated in their neighborhoods.

The 1962 mayoral election in New Orleans appears to be one in which both candidates were essentially conservative (or noncommittal) on economic matters and in which one was slightly more liberal in racial matters. The lower-income whites, faced with a choice at a time when they felt they were bearing the brunt of school desegregation, chose the racial conservative.

That such a voting pattern is not an immutable feature of southern municipal elections is dramatically demonstrated by the results of a council contest in 1967. Rosenzweig considers the election especially noteworthy because it "represents a test of the feasibility

36 *Ibid.*, 63.
37 *Ibid.*, 62.
38 *Ibid.*, 63.

of attempting to build a coalition of Negroes and poor whites."[39] Eddie Sapir, the liberal Jewish candidate, was raised in a New Orleans slum. His image was that of "a well dressed strong-arm man rather than the bright lawyer-politician that he is."[40] He faced Dennis Lacey, who was Mayor Schiro's candidate. Schiro, viewing some of Sapir's wealthy Jewish backers as a future threat to his own organization, went to great expense to insure Sapir's defeat. He obtained for his candidate the endorsements of numerous figures influential in politics, including a well-known Negro leader. Sapir, to counter these endorsements, "sought to win as much support as possible from all white classes by choosing popular issues and by playing the part of the underdog man-of-the-people who was being opposed by a colossal machine."[41] His most spectacular tactic was to conduct a house-to-house campaign in Negro areas of the city. Sapir received 44 percent of the white vote and the black precincts gave him 87 percent, thus repudiating the well-known black leader who supported Lacey. The correlation between class and support for Sapir was −.436. According to Rosenzweig, "the significant achievement is that Sapir's overwhelming majority in Negro precincts did not result in a corresponding drop in support from lower class white areas." Sapir faced a conservative Republican in the partisan council race a month later and won handily with an even stronger alliance between blacks and lower-class whites.

Thus, the issues and strategy in the case of Eddie Sapir were quite different from those employed by Adrian Duplantier in 1962. Unlike the aristocratic Duplantier, Sapir appealed to the economic (and perhaps the psychological) needs of the lower-income whites, although not limiting his appeal to them, and at the same time he made an open, unashamed appeal to the black voters by his door-to-door campaign. He was apparently more liberal on both racial and economic issues than his opponent, and he won, carrying a disproportionately high percentage of lower-income whites with him. His

39 *Ibid.*, 218.
40 *Ibid.*, 219.
41 *Ibid.*, 220.

strategy for working-class support paid off. In other words, when the racial liberal was not an economic liberal, his support came from the more affluent. When he was both racially and economically liberal, his support came from those lower down.

In the two Democratic primaries, Bourbons backed the racial liberal. But the liberal (or less conservative) gubernatorial candidates in these two cases were both economic conservatives. As in Atlanta—and unlike the Houston case—a tradition of combining racial and economic liberalism in the platform of a single candidate or faction has yet to fully develop. However, there is no reason to accept this as unalterable. The present cleavage in the Texas Democratic primaries grew out of a situation in the 1920s and early 1930s that was similar in many respects to the circumstances in Georgia and Louisiana in the 1960s.

What is possible in New Orleans when racial and economic liberalism are combined is seen clearly in the five general elections involving such a combination. In all five a strong negative correlation between class and liberal support emerged—the lowest being —.754 in President Johnson's 1964 race. The highest was —.839 in Hale Boggs's 1966 race. Boggs, according to Rosenzweig, was " 'obliged' to vote against the 1964 Civil Rights Act," but "his record on race was about as liberal as a congressman of his constituency could be."[42] He received 93 percent of the New Orleans Negro vote in 1964. (In 1965 he joined with five other southern congressmen to vote for the Voting Rights Act of that year.) His Republican opponent, riding on Goldwater's coattails, gave Boggs stiff competition, receiving 45 percent of the New Orleans vote. Yet unlike the support for Democratic moderate Charles Weltner in Atlanta that year, Boggs's white backing came disproportionately from the lower-income groups. In fact, according to Rosenzweig,

---

42 *Ibid.*, 196. Whether Boggs was really obliged to cast a negative vote is not certain. Senators Kefauver in Tennessee and Yarborough in Texas, both racial and economic liberals, had previously won reelection despite having supported civil rights measures and openly admitting this in their campaigns. Texas and Tennessee are of course both "rim South" states, whereas Louisiana belongs to the heart of Dixie. Nonetheless it is true that Yarborough carried East Texas, which is in many respects akin to the Deep South.

"only the most impoverished of the city's white precincts gave Boggs a majority of their votes."[43] In the presidential race of 1964 as well, the lower-income whites were disproportionately in favor of Johnson. Although a majority of whites at each socioeconomic level were for Goldwater, the precincts at the lowest level gave him 54 percent, while those at the highest backed him with 68 percent.[44]

SUMMARY

At the beginning of the chapter, this question was asked: Are personality traits or external social circumstances more important in determining the behavior of whites toward blacks? Our study of voting behavior suggests, at the very least, that social circumstances play a significant role in the electoral behavior of whites. For we have discovered a wide variation in the relative support various social strata have given to racial liberals in three southern cities. At times the Bourbons are more likely to support them, but at others lower-income whites are. This fact alone requires an explanation which goes beyond personality factors. What is it, then, that activates the Bourbons and lower-class whites to cooperate with blacks at the ballot box?

Our most noteworthy finding is that when elections other than nonpartisan ones are examined, the Bourbon-Negro pattern is not nearly as typical as writers like James Q. Wilson have suggested. In partisan elections, especially for national office, when the Democrat's platform combines racial and economic liberalism, lower-class whites are usually the blacks' strongest ally. This is also true in primary elections like those in Houston, in which the candidates of the liberal faction combine economic and racial progressivism.

Yet when the racial liberal (or "moderate") is an economic conservative, or when he and his opponent do not even bring economics into the campaign, there is a greater likelihood of Bourbon support

43 *Ibid.*, 198.
44 *Ibid.*, 229.

developing. Primaries in Atlanta and New Orleans fit this pattern, as did nonpartisan elections.

Table 7.9, based on the three sets of elections described in this chapter, shows clearly the impact that economic liberalism espoused by a racial liberal has upon the white electorate. The Bourbon-Negro pattern is far less likely to emerge when the two kinds of liberalism are combined in a single platform. However, the fact should not be lost sight of that even when the racial liberal is not an economic liberal, the Bourbon-Negro pattern does not develop in almost half the cases.

Table 7.9
CONTESTS WITH INVERSE CORRELATION BETWEEN WHITE PRECINCT CLASS STATUS AND SUPPORT FOR RACIAL LIBERAL, THREE SOUTHERN CITIES

Type of Racial Liberal

Economic Liberal	Economic Conservative*
82%	42%
(N = 28)	(N = 12)

* Or economic position is not salient

Although we have examined only three cities in the South, it is unlikely that this is an isolated pattern. Vander Zanden's study of voting in segregationist referenda in fifteen cities, mentioned above, found an inverse correlation between socioeconomic status and liberal support in three, a direct correlation in one, and no clear-cut pattern in the remainder. These were nonpartisan contests in which race alone was salient, and as our data suggest, support from one social class or the other is just about as likely in such elections. So, too, with Meyer's above-cited study of segregation referenda: class was not found to be very useful in explaining the outcome. On the other hand, Parks's study of Nashville elections and Cosman's study of presidential elections in 1960 and 1964 both dealt with racial and economic conservatives confronting racial and economic liberals.

And, as mentioned above, the lower-class whites gave relatively more support to the racial liberals.

It is probable that this phenomenon is not a recent development and that it is not limited to cities. Meyer cites the case of five southeastern Alabama counties which had traditionally joined the northern upland counties in voting for economically progressive candidates, including "Big Jim" Folsom, a gubernatorial aspirant in 1946 who was known as a racial moderate. These same counties gave Folsom a higher than average vote in 1956 in his campaign for national Democratic committeeman, at a time (during the South's "massive resistance") when he was still labeled a race moderate. Yet, three months later they ranked in the bottom third of all Alabama counties in moderate voting in a segregationist referendum.[45]

How should we interpret these findings? The most convincing explanation is this: White Southerners, like white Northerners, can be classified according to their economic interests. Further most of these Southerners are fairly rational political animals, and they identify the national Democratic Party (and the liberal faction of the party in some states) as more attuned to the interests of the ordinary folk. Other things being equal—and they seldom are—the wealthy Bourbons will support the party or faction that best serves their interests, and the ordinary whites will support those that serve theirs. As racial bigotry is distributed fairly equally between the classes, one group is about as likely as the other to support a racial liberal when economics is not at issue.

But when racial and economic liberalism are advocated by the same party or faction, strong cross-pressures develop. Racially liberal voters who are economic conservatives may find themselves appalled by the racial demagoguery of the conservative candidate. Racially conservative voters who are economic liberals will feel great ambivalence toward the liberal candidate. The outcome of the election will depend greatly on whether racial or economic sentiments prevail among the voters.

This would explain, in large measure, the nature of the partisan

45 Meyer, "The Not-So-Solid South," 69.

struggle for the southern vote in the 1960s. The strategy of the Republicans, based on the assumption (as will be shown in the following chapter to be correct) that the South as a whole is more liberal than conservative on economic matters, has adopted a strategy of playing down economic issues and waving the bloody shirt on social issues, such as race and crime. The national Democrats, on the other hand, have stressed economic issues. The resultant cross-pressure among Southerners is predictable. Samuel Lubell wrote in 1964: "My own interviewing has often disclosed voters who threatened to bolt the Democratic Party in racial anger, but who would reverse themselves when asked, 'What if the President came out strong for medical care for older people under social security?'"[46] Gertrude Selznick and Stephen Steinberg discovered the same phenomenon in their analysis of the 1964 presidential election. At every class level they found many people who were torn between conservative views on "social issues" and liberal views regarding economic welfare. Selznick and Steinberg claim that these cross-pressures were usually resolved at the national level by voting Democratic, as the economic views won out. And it was among the workers that the liberal welfare views were most strongly held, which explains why they gave overwhelming support to Johnson.[47] Donald R. Matthews and James W. Prothro found precisely the same thing in their study of the 1960 elections in the South. Southern workers, who were severely cross-pressured, nonetheless stood firmly behind Kennedy. Economic issues loomed larger than the racial ones in the voting booth.[48]

In terms of practical politics, Republicans and Bourbon Democrats have seen quite clearly what this means. Economic issues must be muted and racial issues emphasized. Most Republican candidates in the 1960s in the South acted accordingly. (Governor Winthrop

---

46 Samuel Lubell, *White and Black: Test of a Nation* (New York: Harper & Row, Publ., 1964), 159.

47 Gertrude Selznick and Stephen Steinberg, "Social Class, Ideology, and Voting Preference: An Analysis of the 1964 Presidential Election," in Celia S. Heller (ed.), *Structured Social Inequality* (New York: Macmillan Co., 1969), 216-26.

48 Donald Matthews and James Prothro, *Negroes and the New Southern Politics* (New York: Harcourt, Brace & World, Inc., 1966), 388-89.

Rockefeller of Arkansas was the rare exception.) On the other hand, many southern Democrats with racially liberal inclinations seem not to have seen the situation as clearly as the Republicans. Rather than advocate liberal-to-radical economic reform which would appeal to large sectors of the southern voting-age population, they have allowed their opponents to circumscribe the areas of political discourse so narrowly as virtually to insure liberal defeat. They have lost by default to candidates who define the issues in terms of race alone or to candidates who appeal to a spurious populism. Yet, unless the ordinary southern white voter is effectively cross-pressured by appeals to his economic needs, the racist appeal of the opponent will be far more likely to carry the day.

In the last analysis, then, the shape of southern politics in the future depends largely upon what the candidates have to offer. We have shown that many less affluent whites will vote for the same candidate as do blacks when appeals are made to their economic interest as well as to their sense of justice. A large part of the white southern electorate is presently receptive to progressive change, and the candidate who fails to take account of this fact has no one to blame but himself. His task will undoubtedly be made easier, however, if he can rely upon the institutional support of a formal coalition, such as exists in Houston. It is to this matter that we turn in the concluding chapter.

VIII

Toward a New "Southern Strategy"

The voting patterns so far discussed are compatible with the analysis of southern politics that Key, Heard, and, more recently, Parks, among others, have offered. Its essence is that class conflicts have characterized southern society from the era of slavery to the present. The economic bases of the upper classes are numerous and changing, the form and intensity of the struggles have varied, and unlike the class "contradictions" Marx envisioned, those in the South are not likely to be resolved through violent revolution. Much of the success of the upper classes in maintaining their dominance has its source in their ability to play Negroes and whites in the lower orders against one another. This is possible so long as the race issue clouds economic considerations.

Such an interpretation, although leftist in tenor, has been accepted by some conservative Republican strategists as well.[1] If it is correct, what strategy does it dictate for urban southern blacks who, like those in Houston, have discovered that "politics as usual" is an unlikely instrument to accomplish the goals of racial justice?

Essentially there are two options. On the one hand, the policy of voluntary separatism is advocated by a small but growing minority of writers and activists. On the other, a biracial coalition is urged, with economic goals radical enough to mobilize large sectors

[1] Much of Kevin B. Phillips' chapter on the South in his book, *The Emerging Republican Majority* (Garden City: Doubleday & Co., Inc., 1970), is predicated on this interpretation. Phillips' work, called "the political Bible of the Nixon era" by *Newsweek*, urges the Republicans to continue to soft-pedal economic issues and to exploit "social" ones like race in order to effectively divide the New Deal Democratic coalition.

of the less affluent of both races. The shortcomings of a policy of separatism are well known. One in particular is unanswerable: A very small number of political units even in the South contain a majority of blacks, and a go-it-alone strategy is destined to come to grief because of this fact.[2]

The coalition strategy has also been sharply criticized, especially by blacks who have personally experienced the failure of white allies to support them when the chips were down. Much of this criticism is valid. Yet, taken as a whole, it is not so damaging as to preclude the revival of a militant and essentially new coalition politics, based upon class appeals. Why this is so, however, is not immediately clear. The purpose of this concluding chapter therefore is to suggest, in summary fashion, why a biracial coalition is the preferable option open to both blacks and less affluent whites. The case for such a coalition can be made most cogently by considering the major arguments against it. These consist, in one form or another, of the following objections:

1. A coalition between blacks and whites will result in the compromise of the interests of the blacks and in the co-optation of the black leaders into the "white power structure."

2. Blacks and whites have mutually exclusive interests.

3. Organized labor, the political arm of the working class, is no longer, if it ever was, a suitable ally of blacks.

4. Even if blacks and whites could join together for common purposes, there are too few progressive whites to constitute a majority.

5. A coalition based on class issues would alienate the upper-middle-class whites who are already allies of Negroes.

6. A mass movement with a working-class base would bring into

2 In the eleven southern states, only one major city—Atlanta—is now predominantly black. Of more than 1,000 southern counties, only 102 are at least 50 percent black, according to the 1970 census. Even fewer have a voting-age population the majority of which is black. Sixteen small cities of more than 25,000 population have a population at least 50 percent black. The number of predominantly black cities in the South will probably increase slightly in the 1970s, while the number of black counties will probably decrease, as will the percentage of blacks in the southern states. For a trenchant criticism of the separatist strategy, see Bayard Rustin, "The Failure of Black Separatism," *Harper's*, January, 1970, pp. 25–34.

the active political arena precisely that element of society least capable of responsible political behavior.

7. A mass movement dependent upon the mobilization of the working class is bound to fail because the political enthusiasm of this class is extremely difficult to engender and even more difficult to sustain.

A COALITION WILL COMPROMISE THE INTERESTS OF BLACKS

This proposition is deduced from a theory of political coalition advanced by Stokely Carmichael and Charles V. Hamilton.[3] The argument goes as follows. To attain its goals any party to a coalition must have interests that in large measure coincide with those of the other parties, and it must have an independent base of power so that, in those areas where its interests do not coincide with those of the other parties, such interests will not be compromised. For example, Negroes should enter into a coalition with organized labor only when their economic interests coincide and only when the Negroes as a group are powerful enough so that organized labor, in a bargaining situation, cannot sacrifice interests which are peculiar to the blacks. Carmichael and Hamilton write:

> Viable coalitions therefore stem from four basic preconditions: a) the recognition by the parties involved of their respective self-interests; b) the mutual belief that each party stands to benefit in terms of that self-interest from allying with the other or others; c) the acceptance of the fact that each party has its own independent base of power and does not depend for ultimate decision-making on a force outside itself; and d) the realization that the coalition deals with specific and identifiable—as opposed to general and vague goals.[4]

Lacking either a common interest or parity within the coalition, neither friendship nor moral commitment will prevent the stronger party from compromising the basic interests of the weaker one. If

3 For a full exposition of this theory, see chapter 3 of Stokely Carmichael and Charles V. Hamilton, *Black Power: The Politics of Liberation in America* (New York: Random House, Inc., 1967).

4 *Ibid.*, 79.

the coalition formally continues, the leaders of the weaker faction will be co-opted and its interests sold down the river. If the coalition falls apart, the dominant faction may turn on its former ally with a vengeance, scapegoating it for the failure of the coalition to achieve its goals. Populism is cited as an example of this turn of events.

This theory of coalition politics has also been accepted by writers who disagree with the Carmichael-Hamilton strategy. Martin Luther King's position regarding the requirements for a successful coalition was very close to that of Carmichael and Hamilton. He wrote in his last book:

> A true alliance is based upon some self-interest of each component group and a common interest into which they merge. For an alliance to have permanence and loyal commitment from its various elements, each of them must have a goal from which it benefits and none must have an outlook in basic conflict with the others. Thus we cannot talk loosely of an alliance with labor. Most unions have mutual interests with us; both can profit from the relationship. Yet with some unions that persist in discrimination to retain their monopoly we can have no common ground.[5]

Although King saw the need for manufacturing situations such as the Birmingham confrontation in 1963, the Selma March in 1965, and the Memphis Garbage Workers Strike in 1967—confrontations to appeal primarily to the sentiment of the nation—he understood fully the necessity for a long-term alliance based on the coincidence of self-interest.

The point of contention between separatists and coalitionists, then, lies elsewhere. Essentially the debate is over whether the conditions for a coalition can be fulfilled at present or whether they can only be met at a much later date. Carmichael and Hamilton deny that "in the context of present-day America, the interests of black people are identical with the interests of certain liberal, labor, and other reform groups."[6] (Actually their theory does not

---

5 King, *Where Do We Go From Here: Chaos or Community?* (New York: Harper & Row, Publ., 1967), 151.
6 Carmichael and Hamilton, *Black Power*, 60.

require that the interests of blacks be identical with those of other groups. But at any rate they want to argue that there is not even that degree of coincidence of interest which renders a successful coalition possible.)

The truth of this first criticism of the coalition strategy therefore depends upon the truth of the second criticism, namely, that there are no common interests between blacks and at least some whites—a contention to be considered below. Here, however, it must be pointed out that the Carmichael-Hamilton thesis does not rely for its force upon a demonstration that whites and blacks have no common interests (almost no evidence is presented on this point). Rather, the appeal of their argument stems from their reiteration of the risks blacks run in entering into alliances.[7] Yet advocates of separatist politics tend to gloss over the serious dangers which inhere in their own strategy. According to the Black Power position, at least as it was enunciated in the late 1960s, Negroes must withdraw from coalitions until they have formulated their goals precisely, arrived at an agreement upon strategy, and strengthened their solidarity.[8] To their white sympathizers they allocate the task of radicalizing the white community. When the Negroes have established power bases from which they can act as an independent

7 Carmichael, as a civil rights worker in the Deep South, could speak with authority on the dangers of coalition politics, and his bitterness over the betrayal of the Mississippi Freedom Democratic Party was born of experience, not theory. The examples he cites of coalitions gone awry cannot be wished away or ignored.

For an account of the Johnson administration's attempts to dilute the strength of black militants through coalition politics, see Ronald Radosh, "From Protest to Black Power: The Failure of Coalition Politics," in Marvin E. Gettleman and David Mermelstein (eds.), *The Great Society Reader: The Failure of American Liberalism* (New York: Random House, Inc., Vintage Books, 1967), 278–93. Radosh's argument is quite similar to that of Carmichael and Hamilton, and he concludes that no coalition is possible between militant blacks and the Democratic Party, as constituted *circa* 1967.

8 Some advocates of Black Power do not argue for a complete withdrawal from politics during this regrouping period. At one point Black Power was understood primarily as a withdrawal from national politics to the local level, where, in some cases, blacks constituted a majority. It was argued that once these predominantly black counties and cities were governed by blacks in proportion to their percentage of the population, they would constitute power bases from which blacks could "negotiate from a position of strength" at the national level.

force in a coalition, then they will join with their white radical allies in a full-fledged social movement.

But two questions remain unanswered. First, what happens in the meantime? If blacks withdraw from coalitions—even such unsatisfactory ones as the Democratic Party—who will fill the vacuum created by their pullout? Unfortunately, the political system will not mark time while the blacks withdraw and regroup. The Negro struggle on the national level must go forward or it will go backward. And as blacks know only too well, if they are not on the firing line themselves, no one else is going to be there in their place. The facts are simple: In national politics the blacks are in a coalition they have been part of since the New Deal. It is in many ways an unsatisfactory one at present. But they cannot afford to pull out if by doing so they absent themselves from national politics.

Second, is it reasonable to expect that an effective biracial coalition can emerge ten or twenty years hence, after both races have been politically segregated? On the surface there is some plausibility in the idea of blacks withdrawing from biracial politics to put their house in order, while their white allies do so in the white community. Yet as Thomas Pettigrew has argued, the likelihood of racial cooperation growing out of a segregated situation runs counter to most research findings in the social psychology of racial attitudes.[9] The chances for biracial cooperation are vastly increased by integration on the job, in school, in the residential neighborhood, and in politics. No amount of "book learning" (or of propagandizing by white liberals or radicals, one might add) is as effective in destroying racial stereotypes as actual biracial contact, under the proper conditions. As Harvey Swados puts it: "One personal experience of a Negro standing at your side in a strike instead of scabbing on you is worth a thousand Hollywood movies on the charm of Negro children and the rectitude of 'tolerance.'"[10] In

9 Thomas F. Pettigrew, "Racially Separate or Together?" *Journal of Social Issues*, XXV (1969), 43–69.

10 Harvey Swados, "The UAW—Over the Top or Over the Hill?" in Irving Howe (ed.), *The Radical Papers* (Garden City: Doubleday & Co., Inc., Anchor Books, 1966), 246.

summary, while the dangers of coalition politics are real and should not be minimized, the dangers of separatism are also formidable and outweigh the risks of a biracial alliance, entered into with proper caution.

BLACKS AND WHITES HAVE MUTUALLY EXCLUSIVE INTERESTS

Much confusion arises over the ambiguity of the word "interest." It has at least two broad meanings when applied to aggregates of people, both of which are evoked in Marx's distinction between class *an sich* and class *für sich*. A class ("class in itself") by its very position in the social and economic structure, Marx argued, has certain clearly defined interests, whether or not the members of the class are aware of them. In its early stages of development, a class is unaware of these interests, but as its social consciousness increases, they become evident. That is to say, they take on a psychological reality as well. It is the task of the class leaders, Marx wrote, to discover these interests and bring them to the attention of the class members, who will then unite politically as a "class for itself."

Some political theorists deny the usefulness of the concept of group interest, except when it refers to goals the group members are agreed upon. By this definition "false consciousness" or a group interest of which the members are unaware would be a contradiction. Nonetheless, there are instances in which it is useful to speak of group interests that the members are unaware of. In common usage we often speak of a group—such as a labor union, a political organization, an age group, or an occupational category such as farmers—acting without regard for its own interests. All that is meant by this is that there are possible benefits to the group of which the members are unaware—benefits that may be forfeited because of the group's ignorance.

We can define an "objective interest" as a benefit to a group, whether or not the group is aware of it and whether or not they know how to go about realizing it. Thus, the enactment and enforcement of industrial safety laws in the oil fields would be an objective interest of oil field workers, whether or not they had any notion of such laws and their consequences. Benefits become "subjective interests" when the group becomes aware of them.

In asserting that there are no common interests shared by blacks and at least some whites, the critics of coalition politics may be making one of two different claims. They may mean that blacks and whites have no "objective interests" in common. In other words blacks do not share with any whites enough common characteristics to warrant referring to them as a group, either potential or actual. On the other hand, the critics may simply mean that despite the existence of many similarities in the life situation of blacks and lower-income whites, such as would constitute the basis for group solidarity and a commonality of "objective interests," these interests have not yet been recognized as such by them. "Subjective interests" have not emerged. The two different claims then are that there are no bases for "groupness" among blacks and some whites; or that while the basis for group life exists, the awareness of common interests has not developed.

Some of the extreme separatists, who have argued that the black experience has been fundamentally different from that of any whites, appear to be arguing the former position when they assert that there are no common interests between blacks and whites. But there are other coalition critics, some of them Black Power advocates, who are simply asserting the latter—that awareness of group benefits by blacks and some whites is potential but not yet actual.

A case can be made, on the contrary, that there are common interests between blacks and whites in both senses. There is evidence that lower-income blacks (the majority of the black population) and lower-income whites (at the very least a sizable minority of the white population) share positions in the social structure that are similar enough to provide a basis for group solidarity. Moreover there is evidence of an incipient group consciousness and awareness of common goals that can be sharpened into more explicit forms of solidarity.

If one defines social and economic categories rather broadly, it is an undeniable fact that large numbers of blacks and whites share similar positions in the economic structure. For example, in 1968 more than a quarter of nonwhite families and about a tenth of white families were below the government's minimally defined poverty level.[11] Almost two-thirds of nonwhite families and a third of white families that year had incomes of less than $7,000.[12] If one accepts the Bureau of Labor's 1967 estimate of the minimum income necessary for an urban family of four to maintain a moderate standard of living—$9,076—the glow of American affluence dims appreciably.[13] Almost three-fourths of nonwhite males and half of white males in the labor force were in nonfarm manual occupations (blue-collar and service jobs).[14] More than two-thirds of all Negroes twenty-

11 United States Bureau of the Census, *The Social and Economic Status of Negroes in the United States, 1969*, Bureau of Labor Statistics Report No. 375 (Washington, D.C.: United States Government Printing Office), 16.

There are, of course, numerous critics of the government's definition of poverty. Victor Fuchs, for example, argues that a poverty level defined relative to the median family income is more realistic than one employing fixed income levels, because the popular concept of poverty is relative to the general level of affluence in a society and not fixed. Thus, the family earning $3,000 in 1936 was not considered poor by the standards of that day, even if the dollars had the purchasing power of today's dollars. Fuchs suggests that the gross poverty level be considered one-half of the median family income, in which case approximately 20 percent of the population today, as twenty years ago, is poor. Victor R. Fuchs, "An Alternative Income-Oriented Definition," in Robert E. Will and Harold G. Vatter (eds.), *Poverty in Affluence: The Social, Political and Economic Dimensions of Poverty in the United States* (2nd ed.; New York: Harcourt Brace and World, 1970), 14–18.

12 *Ibid.*

13 In addition to the "moderate" budget, the Bureau of Labor Statistics now has devised a "lower" and "high" model budget. All three budgets are calculated for a family of four, including a father who works, a wife not employed outside the home, a girl of eight and a boy of thirteen. "All three budgets provide for the maintenance of physical health and social well-being, the nurture of children, and participation in community activities. . . . The content of the budgets is based on the manner of living and consumer choices in the 1960's." Jean Brackett, "New BLS Budgets Provide Yardsticks for Measuring Family Living Costs," *Monthly Labor Review* (April, 1969), 3.

The lower budget, calculated for urban areas in the spring of 1967, was approximately $5,900 (and almost $7,000 in 1970). It assumes that the "family lives in rental housing without air conditioning, relies heavily on the use of public transportation, supplemented, when necessary, by the use of an older car, performs more services for itself, and utilizes free recreation facilities in the community." *Ibid.* Such a budget allows less than $32 a week for food, and a maximum of about $40 a month for medical care. Transportation is alloted less than $10 a week. Within the context of American middle-class affluence, this budget surely provides a good yardstick for serious deprivation for a family of four.

14 *The Social and Economic Status of Negroes . . .*, 42.

five years old and above and 43 percent of comparable whites had not completed high school.[15]

Gross figures like these can only be suggestive. Many people in these more or less arbitrarily defined categories are not disadvantaged. Others who are outside of them are. Nevertheless they are sufficient to indicate that a very large number of blacks and whites in the United States today are in serious economic trouble. Included in this category are the family breadwinners working in unpleasant, often dangerous, often profoundly alienating jobs. Concentrated in the unskilled and semiskilled levels, these jobs offer the worker little chance of advancement or personal satisfaction, a good possibility of seasonal layoff, little control over decisions made by higher-ups. Included also are the families hit by the credit squeeze and the inflation squeeze. These are the families who must come to grips with second-rate schools (in a national educational system which is itself second-rate at best), inadequate city improvements, and the leavings of any major public works outlays. Within this aggregrate are the families whose futures are perpetually threatened by the possibility of accident or illness, whose sense of security is undermined by the knowledge that a serious hospitalization would obliterate any chance for long-term solvency. This is the grey America, comprised of people whose lives are stale and unpromising in their own eyes, when compared with the images of middle-class affluence served up daily on television. These are the families not only of the poor but the near poor, wage earners and retirees for the most part, families whose educational background, occupational status, and annual income insure them a marginal position in the economy and the American social structure. And it is grey America in more than one sense: it is a melange of blacks, browns, and whites, but with whites predominating. If many of the whites in this group share some of the "skin privileges" of the white caste generally, they are

---

15 United States Bureau of the Census, *Current Population Reports*, Series P-20, No. 192, "Voting and Registration in the Election of November 1968" (Washington, D.C.: United States Government Printing Office, 1969). Calculated from data on pp. 34–35.

also victims of the extreme social and economic injustices so common to blacks.[16]

At a time when so much is made of the differences between whites and blacks, it is imperative that this fact not be lost sight of. Social and economic inequalities among whites are at least as great in many respects as they are between the white and black populations. A greater number of whites than blacks are poor, for example, and are the victims of economic, social, and psychological deprivation. And yet, however obvious this may seem, writers who should know better overlook this fact.[17]

So far we have considered the charge of irreconciliable black-white interests as a claim that most members of the two populations do not have a similar position in the socioeconomic structure. Now let us examine the charge that no common group awareness exists across racial lines. Black separatists (and white ones) stress the feelings of solidarity which members of each race feel, in varying degrees, with "their own kind." And it is true that the legacy of caste in this country has led to feelings of color solidarity. Blacks, for the most part, do feel more comfortable among blacks, other things being equal. The same "color consciousness" of course exists among whites. But it is also true that people of one class have a group consciousness. They feel more comfortable—again, other things being equal—with members of their own social class. The strain on blue-collar people in a white-collar social setting is obvious. A similar strain is felt by middle-class people in a working-class social environment, although their confidence in their superior social status may enable them better to conceal this uneasiness. This is no less true for blacks than for whites. As numerous writers have pointed out, a chasm exists between the Negro classes and it engenders much dissension within the "movement." Undoubtedly there are situations in which black and white working-class people feel more at ease with one another than they would in the company of middle-class persons of their own race.[18] One such situation is

16 Will and Vatter, *Poverty in Affluence*, 53.
17 *Ibid.*
18 For example, class schisms in the black population came to the surface in

the factory work place, where the workers are often united in their antagonism to management. This is true because, whatever the realities of ethnic hostility, the kind of work one does and one's position in the authority structure of an enterprise, influence his relations with other workers. The continuous attempt by owners and managers throughout the history of American industrial capitalism to use race and ethnicity to drive a wedge between workers, thereby neutralizing the solidarity which develops in common working situations, is testimony to this fact.

Certainly "consciousness of kind" among members of the same class is not always highly developed nor has it ordinarily attained the status of political consciousness. One can feel socially more "at home" with other members of his group, and he can even identify group enemies and group goals in a vague sort of way without translating this knowledge into political terms. S. M. Miller and Frank Riessman write that "an awareness of class differences exists but it is not traditional class-consciousness. The recognition of class differences is not tied to any specific political ideology or platform and most often is implicit (bring a group of college students to an auto plant, and the awareness of class differences on both sides will

---

the spring of 1971 as middle-class blacks joined middle-class whites in several cities to prevent construction of federally subsidized housing projects for low- and moderate-income families. New York *Times*, February 15, 1971.

One of the most suggestive treatments of the conflict between class solidarity and racial solidarity is found in Allison Davis, Burleigh B. Gardner, and Mary R. Gardner, *Deep South* (Chicago: University of Chicago Press, 1941), chapter 21, "Relation Between the Caste System and the Economic System," 454–82. The authors uncovered in "Old City" (Natchez, Mississippi), strong mutual expressions of solidarity between Negro and white businessmen, as well as between the Negro and white poor. There were, of course, antagonisms as well, but the economic basis of solidarity significantly weakened the racial caste barriers in many cases. Negro and white landowners showed a similar contempt for white tenant families—the so-called "poor white trash." Several instances of mutual cooperation and social contact between black and white tenant families are cited.

For a summary of studies showing the similarity of attitudes of blacks and whites of the same social class, see Thomas Pettigrew, *A Profile of the American Negro* (Princeton: D. Van Nostrand Co., Inc., 1964), 33. Also see Herbert H. Hyman's suggestive discussion of the class prejudice of whites as a component of race prejudice, in Hyman, "Social Psychology and Race Relations," in Irwin Katz and Patricia Gurin (eds.), *Race and the Social Sciences* (New York: Basic Books, Inc., Publ., 1969), 9–19.

electrify the air). Workers with a strong 'class-awareness' can be quite conservative or uninterested in politics."[19] Nonetheless this common awareness of class differences, which more and more is coming to transcend the weakening barriers of caste, is a potential foundation for mutually rewarding political enterprises, and it is the matrix for class consciousness in the narrower sense. Arthur Shostak, in his book on working-class whites, cites evidence that what is sometimes mistaken for racial prejudice among this group is really envy of the blacks' recent political successes (real or imagined): "While these same whites vaguely seek answers to their own political and economic problems, they differ from many Negroes in not feeling driven to do so. They are also unwilling to act in a concerted and dramatic way—as they imagine the Negroes they envy are doing. . . . Harboring an old-world or ethnic suspicion of authority, blue-collarites hesitate to bring government into their lives and resent the successes that such action seems to bring to Negroes."[20] No doubt this envy is real, as evidenced by the fact that many whites actually tell interviewers that Negroes at their own social level have better chances for education, good jobs, and even good housing. But white workers envy the imagined success of blacks precisely because they share the blacks' situation, in many respects, and their goals. The logical goal of any liberal-radical movement, therefore, would be to dispel this envy through political education and through working together as a biracial (or multiracial) group.[21]

In summary, the theory that the interests of blacks and whites are irreconcilable seems plausible only when the distinctness and homo-

19 S. M. Miller and Frank Riessman, "Are Workers Middle Class?" *Dissent*, VIII (1961), 516.

20 Arthur B. Shostak, *Blue-Collar Life* (New York: Random House, Inc., 1969), 223.

21 Robert Dahl's observation concerning ethnic cleavages in New Haven is very much to the point. ". . . the very fact that the politician exploited ethnic unities . . . [led to] a self-fulfilling prophecy; by treating ethnic distinctions as fundamental in politics, he *made* them fundamental. Had there been no ethnic distinctions to work with, class or socioeconomic differences would have been more obvious. Politicians would have shaped their strategies in order to appeal to socioeconomic groups or classes." Dahl, *Who Governs? Democracy and Power in an American City* (New Haven: Yale University Press, 1961), 54.

geneity of the racial groups are exaggerated and other social and economic similarities are minimized. There are indeed many similarities in the position of most blacks and that of a large minority of less affluent whites—a fact reflected in a "consciousness of kind" which refuses to disappear completely even under the stress of racial polarization. It is also reflected in many of the voting patterns analyzed in the previous chapter.

ORGANIZED LABOR, THE POLITICAL ARM OF THE WHITE WORKING CLASS, IS NOT A SUITABLE ALLY OF BLACKS.

Among the less affluent whites who share many of the problems and perspectives of blacks, the most politically aware and best organized have traditionally been the unionized. Yet the above criticism is a standard claim not only of Black Power advocates and white radicals, but of liberal intellectuals as well. The unions, it is argued, have sold out. They have become thoroughly middle class in their aspirations and values. Having won their battle for acceptance into the political system, they are now prosperous, so it is claimed, and they have emerged as a new bastion of conservatism. Academic critics such as Harold Wilensky have emphasized the alleged "middle classification" of labor.[22] Julius Jacobson has recently written a stinging indictment of union racism.[23] Labor leaders themselves have lamented the decline of union militance. The late Walter Reuther, speaking to a United Automobile Workers convention shortly before the UAW's split with the AFL-CIO, said: "In the 11 years of the merger we believe that the AFL-CIO has become stagnant and is vegetating. I say, to put it simply and understandably, it has an acute case of hardening of the arteries."[24] More recently Victor Gotbaum, a municipal employees' union official, attacked the leadership of the 1.3 million-member New York City

22 Harold L. Wilensky, "Class, Class Consciousness, and American Workers," in William Haber (ed.), *Labor in a Changing America* (New York: Basic Books, Inc., Publ., 1966), 12–28.
23 Julius Jacobson, "Union Conservatism: A Barrier to Racial Equality," in Jacobson (ed.), *The Negro and the American Labor Movement*, (Garden City: Doubleday & Co., Inc., 1968), 1–26.
24 Quoted in Jacobson, "Union Conservatism," 10–11.

Central Labor Council for its failure to meet the needs of the city's blacks and Puerto Ricans. "Let's not kid ourselves," he said. "They don't like us in the black community.... Labor may be doing as much as other groups, but that isn't enough. We're supposed to be the friends of the underdog."[25] The culpability of the unions with regard to blacks was underlined by the announcement by NAACP officials at their 1970 convention that the organization was sponsoring a national campaign of mass demonstrations to force union hiring of minority groups.

In assessing the potential for a continued but more successful alliance between blacks and organized labor, however, the above observations about the conditions of less affluent whites apply to unionists as well. Contrary to popular assumptions, often fostered by an antilabor press, organized labor still counts among its members the economically less advantaged members of society. It may be true today, as Wilensky asserts, that former labor militants or their sons "peacefully negotiate contracts with employers, serve on community welfare council boards, run for municipal office (and occasionally win), and live the modestly comfortable middle-class life of trade-union officials."[26] But to generalize from this affluence of the labor aristocracy (or some part of it) to the conditions of the rank and file is unjustified. Any announcement of the ascendancy of organized labor as a whole to middle-class affluence is premature, to say the least. Nor, for that matter, does it seem to be true that the values and habits of thought of blue-collar people in general, including those in the highly unionized skilled occupations, are indistinguishable from those of the middle classes.[27]

Voting studies show that union families are still far more firmly

25 New York *Times*, July 13, 1969. A sharp criticism of this picture of American unionism is found in Michael Harrington's article, "Don't Form a Third Party: Form a New First Party," New York *Times* Magazine, September 13, 1970, pp. 28, 128, 132–35.

26 Wilensky, "Class, Class Consciousness," 427.

27 See Richard Hamilton, "The Behavior and Values of Skilled Workers," in Arthur B. Shostak and William Gomberg (eds.), *Blue Collar World: Studies of the American Worker* (Englewood Cliffs: Prentice-Hall, Inc., 1964), 42–57; Norval D. Glenn and Jon P. Alston, "Cultural Differences among Occupational Categories," *American Sociological Review*, XXXVIII (1968), 365–82.

committed to the Democratic Party than the rest of the population. Even in 1968, when labor support dropped lower than at any time since 1936, because of the 15 percent of their vote going to George Wallace, 56 percent of those voters in union families backed the Democrats.[28]

An opinion survey of the AFL-CIO rank and file in 1967 revealed a continuing economic liberalism combined with middling support for civil rights.[29] Polls taken in 1971 revealed that the widely heralded "turn to the right" by organized labor in the late 1960s was mythical. On many issues unionists were somewhat more liberal than non-unionists. They expressed support for the 1954 school desegregation decision by a 58–33 ratio, as opposed to the public's 55–32 approval.[30]

Another fact to be reckoned with is that organized labor is not lily white. It is estimated that about two million union members are black. Moreover, as Martin Luther King pointed out, these blacks are concentrated in key industries. "In the truck transportation, steel, auto and food industries which are the backbone of the nation's economic life, Negroes make up nearly 20 percent of the organized work force, although they are only 10 percent of the general population," King wrote. "This potential strength is magnified further by the fact of their unity with millions of white workers in these occupations. As co-workers there is a basic community of interest that transcends many of the ugly divisive elements of traditional prejudice."[31] King's attitude toward organized labor seems to be shared by large numbers of other blacks. A national opinion survey of blacks carried out by William Brink and Louis Harris for *Newsweek* in 1966 revealed that while 44 percent of the respondents were not

28 Arthur B. Shostak, *Blue-Collar Life* (New York: Random House, Inc., 1969), 90.

29 New York *Times*, July 16, 1967.

30 Houston *Post*, March 25, 1971. Derek Bok and John Dunlap write that while the unions are not much more progressive than the rest of the population—as measured by attitude surveys—they are not much less, either. There has not been a shift to the right among unionists, as many journalists and commentators have been stating recently. Bok and Dunlap, *Labor and the American Community* (New York: Simon and Schuster, Inc., 1970), 47.

31 Martin Luther King, Jr., *Why We Can't Wait* (New York: Harper and Row, 1964), 140.

sure whether labor unions were "more helpful" or "more harmful" to Negro rights, 76 percent of those expressing opinions believed the unions were more helpful. When asked about "white businesses," 50 percent of the respondents were not sure, and of those expressing opinions, only 60 percent believed business was more helpful than harmful.[32] Derek Bok and John Dunlap write: "It is no accident that organized labor began to widen its goals in the thirties after its ranks had been swelled to include more semiskilled and low-wage workers, who had an obvious stake in social insurance and welfare legislation. Nor is it mere happenstance that an AFL union such as the Meat Cutters started to take a more active interest in civil rights after it began to attract many Negro and Puerto Rican workers in the food-processing industries."[33]

The problem, then, becomes realizing this potential through increasing the awareness among white unionists of the interests they share with blacks, and in pointing out that many of the barriers between them are artificial and can be explained by the unplanned nature of the economy. Such political education must be carried out in conjunction with efforts to capitalize on the widespread discontent among unionists not only with their economic situation but also with their conditions of work. For, as Shostak points out: "Only in those rare cases in which labor can link its political efforts to 'wages, hours, and working conditions,' rather than to espousal of 'reform' or 'liberal government' or 'friends of labor,' is there clear-cut rank-and-file response."[34]

Another widespread myth about labor is that work discontent is a thing of the past and no longer provides the basis for union protest. Journalist Theodore White gives expression to this myth in its most exaggerated form in the latest volume of his series on presidential election campaigns: "The white workingmen—at least, the union men—have now all but conquered the conditions of their work. For most, their unions have made their hours in the working places the

---

32 William Brink and Louis Harris, *Black and White: A Study of U.S. Racial Attitudes Today* (New York: Simon and Schuster, Inc., 1967), 234-35.
33 Bok and Dunlap, *Labor and the American Community*, 395.
34 Shostak, *Blue-Collar Life*, 225.

best part of the day—air-conditioned, clean, safe. At the plant, the condition of life is better controlled for American workingmen by their union leaders than in any other country in the world."[35] According to White such problems as remain for the blue-collar workers arise only when they go home from work.

Other writers closer to the work scene than White take sharp issue with this point of view. Harvey Swados, an observer and sometime member of the industrial proletariat, discerns in assembly-line workers a deep disenchantment with their work which is responsive to the slogans of the New Left demanding a humanizing labor movement.

> For many assembly-line workers in America, being dumped into dead-end jobs deepens the gulf not so much between colors as between classes. Their racist bias has hardly diminished in recent months—but as some [radical college] students have been discovering to their surprise—this does not preclude a passionate concern about the human condition, sometimes in concert with those with whom they are willing to work and unwilling to live.
>
> In our bemusement with students dropping out of the hypocrisy machine like mercury slipping from a broken thermometer, not many of us have been paying attention to the parallel phenomenon of workers rebelling against the bureaucracies of both employers and unions. Delegates to recent u.a.w. conventions—among the highest-paid industrial workers in the country—have been holding up placards bearing two words: "Dignity Now."[36]

The image of the typical union man as white, middle aged, lost in reveries of World War II or before, and generally content with his income and his work in an air-conditioned (if not automated) factory badly needs refurbishing. A recent article about Detroit auto workers in *Fortune*, obviously intended to awaken its readers among corporate management to the dangers of worker discontent, makes

35 Theodore White, *The Making of the President, 1968* (1969; New York: Simon & Schuster, Inc., Pocket Books, 1970), 458.

36 New York *Times*, August 30, 1969. In this connection, see Swados' article, "The Myth of the Happy Worker," in Robert Perrucci and Marc Pilisuk (eds.), *The Triple Revolution: Social Problems in Depth* (Boston: Little, Brown and Co., 1968), 234–40. This originally appeared in Harvey Swados, *A Radical America* (Boston: Atlantic-Little, Brown, 1957).

this point emphatically. One central fact emerges from the article: 40 percent of the 740,000 hourly paid workers in the auto industry are under the age of thirty-five. According to the author, Judson Gooding, these younger workers "bring into the plants with them the new perspectives of American youth in 1970. . . . The new attitudes cut across racial lines. Both young blacks and young whites have higher expectations of the jobs they fill and the wages they receive, and for the lives they will lead. They are restless, changeable, mobile, demanding, all traits that make for impermanence— and for difficult adjustment to an assembly line. The deep dislike of the job and the desire to escape become terribly clear twice each day when shifts end and the men stampede out the plant gates to the parking lots, where they sometimes actually endanger lives in their desperate haste to be gone."[37]

Other evidence of this discontent among auto workers is a sharp increase in absenteeism, tardiness, more arguments with foremen, and higher turnover. (The quit rate at Ford in 1969 was 25.2 percent.) Industrial sabotage, in the form of purposely inflicted damage to new cars, is very high.[38] While generalizations to other industries can be risky (70 percent of the auto workers are unskilled compared with 10 percent in all industry), there is reason to believe that younger workers in many sectors of the labor force are not content with their work, and, having been led to expect more satisfaction, they can be mobilized to support numerous humane and egalitarian social and economic policies which are tied to the issue of work alienation.

This is true not only in the industrial sector of the labor force, which is most highly unionized, but in the rapidly expanding service

37 Judson Gooding, "Blue Collar Blues on the Assembly Line," *Fortune*, LXXXI (July, 1970), 69. An article containing similar information is contained in the New York *Times*, June 1, 1970.

38 Almost as an aside, Gooding says (p. 112): "The fact that 100,000 of the 740,000 auto workers were laid off for varying periods this year has, of course, added to discontent." Swados has explained the depth of this discontent as follows: "In former times, when a worker was laid off he took his gun and went hunting, or he drove back down home to the old folks' farm until word came that they were hiring again. If it got really tough, he went on relief and sweated it out until things picked up and he was called back. Now, a layoff may mean that he will *never* work again." Swados, "The UAW—Over the Top or Over the Hill?" 248.

occupations as well, which are almost totally nonunion. As this
sector continues to grow as a proportion of the total work force
and the industrial sector continues to decline, as it has throughout
the century, the labor movement must either establish a beachhead
in the service occupations or decline to the status of one insignificant
pressure group among others, precisely at a time of rapid corporate
concentration. In other words the labor movement must organize
the service occupations or lose ground. There is some indication
that labor leaders, who are not completely blind to their long-term
interests, are beginning to recognize this imperative and to rely upon
the militance of minority groups to give the movement impetus.

For example, the successes of Drug and Hospital Local 1199
throughout the country have gained for it a great deal of respect
and support from its big brothers in the union movement. The local,
which has won important gains for black and white hospital workers
at the very bottom of the pay scale in numerous cities (including
Charleston, South Carolina, the scene of a bitter and successful strike
in 1969), is now approaching the status of an independent force
within its parent AFL-CIO. A. H. Raskin, labor writer for the New
York *Times*, writes:

> So far as the labor hierarchy is concerned, the new union is an off-
> shoot of the Retail, Wholesale and Department Store Union, the
> A.F.L.-C.I.O. international with which Local 1199 itself is affiliated.
> Having a local union sprout a whole treeful of affiliates under a
> distinct national charter is decidely unorthodox, but the prestige
> Local 1199 enjoys and the diversity of the power centers with
> which it is linked made its own international decide it was the
> course of wisdom to bless the new venture rather than fight it. In
> a year or two the fast-growing infant may well dwarf its parent
> international and ask for A.F.L.-C.I.O. to give it the key to a house
> of its own.[39]

Local 1199 is completely integrated racially, and the membership
is preponderantly black and Puerto Rican. Black leaders—and white

39 A. H. Raskin, "A Union with 'Soul,'" New York *Times* Magazine, March
22, 1970, p. 38. For a perceptive and somewhat critical description of Local 1199,
written from a different vantage point, see Elinor Langer "Inside the Hospital
Workers' Union," *New York Review of Books*, May 20, 1971, pp. 25-33.

—of quite different views have lined up in support of the local, for the same reason that a front-running candidate is able to build a coalition of divergent factions: everybody loves a winner. But Local 1199 has not been a winner of empty victories. "What gives Local 1199 its special magic," Raskin writes, "is the extent to which it has coupled the substantial bread-and-butter gains it has brought its rank and file with equally solid progress toward making unionism a way of life, an integral element in the freedom struggle."[40]

The local is a sponsor of a thirty-million-dollar urban renewal project on the Harlem bank of the East River, which will provide cooperative apartments for thirteen hundred fifty families, many of which are headed by hospital employees. The union hopes to turn the development into a center for interracial living through the inclusion of a dozen community facilities. Supporters of the union, at one time or another, have included Malcolm X, Dr. King (who called it his "favorite union"), Roy Wilkins, A. Philip Randolph, Mrs. King, who is now honorary chairman of the national organizing drive, Harry Van Arsdale, Jr., president of New York City's Central Labor Council, George Meany, Walter Reuther, and Thomas Gleason, head of the International Longshoremen's Association. The lesson to be learned from Local 1199, apparently, is that when fundamental economic gains benefiting organized labor and the black population come to be seen as real possibilities worth fighting for, factional squabbles are submerged both within the black community and within the family of organized labor. One can hope that the labor "establishment" under the prodding of mavericks such as Local 1199 will begin to espouse a more militant policy partly out of fear of being upstaged as a spokesman for the rank and file. A sign of what could be in the wind if this happens appeared in the spring of 1970, when the executive council of the AFL-CIO came out with a strong endorsement of a program for national health insurance that would provide comprehensive health

40 Raskin, "A Union with 'Soul,' " 38. For a moving account of some of the activities and successes of Local 1199 in New York, see the Local's documentary film, "Like a Beautiful Child."

care for the entire population and which would be financed largely by employers and the federal government.[41]

Militancy among the union mavericks may be rising, even in the South.[42] A report by Roger Williams in the spring of 1970 claims that public employees in major southern cities are becoming unionized at a rapid rate. In the wake of strikes in Memphis, Charleston, and Atlanta, the American Federation of State, County and Municipal Employees claims some thirty thousand members in southern unions, and one official predicted a membership of two hundred thousand within five years.[43] The progress to date is attributed to several factors, including the decrease in public resistance to collective bargaining and the fact that "racial antagonisms, which long have hampered cooperation among southern workers, are proving to be not so great a problem in public employment as one might expect."[44]

For example, an American Federation representative reported "terrific unity" between black and white water works employees in Little Rock who were striking to gain union recognition. "It's amazed everybody here," she said. A white union leader in Pascagoula, Mississippi, where the municipal union is 60 percent black, is quoted as reporting: "We get along fine. Any time you can talk about your problems together, you can work better together." The state president of the AFL-CIO in North Carolina claimed that "we don't care if the workers are black, white or purple. Shoot, we're

41 New York *Times*, February 18, 1970. The council in effect endorsed a bill introduced in Congress by Representative Martha W. Griffiths of Michigan. According to the *Times* the benefits would include "virtually every kind of medical service for the diagnosis and treatment of disease."

42 As pointed out in chapter VI, cooperation between blacks and organized labor is not without precedent in the South. Alan Samuel Meyer claims that labor supported the Longs in Louisiana, Folsom in Alabama, Rainey and Lyndon Johnson in Texas, and opposed the Byrd machine in Virginia and the "financial and business ruling faction in North Carolina." See Meyer, "The Not-So-Solid South: A Study of Variability in Southern Sentiment in School Desegregation" (Ph.D. dissertation, Columbia University, 1962), 331.

43 Roger Williams, "Southern Cities on Strike," *South Today*, June, 1970, p. 6.

44 At a period when labor is generally characterized as "sick," "stagnant," or in decline, it is interesting to note that the percentage of companies in the Houston

organizing the Lumbee Indians in one part of the state." He believes racial animosity is disappearing among rank and file members. "It's bound to," he says. "It's a threat to any worker to have other workers underpaid and underprivileged. It holds him back, too."[45]

Regarding interracial attitudes within an American Federation local in Memphis that was "born of the historic 1968 garbage strike that claimed the life of Dr. Martin Luther King," Roger Williams wrote in 1970:

> Over 90 percent of the membership is black, but union leaders say that in recent months whites have been joining at a faster rate than blacks. There has been little black-white animosity within the local and no more than the normal amount of white reluctance to join a heavily-black organization. Some members quit last fall after the local began supporting "Black Monday" boycotts, on the ground that the union had no business being involved in a civil rights situation. Overall, however, cooperation between the races within the local is good. Two whites, both employees of the city's auto testing station, sit on the 20-man board of directors of 1733. One of them, 56-year-old Joe Owne, says: "My idea is that if you're going to have a union, it's got to be for the benefit of all the working people, no matter what color they are." The Reverend James Smith, an articulate young Negro who is the local's senior staff representative, charges the white power structure with playing on racial feelings in order to undercut the union: "They've even met with workers, black as well as white, to try to argue them

---

area which recognize union representation has been steadily increasing, as indicated in the following table.

Union Recognition in Sampled Companies, Houston

Time Period	Percentage of Companies Recognizing Union Representation
Prior to 1940	7.5%
1940–1945	18.8
1946–1951	35.8
1952–1957	44.3
1958–1963	50.9
1964–1967	55.7

Source: "Houston Labor: Data Sheet compiled by the industrial development department of the Bank of the Southwest" (Houston. (n.d.).

45 Roger Williams, "Southern Cities on Strike."

out of joining. It's the old divide-and-conquer idea of the power structure."[46]

Another new development in the South, alongside the municipal employees unions, is the push for tenant unions, which is just beginning. The National Tenants Organization, composed of one hundred forty groups in twenty-five states, has recently begun to concentrate on southern targets. At this writing only ten cities in the South have well-organized tenant unions, but National Tenants organizers plan to establish a regional network of such groups. According to one observer, the problems of rising rents, building deterioration, and decreasing services that plague the low-income tenants the group concentrates on are also increasingly common problems for middle-income apartment dwellers. For this reason 25 percent of the organized tenant activities in 1969 were initiated by this latter group. Thus, it is claimed, "the NTO is a unique tenant coalition which cuts across income and racial lines and has the potential for radically changing the housing situation."[47]

Concern among the labor giants over getting their share of the new union members is evidenced by ambitious organizing efforts of the Alliance for Labor Action, which in late 1969 launched its drive to establish a southern base for organized labor in Georgia. The alliance, composed of the 3.7 million-member coalition between the Teamsters and the United Auto Workers after the latter split off from the AFL-CIO, is employing new organizing tactics, such as radio and television propaganda, as well as the traditional techniques.

According to journalist Jon Nordheimer, the payoff for the unions is a portion of the 85 percent of the southern nonfarm work force which remains unorganized.[48] The barriers, however, are also great.[49] Alongside the traditional antiunionism in the area, many in-

46 Roger Williams, "Memphis Municipal Union Now a City Force," *South Today*, July–August, 1970, p. 8. A similar coming together of the lower-income groups may be in an initial stage of development in the North as well. New York *Times*, May 20, 1970.

47 Kitty Griffith, "Rent Strikes Are Heading South," *South Today*, June, 1970, p. 2.

48 Jon Nordheimer, "Labor Organizers Invade South via Madison Avenue," New York *Times*, April 6, 1970.

49 In Pat Watters' words: "Antiunionism ... [in the South] continued to sepa-

dustrial centers continue to suffer from a glut of workers on the labor market that is the result of the influx of blacks driven off the farms by automation. Yet the significance for Negroes of AFL-CIO success in Georgia could be great. Half of the nonfarm workers in the greater Atlanta area, where the Alliance for Labor Action's efforts have been concentrated, are black. And half of the organizers are black as well. "The black man has learned from the gains made in civil rights that there's strength in organization," a Teamster organizer was quoted as saying. "The idea of unions isn't so strange to him today as it once was."[50]

Intentions of course cannot be taken for the act. Attempts at unionizing the South have failed before. The CIO's "Operation Dixie" which spurred the AFL into competition in that region following World War II is a case in point. Moreover the hopeful developments must be balanced against the bigotry of some unionists. Consequently, as King wrote when discussing coalition strategy, blacks should be cautious in choosing their political bedfellows. But a cautious approach will entail not only rejecting some unions out of hand as potential allies, but accepting others.

A COALITION OF THE KIND ENVISAGED COULD NOT POSSIBLY CONSTITUTE A MAJORITY.

To be meaningful any claim about the political attitudes of a majority must specify what electoral population is under discussion.[51] Is it the entire adult population of the United States? Or that

---

rate the poorest of both races from their natural interests. In 1962, only 1,577,000 of 12,200,000 non-agricultural workers in the eleven states belonged to the AFL-CIO. In 1966, the figure was 1,923,000. In no state was union membership even 20 percent of the non-agricultural employment; nationally it was 28.8 percent." Watters, *The South and the Nation* (New York: Pantheon Books, 1969), 81.

50 Nordheimer, "Labor Organizers Invade South."

51 Many authors who make this claim fail to recognize the diversity of electorates which influence policy decisions. "*Nowhere is there evidence*," writes Lewis Killian, criticizing Bayard Rustin, ". . . that the majority of the American electorate is disposed to pay the price for such a feat [i.e., the eradication of poverty]. That the price would be small as compared to the cost of Viet Nam or the space program does not change the fact that the American public is willing to pay for these latter

much smaller one which votes in presidential elections, or the smaller one yet which votes for lesser political offices? This is important to know, because the population becomes more liberal on many issues as it becomes larger. (See below, pp. 256–57.) Does the discussion concern the popular vote for the presidency or the weighted vote which is an artifact of the electoral college? Is the electorate in question the probable voting population of a county, or a city, or a congressional district? These are crucial questions, as the demography of these different populations varies drastically. For example in 1960 at least ninety congressional districts had a population containing 20 percent or more blacks. A smaller percentage of whites is needed in these districts to form a biracial majority than is needed in the nation at large. Significantly at least half of all southern congressional districts are one-fifth or more black. According to current population projections, at least thirteen large cities across the country will have black majorities by the mid-1980s. At least that many more will have black populations large enough to enable blacks to win with only a small percentage of whites as allies. It is all too easy to talk sweepingly about the moods and attitudes of "the" majority. It is quite difficult to know precisely what a given majority at a given moment will support. It is not even possible to know this by examining voting behavior in many instances. For past candidates often have not presented the sorts of alternatives that would allow us to ascertain the electorate's feelings on many matters.

One source of information in this regard is opinion surveys. Although they are open to the criticisms mentioned in chapter 6, they present data that must be considered along with other kinds. The results of a special nationwide opinion poll conducted by the Gallup organization in 1969 are of interest in this connection. Commissioned by *Newsweek*, the survey involved a sample of 2,165 persons representing a cross-section of white Americans, including the large

---

ventures, but not the former. The affluence of the majority of the population accounts in part for this phenomenon." *The Impossible Revolution? Black Power and the American Dream* (New York: Random House, Inc., 1968), 151. Italics added.

stratum in the five-thousand- to fifteen-thousand-dollar-income category—that slice of "middle America" which is popularly reputed to be the most conservative in their opinions. Some beliefs of these whites about Negroes are shown in Table 8.1.

Table 8.1

WHITE EVALUATIONS OF NEGROES' CHANCES

QUESTION: Do Negroes today have a better chance or worse chance than people like yourself?

	Better	Worse	Same
To get well-paying jobs?	44%	21%	31%
To get a good education for their children?	41	16	41
To get good housing at a reasonable cost?	35	30	27
To get financial help from the government when they're out of work?	65	4	22

Source: *Newsweek*, October 6, 1969, p. 45.

Caution is necessary in interpreting these data. It does not follow from the indicated responses that the majority of whites questioned are unreceptive to policies that would benefit whites and blacks alike. Surely, too, there is some hope to be gleaned from the fact that in response to all but the last question, only a minority of the sample believed Negroes had better opportunities. One must even be careful in interpreting the meaning of this minority response. The question, as worded, is ambiguous. It does not, after all, ask if the average Negro has a better chance than the average white. It asks, rather, if "Negroes" have a better or worse chance than "people like yourself."[52] It is a fact that as the socioeconomic status of whites decreases, there is a greater similarity between their life chances and those of most blacks. At the extreme the life chances of poverty-stricken whites are in many respects less than those of middle-class Negroes. For this reason the judgment by some whites that "Ne-

---

52 The wording of this question is flawed for a second reason. As reported in *Newsweek*, it did not give the respondent a chance to answer "the same" instead of "better" or "worse". Presumably those respondents who answered "the same" did so in spite of the question's wording.

groes today" have a better chance than they do may reflect realities that affluent whites (including sociologists) tend to overlook.[53]

Turning from racial attitudes to the sample's receptivity to a reordering of priorities on government spending (Table 8.2), an unexpected pattern is seen, one that calls into question the alleged conservatism of the white population. It is obvious that the strongest support is expressed for increased spending on what can be characterized as "welfare state" measures. One of the two highest items on the list for which more money was thought necessary was job training. This suggests that the majority of respondents believe it is within the legitimate scope of the government's activities to provide job skills for those who need them. Only 7 percent believed that less money should be allocated to job training. The overwhelming ratio of "more money" to "less money" advocates on such questions as medical care for the old and needy, improving schools, providing better housing for the poor (including the ghetto poor), and fighting pollution challenges the conventional view of conservatism in white America. It also challenges the assumption that people who put a high priority on fighting crime in the streets (usually taken as an index of "conservatism") must eo ipso put a low priority on increased welfare state measures (which are usually taken as an index of "liberalism").

The extremely low priority put upon increased defense expenditures, space exploration, and foreign aid is especially noteworthy. The survey was made at a time when the issue of ABM deployment was being debated in Congress and when the Nixon administration was invoking the presumed mandate of the so-called "silent majority" to legitimize not only vastly increased expenditures on such advanced weapons systems as ABM and MIRV, but higher levels of defense spending in other areas as well. Most remarkable of all is that the poll was taken shortly after the first landing of men on the moon. Yet only 10 percent of all white Americans sampled felt that more money should be spent in space exploration, while 56 percent felt

53 A recent description of the extent of white poverty in the rural South is found in Paul Good, *The American Serfs: A Report on Poverty in the Rural South* (New York: Ballantine Books, Inc., 1968).

that less should be allocated for this purpose. Only one in six persons believed more money should be spent on defense, while one in four was for cutting expenditures.

One might argue that the order of priorities reflected in Table 8.2

Table 8.2

WHITE PREFERENCES FOR NEW PRIORITIES ON UNITED STATES SPENDING[54]

QUESTIONS: On which, if any, items on this list do you think the government should be spending *more* money than it is now? Any others?

On which, if any, do you think the government should be spending *less* than it is now? Any others?

	More Money	Less Money
Job training for the unemployed*	56%	7%
Air and water pollution	56	3
Fighting organized crime	55	3
Medical care for the old and needy	47	5
Fighting crime in the streets	44	4
Improving schools	44	7
Providing better housing for the poor—especially in the ghettos	39	13
Building highways	23	14
Defense expenditures*	16	26
Space exploration	10	56
Foreign economic aid	6	57
Foreign military aid	1	66

Source: *Newsweek*, October 6, 1969.

*Subsequent Gallup polls indicate that the sentiment expressed in the above table is not evaporating or shifting to the right. A poll in late 1970 indicated that 61 percent of the respondents agreed that "Congress should vote more money to improve the living conditions of poor people in the cities." New York *Times*, November 4, 1970. One taken in early 1971 revealed that half of the national sample believed that the United States should reduce spending for national defense and military purposes. Only 11 percent felt that too little was being spent. Eight percent had no opinion. New York *Times*, April 15, 1971.

54 Here too the wording of the question upon which the data in this table are based leaves something to be desired, for the respondent was not able to indicate that he felt spending should continue at the same level.

would have been quite different if the respondents had been aware of the personal economic sacrifice that added spending in the areas indicated would require. It is not clear, though, that this reordering of priorities would require additional taxes for most citizens. It is entirely possible that a simple reallocation of existing revenues would go a long way to alleviating some of America's more pressing needs. Furthermore, a fundamental restructuring of the present tax system would preclude imposing additional taxes on large sectors of the population.

But even assuming that the desired changes would mean higher taxes for many, there is no compelling evidence that most whites would reject these changes simply because of the added sacrifice. Indeed there is evidence to the contrary. A question bearing on this issue was asked of a representative sample of whites in fifteen American cities in 1968. (No southern cities were included.) The survey was carried out by the University of Michigan's Survey Research Center at the request of the National Advisory Commission on Civil Disorders.[55] Table 8.3 presents the results relevant to our discussion. Answers to all five questions indicate that a solid majority of whites in the fifteen cities favored increased government expenditures to meet the urban crisis. Question 4 is designed to ascertain white attitudes toward increased government spending to alleviate Negro needs, and Question 5 mentions a hypothetical monetary sacrifice that such increased spending would require of the respondent. When the actual sacrifice is spelled out, willingness to support the program decreased. But it was only a 13 percentage point drop and still a majority of the white population expressed support for the program.

The data in the tables above are based on interviews with whites alone. As the Negro population is significantly more liberal on economic matters than whites, the combined percentage favoring the measures mentioned in the surveys would be even higher. Thus, the results of one survey indicate that a large proportion of Americans are receptive to certain kinds of progressive social change. The results of another indicate that the majority of residents in many

55 Angus Campbell and Howard Schurman, *Racial Attitudes in Fifteen American Cities* (New York: Frederick A. Praeger, Inc., 1968).

northern cities are likewise receptive. But assuming that these findings are valid, can these majority opinions be translated into electoral
majorities? This question is best answered by considering a further
criticism of a class-based coalition.

Table 8.3

WHITE SUPPORT FOR GOVERNMENT EXPENDITURES IN FIFTEEN
AMERICAN CITIES, 1968

Question	Government Should Do This	Government Should Not Do This	Don't Know
1. Some people say that if there are not enough jobs for everyone who wants one, the government should provide the extra jobs needed. Others say that the government should not do this. What is your opinion?			
	59%	37%	4%
2. Some neighborhoods in and around (Central City) have public schools with better buildings and more trained teachers than others. Do you think the government should provide money to bring the poorer schools up to the standard of the better schools, or that the government shouldn't do this?			
	78%	15%	7%
3. There are areas in cities like (Central City) where the housing is rundown and overcrowded. Some say the government should provide money to help improve housing in such places. Others don't think the government should do this. What is your opinion?			
	59%	36%	5%
4. If top government officials in Washington said that a program of spending more money for jobs, schools, and housing for Negroes is necessary to prevent riots, would you go along with such a program or would you oppose it?			
	66%	28%	6%
5. Suppose the program increased your own taxes by 10 percent—that is, if you were paying $300 last year, you would pay $330 this year, and so forth. Would you be willing in that case?			

Oppose Program 28%   Yes 53%   No 13%   Don't Know 6%

Source: Angus Campbell and Howard Schurman, *Racial Attitudes in Fifteen
American Cities* (New York: Frederick A. Praeger, Inc., 1968), 37.

A COALITION BASED ON CLASS ISSUES WOULD ALIENATE THE
MIDDLE-CLASS WHITES WHO ARE NECESSARY ALLIES OF BLACKS
IN INFORMAL COALITIONS AT PRESENT.

It is reasonable to expect a defection from the ranks of well-to-
do supporters of civil rights when lower-income whites and blacks
ally themselves to demand economic rights. Having admitted this,
three questions arise: How many affluent whites are now firmly
committed to the cause of Negro economic justice? How many
would defect in the face of increasing militance? Can these defections
be compensated for with new recruits? None of these three questions admits of a decisive answer, but analysis reveals that the above
criticism is not as damaging as it might at first seem.

Part of the force of this criticism rests on an exaggeration of the
extent to which better-off whites are allies of Negroes. In previous
chapters it was pointed out that often a very high percentage of
wealthy whites vote for and finance either the racist wing of the
Democratic party, or the more racist of the two national parties, or
in some cases both. The business elites who put together local Bourbon coalitions with Negroes in cities like Atlanta are seldom willing to tolerate more than token gains by the black community.
When they feel their economic interests threatened or when they
finally find their own families and their own segregated milieux
"threatened" by the process of desegregation which they have
magnanimously sanctioned for lower-income whites, their racial
moderation suddenly disappears.[56] Roy Reed, a New York *Times*
reporter, wrote in the spring of 1970:

> The people of Charlotte and Atlanta like to think of their cities
> as the most racially progressive in the South. In both cities, the

56 There is some evidence in the social science literature which bears out the
charge of middle- and upper-class inconstancy. Charles H. Stember, reviewing
studies of the relationship between education and prejudice, found the educated to
be "more labile than the others, and more responsive to changing values and beliefs.
... The Supreme Court's school desegregation decision of 1954 at first found its
most enthusiastic support among educated groups; but as resistance in the South
stiffened, many of the educated withdrew their backing and became the staunchest
supporters of the emerging doctrine of gradualism." Stember, *Education and
Attitude Change* (New York: Institute of Human Relations Press, 1961), 169.

reputation rests largely on timely efforts by the business and political establishment. During racial crises of the last 15 years, these leaders have always pitched in at critical times and helped the towns to accept the demand for change. Now, both cities are being pressed to finish the job of desegregating their public schools. The children of the prosperous white middle class will finally be affected. Passions are running higher than ever. And this time, with the cities crying for leadership, most of the leaders are nowhere to be found.[57]

At the outset, therefore, we must question whether the proportion of the middle and upper classes who are firmly committed to socioeconomic justice for blacks, rather than tokenism, is significant. Nevertheless, in a political system where winning margins are usually small, coalitionists cannot afford to take the prospect of defections lightly. Indeed it is this fact that accounts for the influence the Negro bloc now wields within the Democratic Party. So we must treat seriously the second question: How many defections from the ranks of current supporters would a class-based coalition entail?

Defections would depend on the perceived gains and losses resulting from the changes one could expect in the event that such a coalition achieved a measure of success. That we have no idea of what these gains and losses might be for the different sectors of the population is itself a significant political fact. It is, of course, possible that until rather precise programs for reform are put forth by advocates of change, a new coalition would lead to many defections among those in the middle classes. Yet studies of the effects of economic reallocation, once completed, might reveal that few people in the middle classes need suffer loss of status, income, or wealth. It is well known today that the nation's corporate wealth is concentrated in the hands of a very small percentage of families and that

57 New York *Times*, February 23, 1970. A similar phenomenon was observed in 1971 in Houston. In the latter city, upper-middle-class parents led a fight to create a new school district in the fashionable Westheimer area. The move came on the heels of the Supreme Court's Charlotte-Mecklenburg ruling approving school busing as a means of creating racial balance.

the gross inequities in the tax structure are primarily for the benefit of those at the top.

Let us assume, in any case, that a class-based coalition leads to middle-class defections, or worse, a policy of reaction similar to that which followed the demise of Populism. The obvious strategy is to offset the defections with new recruits. But where would they come from? Could they be counted on for consistent support? The insight of V. O. Key once more provides some suggestive hypotheses. One of the central features of southern politics at the time he studied it in the 1940s—and even today—is the region's low rate of political participation. It is true that the rate is low for the nation as a whole. But the South has consistently fallen below the North and West in this respect.[58] Moreover the lower participation rates cannot be explained by southern Negro disfranchisement alone. Southern whites also participate at lower levels than their northern counterparts.[59]

The extent of southern nonvoting is obvious in Figure 8.1, which contains data on presidential elections. Southern participation rates in primary elections are also extremely low.[60] In the period from 1900 to 1960, the mean turnout was less than a third of the southern adult population. In Texas, as in the rest of the South, there has been a gradual upswing in presidential turnout, but at the highest point in this century, it came to a mere 52 percent in 1968 (Table 8.4). In the Texas gubernatorial generals, potentially very important elections, the turnout in presidential years now seems to be in the 40 percent range, while in off-years, it is less than 30 percent. The highest turnout for governor in a Texas Democratic primary in recent years came in 1956, when 31 percent voted. A slight decline in the 1960s is evident and increased voting in the presidential generals has not affected this trend. This means, in effect, that the

58 For recent information on voter turnout, see Walter Dean Burnham, "The Changing Shape of the American Political Universe," *American Political Science Review*, LIX (1965), 7–28.

59 V. O. Key, Jr., *Southern Politics in State and Nation* (New York: Alfred A. Knopf, Inc., 1949), 495–96.

60 *Ibid.*, 493.

Table 8.4

VOTER TURNOUT IN TEXAS, 1944–1968
(AS PERCENTAGE OF VOTING-AGE POPULATION)

Type of Election	1944	1948	1952	1956	1960	1962	1964	1966	1968
General									
President	28%	26%	44%	38%	42%		44%		52%
U.S. Senator						16%	42%	25%	
Governor				34%	40%	28%	43%	24%	46%
U.S. Representative				33%	37%	28%	45%	21%	39%
Democratic Primary									
Governor				31%	28%	26%	28%	22%	23%

Sources: Democratic National Committee, "That All May Vote: A Report on the Universal Voter Enrollment Plan"; and Clifton McCleskey, *The Government and Politics of Texas* (3rd ed.; Boston: Little, Brown, and Co., 1969), 38.

governor of Texas needs only 12 or 13 percent of the state's adult population for a majority in his crucial primary race.[61] Figures for Houston reflect a similar rate of turnout, with even less interest shown in the mayoral race than in statewide races. Black turnout

61 The importance of a relatively small number of voters is well understood by precinct workers, as the following excerpt from an AFL-CIO publication, *How to Win*, illustrates:

Take 100 voters in a normal American precinct. Only about 50% of those turn out in a typical election. These 50 voters will fall into a pattern whereby some 25 are regular backers of the majority party; some 15 will back the minority party; and the other 10 will scatter their votes as unenrolled voters of either party.

In the typical district, then, the victory for the predominant party is generally predictable; it starts with a majority, and usually ends up with 55 to 60% of the vote.

The 25 regular voters of the majority party, then, are the decisive voting bloc in this electorate of 100.

When it comes to the primary, however, not all 25 regular supporters of the majority party will turn out to vote.

As a matter of fact, if 20 to 30 percent of these come out for the primary, it's a high percentage.

That means that of the 25 voters we're talking about, only five or six— or, at the most, 10—will vote in the primary.

To win the primary, then (which is almost identical with winning the election in some 300 out of 435 Congressional districts across the country)

is lower than white, although this is probably more a function of class than of color (Table 8.5).[62]

Key asked whether the vast population of nonvoters differed in significant respects from the much smaller proportion of voters—the

Table 8.5

VOTER TURNOUT IN HOUSTON AND HARRIS COUNTY, 1960–1966
(AS PERCENTAGE OF VOTING-AGE POPULATION)

Type of Election	1960	1961	1962	1963	1964	1965	1966
			WHITES				
General Elections							
President	48%				49%		
Governor			29%				29%
Mayor		18%					
Primaries							
Governor	25%		21%		25%		19%
			BLACKS				
General Elections							
President	27%				35%		
Governor			21%				16%
Mayor		16%					
Primaries							
Governor	13%		19%		20%		17%

AVERAGE TURNOUT IN NINE ELECTIONS
Whites: 29%   Blacks: 20%

Source: Computed from voting returns, using population projections based on the 1960 census.

you must get a majority of the five or six—or, at the most, 10—out of 100 eligible to vote in the election. That means you must get at the most six in this electorate of 100.

62 These participation rates are similar to those in Austin, Texas, during a comparable period. See Harry Holloway and David M. Olson, "Electoral Participation by White and Negro in a Southern City," *Midwest Journal of Political Science,* X (1966), 99–122.

Figure 8.1. Presidential Turnout: United States, 1860–1964, by region.
Reproduced by permission of Walter Dean Burnham.

actual electorate. In *Southern Politics*, his ecological data led him
to surmise that the nonvoters, both black and white, were on the
average quite a bit lower on the socioeconomic ladder than
the voters: "In effect low participation slices from the electorate the
persons who would form the basis for a large faction or, in a two-
party state, the basis for a party.... In some areas of the South the
electorate resembles, for example, what the upstate New York
electorate would be with the disfranchisement of a large proportion
of those people not disposed to vote Republican."[63] This, he believed, resulted from the fact that "a decline in electoral interest
generally operates to a much higher degree among the less prosperous than among the more substantial elements of the community."[64]

As lower-income groups are more liberal on economic issues and
as blacks, obviously, are more liberal on racial issues, Key reasoned

63 Key, *Southern Politics*, 507.
64 *Ibid.*

that the underrepresentation of these groups in the electorate was responsible for the conservatism of the region's politics. "The singular governmental neglect of the Negro can be matched by parallels among white groups. Their elementary rights . . . are weak indeed. Contrast the status of the southern white tenant and sharecropper with that of the northern industrial worker who is unquestionably more active politically. . . . Public policy relative to southern industrial labor likewise is partially explained by the political abdication of a larger proportion of southern wage earners than of other classes."[65]

In a later work, Key was able to show by the use of survey data that the adult population of the South (including the border states) was at least as liberal on economic issues as the non-South.[66] His findings have been confirmed more recently by Richard Hamilton, using data from the Survey Research Center's 1964 election study.[67] A majority of white Southerners favored Medicare (of those respondents who had an opinion), and if blacks are included, a sizable majority did. Hamilton concludes that "the South (including the border states as in Key's procedure) is either as liberal as the rest of the nation's population [on certain economic questions] or slightly more liberal [on certain others]."[68]

Key's suspicion that the economic conservatism of southern senators and representatives stemmed from the underrepresentation of the lower classes in the electorate seemed to be borne out by the relatively greater gap between blue-collar and white-collar participation in the South than in the North. He predicted that if this gap were narrowed significantly in the South, the conservative complexion of the region's politics would change.[69]

The absence of such a large bloc of lower-income voters from the electorate is not, of course, the sole reason for southern congres-

---

65 *Ibid.*, 527–28.
66 V. O. Key, Jr., *Public Opinion and American Democracy* (New York: Alfred A. Knopf, Inc., 1961), 104. Based on University of Michigan Survey Research Center Data, 1956.
67 Richard Hamilton, *Class and Politics in the United States*, in press. See his chapter dealing with southern politics.
68 *Ibid.*
69 Key, *Public Opinion and American Democracy*, 105.

sional conservatism. George Boynton has presented evidence that the more affluent southern whites are not only more likely to vote, but to communicate with their representatives. Moreover the average southern congressman, economically conservative himself, is more likely to heed the views of conservative constituents, thereby reinforcing their already inordinate influence.[70]

The evidence suggests, then, that the nonvoting population is economically more liberal than the actual electorate. And in fact Hamilton has demonstrated that on some issues, nonvoting whites in the South are more liberal than their counterparts who participate. It is especially interesting to note that nonvoting whites in the South were more opposed to Goldwater in 1964 (62 percent against) than the actual white voters (58 percent against). Had the nonvoters—whites and blacks—gone to the polls and voted their expressed preferences, according to Hamilton's calculations, Goldwater would not have carried the Deep South.[71]

We return now to our earlier question: Where would a class-based coalition pick up new recruits to compensate for middle- and upper-class losses? The data examined by Key and Hamilton suggest that the disfranchised groups in the South are one possible source. Today this pool of nonvoters comprises more than half the adult population, and on many economic issues these nonvoters do not have to be converted to a progressive point of view. They simply have to be mobilized.

The danger of the nonvoters to the status quo is clearly recognized by many southern politicians, and it is reflected in the restrictive election laws of the region. But it is not conservative politicians alone who are worried about the nonvoters. Many social scientists have come to believe that nonvoters are a threat to democratic values and should not be encouraged to enter the electorate: Better to let a sleeping dog lie. This attitude finds expression in the following criticism.

70 George Robert Boynton, "Southern Conservatism: Constituency Opinion and Congressional Voting," *Public Opinion Quarterly*, XXIX (1965), 259–69.

71 Hamilton, *Class and Politics*. Here, too, the South is defined to include the Border states. The Deep South, on the other hand, consists of Mississippi, Alabama, Georgia, South Carolina, and Louisiana, the so-called "Goldwater states" of 1964.

A MASS MOVEMENT WITH A WORKING-CLASS BASE WOULD BRING
INTO THE ACTIVE POLITICAL ARENA THE ELEMENT OF SOCIETY
WHICH IS LEAST CAPABLE OF RESPONSIBLE POLITICAL BEHAVIOR.

The answer to this claim is two-fold. First, there is the theoretical question of whether democratic principles are consistent
with the systematic exclusion of a large part of the adult population
on the basis of its real or presumed incompetence. Any notion of
popular democracy dictates that this question be answered with a
firm and unequivocal no. Even the theory of democratic elitism
does not deny the importance of mass electoral participation. But
there is also the practical question of whether the entry into the
electorate of the presently apolitical masses would do more harm
than good to the polity as it now exists, whether it is democratic
or not.

Bernard Berelson and his colleagues have argued that high participation can be positively dangerous. "Extreme interest goes with
extreme partisanship and might culminate in rigid fanaticism that
could destroy democratic processes if generalized throughout the
community."[72] Robert Lane, however, has cited numerous instances
of high participation, only some of which are associated with the
decline of democratic procedures, suggesting that the rate of participation may not be a crucial variable.[73]

Seymour Lipset, on the other hand, relies on his theory of
working-class authoritarianism to raise doubts about the reliability
of nonvoters. He claims: "Studies based on survey and questionnaire data ... indicate that nonvoters differ from voters in having
authoritarian attitudes, cynical ideas about democracy and political
parties, intolerant sentiments on deviant opinions and ethnic minorities, and in preferring strong leaders in government."[74] Lipset seems

72 Bernard R. Berelson, Paul F. Lazarsfeld, and William McPhee, *Voting: A
Study of Opinion Formation in a Presidential Campaign* (Chicago: The University
of Chicago Press, 1954), 314.

73 Robert Lane, *Political Life* (Glencoe: The Free Press, 1959), 349–50. Lane's
chapter 22, pp. 337–57, is a good introduction to the controversies surrounding the
issue of high political participation.

74 Seymour Martin Lipset, *Political Man: The Social Bases of Politics* (Garden
City: Doubleday & Co., Inc., Anchor Books, 1963), 228.

to imply at one point that when nonvoters are "authoritarian," it may be better for a political system if they remain outside the electorate. He goes on to say that "neither high nor low rates of participation and voting are in themselves good or bad for democracy," indicating that when "the lower strata have been brought into the electoral process *gradually* (through increased organization, an upgrading of the educational system, and a growth in their understanding of the relevance of government action to their interests), increased participation is undoubtedly a good thing for democracy."[75] (There is a remarkable similarity between this argument and that employed, until quite recently, by the "better" sort of southern whites in denying Negroes the franchise.)

Thus, although Lipset displays a curious ambivalence on this issue, he seems to come out finally not for exclusion of authoritarians (or those he perceives as authoritarians), but for regulating their rate of entry into the electorate. Presumably if the nonvoters are brought in slowly and acculturated adequately to the norms of the electorate, the system will not be threatened. But if there is a rapid entry, the "authoritarian attitudes," "cynical ideas," and "intolerant sentiments" of the nonvoters will not have time to be modified or eradicated. Even so, given Lipset's belief that authoritarianism is a deep-lying configuration of attitudes, one wonders how long a period of political acculturation might be required.

It is likely that neither rapid nor slow assimilation of nonvoters into the electorate is in itself good or bad. Support for this proposition is provided by the case of the sudden rise in voter participation among southern blacks in the 1960s. Surveys of the opinions and political attitudes of the South's nonvoting blacks in the late fifties painted a hopeless portrait of apathy and ignorance.[76] Yet only a short while later, the efforts of the southern-based civil rights

75 *Ibid.*, 229.
76 Philip Converse, after having read through Survey Research Center interviews conducted with a sample of these Negroes, described them in the main as "extremely ignorant, disoriented, and in the most utter confusion about politics." Converse, "On the Possibility of a Major Political Realignment in the South," in Angus Campbell, Philip E. Converse, Warren E. Miller, and Donald E. Stokes, *Elections and the Political Order* (New York: John Wiley and Sons, Inc., 1966), 234.

movement began to be felt and electoral participation among southern blacks shot upward.[77] The new voters rallied overwhelmingly to the Democratic candidates in 1964 and 1968. In those two years, when the Republicans represented the more conservative alternative, the total black electorate gave them less than 10 percent of the vote. The southern Negroes were no less disciplined than their northern brothers. The sophistication of the newly enfranchised southern black was demonstrated in numerous gubernatorial, congressional, and lesser elections throughout the Old Confedcracy from 1964 on.[78] This was due in large measure to the aggressive and intelligent organization of the new electorate by such groups as the Voter Education Project and numerous local groups that capitalized on the experience and manpower of the older civil rights organizations that have been concerned with voter education since the early 1940s. Therefore, despite the extremely rapid increase in the Negro electorate—possibly a growth of a 100 percent or more in a four-year period—the transition was in the best democratic tradition. The tragedy is that this remarkable event has not yet been accompanied by the fruits the civil rights enthusiasts hoped it would achieve.[79]

77 The following registration figures suggest the extent of increase in Negro electoral participation in the 1960s.

Negro Registration in Eleven Southern States

Year	Estimated Number Registered	As Percentage Of Southern Negro Voting-Age Population
1960	1,414,052	28%
1964	1,907,279	38
1966	2,620,359	52
1969	3,248,000	65

Source: Southern Regional Council, Atlanta, Georgia.

78 There is evidence that previously nonvoting Negroes who migrated North before the civil rights movement also became politically "acculturated" very quickly. Nathan Glazer and Patrick Moynihan remark that the rationality of the Negro vote in New York was especially noteworthy in light of the fact that "in 1960 half of the entire nonwhite population of the city above the age of 26 had come from the South." See Glazer and Moynihan, Beyond the Melting Pot (Cambridge: M.I.T. Press, 1963), 26.

79 Converse, in an effort to square his earlier finding of ignorance and lability among southern blacks with the sophistication of the newly enfranchised, offers a convincing explanation: The lack of awareness among the black population in

The case of the southern blacks challenges the type of theory that accounts for the "irresponsible" attitudes of nonvoters by positing a more or less permanent psychological syndrome. In this connection recent research suggests that common characteristics of people in the lower classes that have been described in clinical terms can often be explained simply by making the usual assumptions of rationality. Elliot Liebow, for example, makes a persuasive case that the "present-time orientation" of low-income Negro males is not a psychiatric peculiarity, but an attitude based on a realistic appraisal of future opportunities. "In many instances, it is precisely the street corner man's orientation to the future—but to a future loaded with 'trouble'—which not only leads to a greater emphasis on present concerns ('I want mine right now') but also contributes importantly to the instability of employment, family and friend relationships, and to the general transient quality of daily life."[80] He also points

---

the late 1950s was a fact. So, too, is the black voter's new-found sophistication. Data in the past three or four years, he writes, attest to a "stunning" political awareness and high level of information, at least with respect to issues directly connected to black leadership and black problems. He concludes that there has been a "true revolution" in political awareness among blacks during the 1960s. Referring to his earlier interpretation, he says: "If I were rewriting [these] phrases, I think I would with the benefit of hindsight want to take out any flavor suggestive of educational horizons so constrictive that politics simply could not be understood, even if the situation so changed that politics became suddenly both accessible and 'relevant.' In other words, adjectives suggesting utter inattention or disengagement from the political process at that time would have worn better than anything suggesting a permanent state." Personal correspondence, February 27, 1970.

80 Elliot Liebow, *Tally's Corner: A Study of Negro Streetcorner Men* (Boston: Little, Brown and Co., 1967), 68–69. Suggestive here is psychiatrist Robert Coles's testimony before a Senate subcommittee in 1966: "I have found in the most apathetic or lawless people enough unused energy and sidetracked morality to make of them different people, given different circumstances in their actual, everyday life." Quoted in Michael Harrington, *Toward a Democratic Left*, (New York: Macmillan Co., 1968), 24.

Arnold S. Kaufman also provides insight into some of the mechanisms of apathy. He describes the "rank-and-file" poor, who, after great struggle in the political arena, are able to wrest token gains from the established powers. In contrast to the leader, who is elated by the symbolic achievement, their "elation soon wears off. They are left very tired warriors. They wonder whether the modest gain was worth such enormous effort. Perhaps they grow even more angry; even more disaffected. Or perhaps they lapse into quiescence. Why struggle? To the outside world it appears that they have become apathetic. It is, however, a *functional apathy*

out that the practical philosophy of *carpe diem* is not peculiar to lower-class individuals, but to many social aggregates, such as war-time populations who find themselves confronting an uncertain future.

Similarly "apathy," "lability," "ignorance," and "cynicism" among nonvoters may be expressions of a realistic appraisal by the lower-income groups of the futility of electoral politics. If an individual believes that politics cannot make a difference in his life, he will not pay it much attention, and consequently he will not be very knowledgeable about it. His expressed preference for a party, a candidate, or a policy may change frequently, compared to that of someone who has decided to play the game. This is not necessarily an indication of a basic psychological instability. If one is not a football fan, he may change his allegiance from the Rams to the Eagles and back again half a dozen times during the game, whereas a serious buff with money on the outcome will be strongly and consistently partisan throughout.[81]

The effects of mobilizing southern nonvoters is not an academic question. The region's political apathetics are predominantly white —an often ignored fact.[82] The rise of Negro voting in the 1960s has been accompanied by a concomitant rise among the white popula-

---

rooted, not in genuine indifference, but in futility bred of impotence." Kaufman, "Democracy and the Paradox of Want-Satisfaction," *Personalist*, LII (Spring, 1971), 202.

81 Edward Banfield suggests three types of "present-time orientation": that resulting from not being able to take account of the future or to control impulses; that resulting from one's perception of the future as not offering acceptable possibilities (this seems to be Liebow's primary interpretation); and that resulting from one's freely adopting the values of *carpe diem* and eschewing a future-oriented approach. These are valid distinctions but so far, unfortunately, we have no knowledge of which type predominates. Suffice it to say that many students of voter apathy and of poverty have tended to play down the importance of situationally determined present-time orientation and to favor the other types, usually without any supporting evidence. See Banfield, *The Unheavenly City* (Boston: Little, Brown and Co., 1970), 216–18.

82 An encouraging sign that this fact is not lost upon black strategists was the announcement in 1970 by John Lewis of the Voter Education Project, a southern-based voter registration organization, that for the first time it is giving special attention to registering poor whites (and Mexican-Americans in Texas). New York *Times*, June 7, 1970.

tion. Racial conservatives like George Wallace have made it clear that they intend to take the lion's share of the newly voting whites. Wallace's political message and his campaign style are directed especially to the lower socioeconomic strata. There is evidence that this strategy is paying off in votes, and these votes may well be going to Wallace by default. An analysis by Richard Hamilton of the support for the American Party in the 1968 election reveals that while there was no class differential (between manual and nonmanual occupations) in Wallace support in the non-South, there was a great deal in the South, where manual workers gave him significantly greater backing.[83] An analysis of the same election by Seymour Lipset and Earl Raab revealed that nearly half of the southern nonvoters in the 1964 election who voted in 1968 supported Wallace.[84] Several political observers have remarked on the significantly different backing Wallace got in the South compared to Goldwater. Both were issue oriented and in some sense right-wingers. But although Wallaceites were more favorable to segregation, to a "hawkish" position in Vietnam, and to the appeal for "law and order" than either Nixon's or Humphrey's followers, they differed sharply from Goldwaterites four years earlier as regards social welfare issues. In this respect "Wallace voters were more favorable to the 'liberal' label than Nixon voters, and almost matched the liberalism of Humphrey voters," which was reflected in Wallace's "frequent appeals to the underdog and the working man, in the tradition of Southern populism."[85] In the words of Roy Harris, the outspoken Georgia segregationist: "Between him [Nixon] and Hubert Humphrey, I would have taken Humphrey—although I managed George Wallace's campaign in Georgia."[86]

83 Hamilton, *Class and Politics.*
84 Seymour Lipset and Earl Raab, "The Wallace Whitelash," *Trans-action,* VII (December, 1969) 27.
85 Philip E. Converse, Warren E. Miller, Jerrold G. Rusk, and Arthur G. Wolfe, "Continuity and Change in American Politics: Parties and Issues in the 1968 Election," *American Political Science Review,* LXIII (1969), p. 1,100.
86 "A Surprising Talk Between a Black Leader and a Top Segregationist," New York *Times* Magazine, April 27, 1970, p. 109. Another interesting case of politics making strange bedfellows is Henry Howell's 1969 gubernatorial campaign in the Virginia Democratic primary. Howell is described as an "urban populist," running on a platform of opposition to increases in electricity rates and automobile in-

The Wallace mobilization of white nonvoters is not an inevitability. A movement for radical economic reform without racist appeals would provide the newly enfranchised southern voters with an alternative. But if Wallace and others of similar persuasion are able to mobilize and hold a large sector of newly voting whites, the effects of Negro enfranchisement in the 1960s would in many respects be nullified. It is a disturbing prospect and not an impossibility.

To recapitulate, the effects of mobilizing current nonvoters, even in the South, will depend on who does the mobilizing, how they are mobilized, and what alternatives they confront when they are mobilized. If the political leaders and the already voting masses support an anti-democratic alternative, the nonvoters, who are perhaps vulnerable to the "bandwagon effect," will swing in behind them.[87] This is what George Wallace would like to be able to achieve in the South. If, on the other hand, the structural and psychological barriers to voting are let down at a period when two bland, quasi-democratic, quasi-elitist parties represent the effective alternatives, the newly enfranchised will back the party which most nearly meets their needs. In the arena of American politics during the past decade, this has meant that blacks have rallied to the Democrats.

But a major thesis of this book has been that neither party represents an acceptable alternative for blacks, who are demanding full political assimilation. What is the purpose of mobilizing black and less affluent white nonvoters into the Democratic Party as it is now

---

surance premimums (appeals to the "little man") and specifically appealing to blacks as well. Although he failed to attain the nomination by a small margin, he received his greatest support among urban blacks, followed by white, urban, blue-collar workers, and then by white, rural, blue-collar workers. He received more than 50 percent of the black vote, along with nearly 50 percent of George Wallace's Virginia supporters. See James Clotfelter, William R. Hamilton, and Peter B. Harkins, "In Search of Populism," *New South*, XXV (Winter, 1971), 13.

National survey data in the summer of 1971 led Louis Harris to write that "it has now become clear that it is something of a myth to assume that the bulk of George Wallace's vote would normally go to Richard Nixon." Houston *Post*, May 13, 1971.

87 See Angus Campbell, Philip E. Converse, Warren E. Miller, and Donald E. Stokes, *The American Voter* (New York: John Wiley and Sons, Inc., 1960), 111–12.

constituted, and, practically speaking, would it be possible anyhow? Can the nonvoters be shaken out of their apathy by any political program feasible in twentieth century America? This leads to the last and perhaps most serious criticism of the coalition alternative to be examined.

A COALITION DEPENDENT UPON THE MOBILIZATION OF THE WORKING CLASS IS BOUND TO FAIL, BECAUSE THE POLITICAL ENTHUSIASM OF THE CLASS IS EXTREMELY DIFFICULT TO ENGENDER, AND EVEN MORE DIFFICULT TO SUSTAIN.

Can the "silent majority" of nonparticipants in the South be brought into active political participation, along with the "silent minority" of nonvoters in the North? The apathy signified by this nonparticipation is a formidable obstacle to social reform. "The concentration of socially deprived characteristics," Burnham writes, "among the more than forty million adult Americans who today are altogether outside the voting universe suggests active alienation— or its passive equivalent, political apathy—on a scale quite unknown anywhere else in the Western world."[88] There is evidence that alienation is even greater among lower-income whites than among comparable low-income Negroes. William Brink and Louis Harris found, in a nationwide poll conducted in 1966, that 40 percent of the low-income Negro respondents agreed with the statement, "What you think doesn't count much," while 60 percent of the low-income whites agreed (compared with 39 percent of the total public).[89]

Lewis Killian, a critic of the coalition strategy, writes:

In addition to the doubt of whether a radical program of political and economic reform would be supported by the white majority,

88 Burnham, "The Changing Shape of the American Political Universe," 27. Burnham, however, is not fatalistic about the possibility of eradicating this alienation. "Unless it is assumed as a kind of universal law that problems of existence which can be organized in political terms must fade out below a certain socioeconomic level, this state of affairs is not inevitable. And if it is not inevitable, one may infer that the political system itself is responsible for its continued existence."

89 William Brink and Louis Harris, *Black and White* (New York: Simon and Schuster, Inc., 1966), 134.

there was the question of whether it would gain the support of Negroes themselves. Gradualism is an inherent feature of a program building a viable political coalition and then reforming a society through social engineering. Maximizing voter registration, winning victories at the polls, and then translating votes into policy is a tedious, often discouraging task lacking the drama of a demonstration.[90]

Whether the apathetics can be politicized depends, in the final analysis, upon the nature of their apathy. One common interpretation, as we have seen, is that they are in the grip of an immobilizing psychological syndrome, whose prognosis is poor. Another view interprets this apathy as a sign of basic satisfaction with the system. Robert Dahl takes this position in his book on New Haven politics.

A third possibility is that much of the apathy in America today signifies neither psychiatric abnormalities nor basic satisfaction with the status quo, but a belief that voting and other traditional modes of political participation are useless as tools for changing one's life situation. In the case of Houston blacks, this is in many respects a well-grounded belief. Research indicates that this holds for Negroes in Philadelphia, Durham, New York, Chicago, and presumably all other cities with a large ghetto population.[91] Change for the better, when it has occurred, has been agonizingly slow, uneven in its effects, and not connected in an obvious way with political efforts. Indeed some of the Negroes' most significant gains seem to have resulted fortuitously from economic booms brought on by war.

Not much is known about the process of conversion from political apathy to activism, a fact that reflects upon the predominant values within the academic disciplines of political science and sociology. But in any case, it is simply untrue that the apathetic cannot be mobilized to participate in politics. The case of the southern blacks

90 Killian, *The Impossible Revolution*, 152. Killian (p. 153) doubts the wisdom of discarding protest for electoral politics, for protest provides Negroes with "their chief source of pride in the present time."

91 John H. Strange, "The Negro in Philadelphia Politics: 1963–1965," (Ph.D. dissertation, Princeton University, 1966); William R. Keech, *The Impact of Negro Voting* (Chicago: Rand McNally & Co., 1968); Glazer and Moynihan, *Beyond the Melting Pot*; Harold M. Baron, "Black Powerlessness in Chicago," *Trans-action*, VI (November, 1968), 27–33.

gives the lie to that myth. So does the rapid mobilization of nonvoters which occurred in Louisiana under the regime of Huey Long. Surprisingly this occurred during the depression, a period that, although involving fundamental voter realignments, did not witness an increase in the nation's electorate as a whole. From one point of view, the "Kingfish" was simply a demagogue who employed the rhetoric of populism to further his own ambitions. A more accurate description would include not only his demagogic tendencies, but his programs of genuine economic reform—programs that made a substantial difference in the everyday lives of the "little people" of Louisiana. Unlike the rhetoric of a Blease or a Ferguson, "his program held more than words and sympathy," wrote Key. "He kept faith with his people and they with him. He gave them something and the corporations paid for it. He did not permit himself, in an oft-repeated pattern, to be hamstrung by a legislature dominated by old hands experienced in legislation and frequently under corporate retainer."[92]

His accomplishments included free school book legislation, highway and bridge construction, the abolition of toll bridges and ferries (a major reform in southern Louisiana, which is interlaced with myriad waterways), and hospital construction—this in a state whose people were abysmally poor and illiterate and until then whose government was tightly controlled by rapacious corporations, especially the major oil companies. Long was a southern progressive in two senses. He financed his major reforms by taxing the corporations, and his policy was by virtue of this truly a "share the wealth" one. Second, unlike most southern demagogues, he did not use the race issue in his climb to power. As Wilbur J. Cash put it in *The Mind of the South*, Long was "the first Southern demagogue largely to leave aside nigger baiting and address himself mainly to the irritations bred in the common white by his economic and social status."[93] For

92 Key, *Southern Politics*, 157.
93 Wilbur J. Cash, *The Mind of the South* (New York: Alfred A. Knopf, 1941), 287. T. Harry Williams' portrait of Long is similar, but not identical. According to Williams, Long rarely exploited the race issue while rising to power. When governor and senator, though, "he discussed the racial problem on frequent oc-

all his accomplishments, Long became a virtual dictator, and the political structure of Louisiana in his heyday was no more democratic than it was under the rule of the corporate oligarchs.[94]

Concomitant with Long's rise to power was a significant swell in the electorate, reaching a peak of voter participation in 1936, the year after his assassination, "unmatched in the recent history of any southern state."[95] White turnout in gubernatorial primaries was slightly more than 40 percent in 1928, but it rose almost to 70 percent in 1936 following Long's assassination and the battle over succession. Key surmised that this rise was not, as Long's critics claimed, simply the result of fraud. Although the repeal of the poll tax in 1934—itself a Long-instigated measure—was in part responsible for the 1936 turnout, "the extraordinary increase in the number of voters must be attributed chiefly to the issues, leadership, and organization that Long introduced."[96] A recent analysis of Long's electoral backing suggests that he received disproportionate support from parishes that ranked low in terms of socioeconomic status. Allen Meyer interprets his data to signify that both poor white farmers and industrial workers were aligned with Long and his economic program.[97]

---

casions. In these pronouncements he seemed to be a typical white Southerner—he was for segregation and white supremacy all the way." But, according to Williams, "his whole racial stance was...a strategy. By seeming to be a complete segregationist, he reserved for himself a freedom of action on racial matters. He could then do some things that breached the patterns of segregation; he could give the Negroes certain rights that he believed they should have. The rights that he would extend were economic ones." And as Williams points out, Negroes shared in the benefits of the Long program. "Indeed, because they were poorer than the poorest whites, they benefited more from the program. Thus the homestead exemption law exempted 77 percent of the homes of white people from taxation but 95 percent of the homes of black people. Huey realized the racial implications of his program. As one of his leaders explained his reasoning: 'You can't help poor white people without helping poor Negroes. It has to be that way!'" T. Harry Williams, "Huey Long and the Politics of Realism," in Harold M. Hollingsworth (ed.), *Essays on Recent Southern Politics* (Austin: University of Texas Press, 1970), 111–12.

94 Key, *Southern Politics*, 156.
95 *Ibid.*, 523.
96 *Ibid.*, 524.
97 Meyer, "The Not-So-Solid South," 281–83.

Was it Long's program of genuine economic reform or his demagoguery that succeeded in mobilizing the nonvoters in his cause? Or was it a combination of the two? To put the issue bluntly: Can the apathetics be moved to support a political program that is in their interest without making use of the strong-arm tactics and corrupt practices characteristic of bossism?

This question goes to the heart of any serious discussion of the possibility of economic reform in a quasi-democratic system such as ours. An unpleasant fact of American political life is that the successful candidate, party, or program requires large sums of money that do not flow easily from the pockets of the ordinary people. In the era of corporate capitalism, this money is available primarily from big business and to a much lesser extent from "big labor." Adequate political financing based on small contributions from the lower strata is hard to come by and even more difficult to depend on as a steady source of funds. As a result the candidates who are willing to look after the interests of the large corporations —or who at least will not threaten them—are the beneficiaries of corporate largesse. Those who refuse to fall into line must look elsewhere. Long's need to finance his organization led him down dark alleys and involved him in unsavory practices. The irony of American politics is that big business, whose profits are extracted in a social and economic system that is basically unjust, can finance its chosen brand of politics by observing all the punctillios of "good government" ethics, while the leaders of class-based reform movements are forced by the rules of the game to resort to the shady practices which characterize machine financing. It is no accident that the conflicts in the twentieth century between "good government" reformers and the machines have often been superficial manifestations of a more basic class struggle. The machine politicians have ultimately lost these battles because the cards were stacked against them from the beginning. The configuration of wealth and politics denied them access to "legitimate" financing, and they were forced to resort to a Robin Hood morality whose distinctions, however, "were hard to maintain and personal finances became mixed, with the inevitable results in neglect of politics through the pursuit of private advantage."[98] The American system of corporate democracy encourages the corruption of lower-class reform movements.

To demand a return to unashamed class politics, then, is to run the risk of Longism, especially in the South. Yet to trust in corporate capitalism to allow the fundamental economic changes that would lift millions of Americans, black and white, out of their materially and spiritually precarious position at the margins of our society is naïve. In the face of this dilemma, the risk of Longism is less dangerous than the risk of status quo politics. A risk, after all, is not a certainty, and the essence of politics is to take risks, hoping that one's awareness of the dangers run will serve as the rational man's talisman and ward them off.

The task of converting the politically apathetic to activism would proceed simultaneously on two fronts. An effort would be made to break down the formal barriers to voting which still discourage lower-income people of all races. At the same time, programs stressing social justice and basic economic reforms for blacks and whites alike would be taken to the people and explained to them in words which relate to their personal experience. In the words of C. Wright Mills, their "troubles," couched in terms of milieux, would have to be translated into public issues, couched in political language. This would not be an easy task, for it requires translators who not only can speak the language of milieu but also are versed in the mysteries of public issues.

If election rules were magically abolished tomorrow, however, it is doubtful that dramatic changes would occur. This is not because such rules are without a force of their own in restricting the electorate, but because changes in election rules usually reflect underlying and more profound changes. For example, the drastic decline in Texas voter participation following the high tide of Populism in 1896 was not simply the result of the poll tax. The tax was instead the seal of approval which the legislature stamped upon an already restricted electorate.[99] So, too, the abolition of the tax in Louisiana in 1934 was a manifestation of Long's rise to power and an increased

98 Key, *Southern Politics*, 163.
99 *Ibid.*, Chapter 25.

electorate, although it may have spurred turnout afterward. The main task for radical reformers, therefore, is to create a popular mass base, and in the process the legal changes will come as well.

What sorts of changes are envisioned and how can they be brought about? They would be firmly grounded in modern economics and sociology, but they would have to speak to the personal experience of lower- and middle-income America. Most of these changes have already been advocated by radicals or liberals, but they have yet to be taken up by the politicians. They include the guarantee of a satisfying and remunerative job for everyone who wants one (this entails community nurseries for working women); a health care system financed by and planned for the public; enforcement of antidiscrimination laws; a program for building new cities and rebuilding old ones; a radical restructuring of the tax system, so as to lift the tax burden off the lower two-thirds of the population;[100] a full-scale effort to restore the ecological balance of the natural environment; the eradication of the public school behemoth and its replacement by humane centers of learning; and the restructuring of corporate power.[101]

In urging a politics that focuses on the economic deprivation of whites and blacks, one risks giving the impression of simply advocating a pragmatic if not cynical "politics of the pocket book" as a panacea. But clearly, a coalition based on a narrow economic appeal would have no chance of success. The economic argument has been belabored in this chapter only because the point has too often been ignored that America's affluence has so far been limited to a relatively small part of the population. But economic appeals are not enough. Social movements come to fruition only if large masses of people are imbued with an ideal. Martin Luther King could never have rallied the southern blacks to the cause of civil rights if he had not managed to identify his movement with a holy cause—the cause of freedom and of human dignity. By the same token, an appeal to

100 The regressive nature of the southern tax structure has been documented most recently by Eva Galambos in her booklet, "The Tax Structure of the Southern States: An Analysis" (Atlanta: Southern Regional Council, 1969).

101 For a list of similar priorities, enunciated by officials of the Institute of the Black World in Atlanta, see New York *Times*, December 23, 1970.

the self-interest of the working man, if not cast within the framework of a larger humanitarian vision, must ultimately fail.

How does a social movement come to be invested with a vision? One might as well devise a formula for attaining wisdom. Undoubtedly it requires charismatic leaders—some would say demagogues— who have a vision whose force can be communicated to great numbers of people. But equally as important, such leaders, if they are to succeed in creating a democracy in America, must be democratic. This truism might seem obvious, were it not for the fact that part of what passes currently for radical politics is shot through with a contempt for the people it is out to save. If the leaders of a mass-based coalition are to succeed, they must be convinced of the truth that democracy cannot be imposed from the top down.

We are now in a position to describe more precisely what sort of coalition is feasible today. First, the term "coalition" implies a formal and on-going alliance, involving an agreement among the constituent elements that they will work together for common goals. Not only would they agree to work for these goals, they would officially organize to obtain them. The advantages of formal organization are twofold: they allow for the rational deployment of members, and they encourage solidarity through personal contact.

It has been demonstrated in the preceding chapter that blacks and lower-income whites in the South have cooperated at the voting booth. This is the minimal cooperation that is possible, and to the extent that it is more or less spontaneous, it is subject to the vicissitudes of all such happenstance cooperation: it breaks apart easily under strain. It is possible that a South-wide coalition is in the offing during the 1970s. But barring this, every effort should be made to establish local ones, improving upon the Houston model.

Second, such a coalition must be biracial. Blacks, most of whom still favor working through "the system,"[102] have cooperated with whites in many different situations—formal electoral politics, union

---

102 A poll in the spring of 1970 by Louis Harris, conducted for *Time*, revealed that the great majority of blacks still wanted to work through the existing structures to achieve their ends. However, 9 percent of the nation's blacks—more than two million—describe themselves as "revolutionaries" and believe that only "a readiness to use violence" will get them equality.

organizing activities, public demonstrations, community action groups, and within educational settings. Usually only a minority of whites have been willing to cooperate. But in many situations, a minority of whites combined with a majority of blacks are sufficient to provide a decisive force for change. While there are very few political units in the South where blacks constitute a majority (one hundred two counties of more than a thousand in 1970, for example), there are numerous units where a unified black population combined with 30 percent of the whites constitute an effective majority.

Third, the coalition is to be class based. This means no more than that the immediate issues around which the coalition would rally are the traditional "class" issues of (1) redistribution of income and wealth; (2) the redistribution of opportunities, including the opportunity for everyone who so desires to hold a decent job, obtain a living wage and adequate retirement income, have access to sufficient, inexpensive public services, educational facilities, and health care; and (3) therefore a sharp curtailment of the power of large corporations to make decisions which properly fall within the public realm.

To describe this coalition as class based is not to imply that it would appeal only to those at the bottom rungs of the class structure. As statistics cited above reveal, large segments of "middle America" are willing to support the expansion of the present system of economic and social justice.

Even though the economic progressiveness of the middle and upper classes should not be exaggerated, it is equally as important not to minimize it. Some writers have spoken of the middle-class progressives as a "conscience constituency," including large numbers of university people,[103] "whistle blowers" within the white-collar in-

---

103 Although much is made of the antagonism between university people and labor unions, there are goals which are common to many members of both groups. The tentative coming-together of peace radicals and some unionists is a significant development. (For an account of one such attempt to reach a mutual understanding, see the Houston *Chronicle*, November 29, 1970.) Tenants' unions provide an ideal vehicle for students and lower-income people to work together for common goals. Recently, The National Tenants Organization, a confederation of tenant

stitutions, the traditional racial liberals, the growing middle-income supporters of tenants unions, the largely middle-class feminists, and the equally middle-class peace groups, environmentalists, and other liberal-radical reformers. While they may constitute a minority of white-collar America, their activism, enthusiasm, courage, and edu-cation—as well as their sometimes influential connections—make them a necessary partner in any coalition of the sort here described.

Fourth, the coalition would be radical. Its goals, while building upon traditional American values, would constitute significant de-partures from the elitist liberalism of the 1950s and 1960s. Other-wise it would be unable to excite the 40 percent of the American adult population (and the 60 percent of the southern population) which does not even vote in presidential elections. Any coalition which attempts to stir the alienated to action would of necessity be radical. The classic weapons of mass movements in quasi-democra-cies would almost certainly be relied upon: strikes, political rallies, disruption and harrassment of corporate and governmental routine, and above all, grassroots education and propaganda. The failure of most mass protests in the 1960s resulted from the lack of a popular base which political education alone makes possible.[104]

A program such as this would undoubtedly face numerous diffi-culties. However, there is reason to believe that it is preferable to others now being seriously proposed. "Normal politics," I. F. Stone recently declared with characteristic acumen, "will no longer do. Normal politics is the Southern Strategy." On the other hand, a reform movement dependent for its financial support upon the largesse of northeastern corporate wealth, as in the case of the Ur-ban Coalition and its successor, Common Cause, seems an unlikely vehicle for basic social and economic change. Finally, as has been argued, the ultimate costs of black separatism most certainly

---

organizations, approved the formation of a special student office. New York *Times*, March 1, 1970.

104 This is not the place to debate the merits of the argument favoring a new political party, as opposed to that advocating a reconstruction of the present Democratic Party. This is an issue, however, which will have to be faced squarely. For a reasoned argument for working within the Democratic Party, see Arnold S. Kaufman, "New Party or New Democratic Coalition?" *Dissent*, XVI (1969), 13-18.

outweigh the benefits. If one accepts our earlier thesis, therefore, that justice for blacks remains ahead of us in the indefinite future, then the option of class-based coalition politics in the South and in the rest of the nation is the one most likely to achieve success.

Appendix A

METHODS FOR CALCULATING
THE NEGRO VOTE

Numerous problems make analysis of Houston and Harris County voting returns difficult. The boundaries of several voting precincts are redrawn annually. Consequently during a decade a large number of the precincts in the county have been changed, abolished, created anew, or merged with others. The study of Negro-white voting behavior is particularly difficult because there is no indication on the ballot or registration form of a person's race. Until a few years ago, the race of a registrant was marked on his poll tax form, but the county tax assessor did not make public a tabulation of voters by race. Therefore all figures, past and present, concerning Negro voting and registration are estimates. The standard procedure, used by the newspapers and the county officials in reporting election returns, is to define the Negro vote as that which is cast in the so-called "predominantly Negro precincts." These are the ones that have Negro precinct judges and in 1966 numbered forty-three of a total of two hundred eighty in the county. Exactly how great a proportion of the qualified and actual voters in these forty-three precincts is Negro is unknown. Census data are not useful here because the precincts are seldom coterminous with census tract boundaries. Only twelve precincts with Negro precinct judges in 1966 fell somewhere within the boundaries of census tracts that in 1960 had a population 90 percent or more Negro.

To make the matter more confusing, there are several "mixed" precincts that contain a sizable proportion of Negroes but are not yet "predominantly" black. W. C. Day, the chairman of the Harris County Council of (Negro) Organizations, listed forty-four mixed precincts for 1964. He refused to estimate the average proportion of Negroes in these precincts but said that in the predominantly black precincts, the proportion was generally "way above 50 percent" and usually at least 90 percent. A source in the county tax assessor's office suggested that "mixed" should be interpreted as meaning from 5 to 50 percent Negro.

Therefore the common practice of simply estimating the Negro vote on the basis of the total vote cast in the predominantly Negro precincts, and counting the mixed precincts as white, rests on the assumption that the number of whites in the predominantly Negro precincts roughly cancels out the number of Negroes in the mixed precincts. For the purposes of the present study, this assumption was accepted if for no other reason than that it is generally shared by knowledgeable politicians and newspapermen. Furthermore it provides a single, easily applied standard. However, this is no more than a rough estimate. This writer's intuition is that the present method of estimating the Negro electorate probably underrepresents the extent of Negro registration and voting by a few percentage points. The following table contains a comparison of county Negro registration estimates over the years and should amply demonstrate the wide disagreement among "experts" over basic data.

Table A.1
Comparison of Estimates of Negro Registration in Harris County

Year	1944	1948	1949	1952	1954	1956	1958	1960	1961	1962	1963	1964	1965	1966
	8,500[a]	9,500[a]	8,500[c]	11,000[a,d]		26,725[a]	46,000[f]	45,000[a]	50,000[j]	75,000[m]	58,378	75–90,000[a]	61,163	91,000[q]
	5,000[b,*]					42,000[e,*]		60,000[g]	55,000[k]	64,000[n]		70–80,000[o]		78,438[*]
								51,871[h]	60,000[l]	55,553[*]		72,297[p]		
								50,220[l]	53,293[*]			70,747[*]		
								48,250[*]						

[a] Holloway

[b] Houston *Post*, July 25, 1944

[c] *Forward Times*, June 15, 1963

[d] Meltzer, citing the Houston *Informer's* 1952 post-election estimates, claims 21,516 Harris County Negroes *voted*. Moon claims 25,254 *major party* Negro votes in the same general elections.

[e] W. C. Day, Harris County Council of Organizations registration committee.

[f] U. S. Commission on Civil Rights. This figure may be high.

[g] Gray

[h] Day

[i] Bullock

[j] *Forward Times* (April)

[k] Wickliff

[l] *Forward Times* (August)

[m] *Forward Times* (May)

[n] *Forward Times* (June)

[o] *Forward Times* (May)

[p] Jordan campaign organization

[q] Carr

[*] These are the figures the author believes most accurate. As can be seen, in recent years they tend to be lower than the average estimates. Unless otherwise indicated, they are calculated by the author.

Appendix B

THE SELECTION OF NEGRO
ACTIVISTS FOR INTERVIEWS

"Leadership" is a term that has been used to classify many different types of qualities and relations. Although at least four books concerned primarily with Negro political leadership were published in the 1960s, no two authors defined leaders or leadership in the same way.[1] James Q. Wilson does not give an explicit definition of either term. He says, rather: "We shall not begin with definitions, as the leaders selected for research in Chicago were not chosen by the application to the Negro community of a single concept of leadership."[2]

Daniel Thompson's definition of a leader is "one who for some period of time identifies overtly with the Negro's efforts to achieve stated social goals. . . . [Leaders] are, or have been, actively engaged in the solution of some common problem or the achievement of specific social goals."[3] Elaine Burgess, on the other hand, says: "I defined the *leader* as an individual whose behavior affects the patterning of behavior within the community at a given time."[4] The

---

1 James Q. Wilson, *Negro Politics: The Search for Leadership* (New York: The Free Press, 1960). Daniel C. Thompson, *The Negro Leadership Class* (Englewood Cliffs: Prentice-Hall, Inc., 1963). M. Elaine Burgess, *Negro Leadership in a Southern City* (Chapel Hill: The University of North Carolina Press, 1960). Everett Carll Ladd, Jr., *Negro Political Leadership in the South* (Ithaca: Cornell University Press, 1966).

2 Wilson, *Negro Politics*, 10.

3 Thompson, *The Negro Leadership Class*, 5–6.

4 Burgess, *Negro Leadership*, 77.

280

following is Everett Ladd's definition: "Little effort was made at the outset to develop any full and precise definition of Negro leadership, because the study as a whole is centrally concerned with defining it. But in general Negro leaders were thought of as persons able to make decisions affecting the choice of race objectives and/or the means utilized to realize these objectives."[5]

Aside from the obvious differences among the above definitions, none of them, as explicitly stated, does justice to ordinary usage. For, although leadership implies influence over others, or "the ability to get others to act, think, or feel as one intends," it is not true that everyone who is influential exercises leadership.[6] One Houston respondent illustrated this point by citing the name of an influential white's Negro maid. "That woman isn't a leader," he said. "She's not known outside the small circle of her family and friends. But she can exert a lot of pressure on her boss's thinking, and in this way may be able to influence the outcome of important political decisions in a more direct way than the recognized Negro leaders." Clearly the maid was influential, but not a leader. To be a leader, one must exercise influence over a group of followers. The ironic phrase "a leader without any followers," is the exception which proves the rule. According to common usage, then, influence is the generic term, leadership the specific one. Leadership is that type of influence exerted by someone over a group of people in a movement, organization, association, or informal grouping who look to him for direction.

Strictly speaking, leadership is not a more or less permanent quality of an individual, such as his height or his moral character. Rather, it is a role. An individual may be a leader in one situation, but only an "influential" in another, and neither in a third.

If this interpretation of leadership is correct, then the more appropriate term for describing the subjects of all four authors' investigations is probably "influentials"; for these studies are concerned

---

5 Ladd, *Negro Political Leadership*, 4.
6 This is Banfield's general definition of influence. See Edward C. Banfield, *Political Influence* (New York: The Free Press, 1961), 3.

not only with influential Negroes with followings, but those who wield power over others without assuming the role of a leader. However, even the term "influential" as it is used in community studies can be misleading. For there is no single, easily applied measure of individuals' influence, even within a limited sphere of activity. It follows that any roster of "the" influentials in a community will probably exclude some persons who are more important than some others who are on the list. Thus, there is good reason for being cautious in generalizing about the characteristics of influentials on the basis of the characteristics of the people whose names are on the roster.

In order to emphasize this necessary imprecision, the subjects discussed in chapter 2 are referred to as activists rather than influentials. There is no doubt that those people on my list were activists. They all participated in numerous political activities. They wished to be influential and to project an image of influence. Most of them were in fact relatively influential in the city's Negro political life. Nevertheless, interviews and observation revealed that some of those who presented an image of influence to an outsider actually played inconsequential roles. It became evident, too, that there were many people in the community who, though publicity-shy, wielded a great deal of influence in certain circumstances.

The list of activists was compiled in the following manner. In the summer and early fall of 1966, on arriving in Houston, the author talked to many Negroes and whites who were widely known for their involvement in city politics in recent years. All available articles, pamphlets, and books relative to the politics of Houston, and especially the Negro's role in it, were read. The author began to attend meetings of organizations concerned with race relations, politics, and civil rights, and participated actively in two of them. The back issues of one of Houston's two daily newspapers were read closely for the period beginning in January, 1966, and the issues dating back to the late 1940s were scanned. Back files of the *Texas Observer*, a weekly political publication often carrying information on Houston, were scanned as far back as the early 1960s. The editor of *Forward Times*, a weekly Negro newspaper that began publication in January, 1960, made available all the back issues of the paper, which are kept at its editorial offices. A card file was constructed, into which was entered local information concerning race relations, politics, and civil rights. Subscriptions to both local Negro newspapers, *Forward Times* and the *Informer*, were bought in August, 1966, and new entries were continually made in the card file throughout the study.

On the basis of participant observation, numerous informal conversations with political observers, and the data obtained from published sources, one hundred seventy names of well-known Negro activists in the city and county in the 1960s were collected. Later this list was reduced to fifty-seven names of people all of whom had been connected with a number of important political events reported in the newspapers. Of these fifty-seven, five preferred not to be interviewed and three were no longer Houston residents. The remaining forty-nine persons were asked to respond to a formal questionnaire, followed by an open-ended interview.

There is reason to believe that many of Houston's most influential Negro activists were included on the list. Each interviewee was given the following instructions, among others:

> I want to find out who are the most influential Negroes in the Houston area in the field of race relations. In other words, which individuals have a significant influence on the course which race relations have taken in the Houston area?
>
> This includes people who have engaged in an important way in politics—either as candidates for office, or as strategists or decision-makers in party organizations, or as get-out-the-vote workers—as well as Negroes who have used their influence to bargain with whites, or who have headed organizations for race betterment, led protests, or otherwise engaged in activities within the area of race relations affecting large segments of the Houston Negro community.
>
> Such persons are usually recognized by numerous other Negroes as influential in race relations, although they *need not* be so recognized by whites.

DIRECTIONS:

On the next page is a list of Negroes who are thought to have exercised such influence in recent years.

(1) Please draw a line through any name or names you feel should not be on the list.

(2) Please add any name or names you feel should be on the list. Try not to let the fact that you like or dislike individuals, or the fact that you agree or disagree with their strategy or "politics" influence your decision of whether or not they are influential.

(3) Please put an "X" in front of the names of the people you think are the 15 most influential on the list.

Forty-six additional names were listed as "influentials" who were not included on my roster. However, the large majority of these names were only mentioned by one respondent. Only seven of the additional names were mentioned by more than one, and only three of them by more than two. Further only fourteen of the forty-six additional names were estimated by the respondents who listed them to be among the "fifteen most important" influentials. A subsequent comparison of the list with that of Professor Wilhelmina Perry, a sociologist who took several panel surveys of the Houston Negro community in the 1960s, revealed that each of those individuals her inquiry had shown to be a community-wide "opinion leader" in the city was on my list.

The following positions or roles had been occupied by the forty-nine interviewees at one time or another: a member of the state advisory committee of the United States Commission on Civil Rights; twelve officers of the NAACP; two delegates to the Democratic national convention; five members of a county grand jury; seven officers of the Harris County Council of Organizations; two members of the statewide Texas Council of Voters; nine voting precinct officers; two civic club presidents; five officers of the local liberal Democratic club, Harris County Democrats; ten board members of the Houston Council on Human Relations; seven holders of appointive political offices; five members of the Harris County Campaign Committee for Kennedy-Johnson in 1960; five members of the Harris County Democratic executive committee; a district chairman of United Political Organization, the statewide Negro group backing Governor John Connally; a member of Lyndon Johnson's exclusive President's Club; two persons who were on close personal terms with President Johnson; one officer of the Student Non-Violent Coordinating Committee; two newspaper publishers; two former officers of the Progressive Youth Association, the student sit-in organization which desegregated numerous public accommodations in the early 1960s; one participant in the James Meredith march through Mississippi in 1966; two persons intimately connected with the white primary lawsuits in the 1940s; eight invitees to the White House; three members of the board of directors of the local United Political Organization affiliate; four candidates for city council; two candidates for the state legislature; six elected officials; one board member of the Southern Regional Council; three board members of the local "war on poverty" organization; six organizers of mass demonstrations; one leader of the short-lived Texas Democratic Coalition; five plaintiffs in recent civil rights suits; two members of the county Republican executive committee; one representative to the African Economic Conference; one newspaper columnist; and a campaign chairman for a Negro candidate.

The great majority of the forty-nine interviewees were obviously connected with established—if not "establishment"—political institutions. Only about ten, or a fifth of the total number, could be considered "young Turks," and even among this group the radical, more or less free-floating militants were underrepresented.

The majority of the forty-nine were between thirty and sixty years old. Only four were under thirty. Eleven were sixty or over. All but eight were in white-collar occupations. Thirty-four were born in Texas, but only fourteen received their primary and secondary education in the Houston schools. Many had moved from small towns in East Texas into the city at a relatively early age. This is not to suggest that there were many "newcomers" in the group. Thirty-one had resided in Houston at least fifteen years. Only two had moved there fewer than six years previously. Their party identification is shown below.

PARTY IDENTIFICATION OF ACTIVISTS

Party	Number
Democratic	28
Republican	2
Independent	3
Independent Democrat	1
Independent Republican	14
Other	1

Further, twenty-eight of the forty-nine professed identification with the liberal wing of the Democratic Party in Texas. As for membership in religious denominations, forty were Protestants, four were Catholics, one was a Moslem, one an atheist, and three were not classified.

Appendix C

THE SAMPLE OF ALL-WHITE PRECINCTS

In order to analyze the voting characteristics of all-white precints in chapter 7, a sample of them was selected in the following manner.

(1) Using two voting precinct maps, one for 1960 and one for 1966, all precincts in the 1960 Houston city limits whose boundaries remained substantially unchanged during this period were isolated.

(2) Of these, all precincts whose boundaries were inside, or almost totally inside, the boundaries of a single census tract were isolated. This is not to say that the boundaries of precincts and tracts were coterminous. In all cases the precincts constituted geographical subsets of census tracts. In a few cases, two or more precincts were located within a single tract. There were 64 precincts that met criteria 1 and 2, of a total of approximately 150 predominantly white precincts in the city in 1960.[1] (There were 185 precincts in Houston in 1959 and 200 in 1966. Thirty-four were predominantly Negro in 1960 and 37 were in 1966.)

(3) Of the sixty-four precincts left, thirteen were predominantly Negro and another eleven contained a significant Negro population, although the majority of voters were white, according to data compiled by the Harris County Council of Organizations. These twenty-four precincts were removed from the sample.

1 See Appendix A, pp. 277–78 above, for a definition of "predominantly" white and Negro precincts. "Mixed" precincts are classified as predominantly white; yet they are excluded from the sample of "all-white" precincts in Step 3, along with the predominantly Negro ones.

(4) The selection of only those precincts that were inside, or almost inside, a single census tract was for purposes of ranking by income. For the analysis of the data, it was assumed that the median family income of the precinct in 1959 was the same as that of its parent tract. This assumption is based on the description of census tracts by the Bureau of the Census as "small areas into which large cities and adjacent areas have been divided for statistical purposes," the boundaries of which "were generally designed to be relatively uniform with respect to population characteristics, economic status, and living conditions."[2] The basic assumption, then, that underlies our analysis is the *relative uniformity* of the tract population with regard to relevant socioeconomic characteristics. But, two of the remaining forty white precincts were located in tracts where Negroes constituted 16 and 18 percent of the total tract population, respectively, according to the 1960 census. As Negro income is in general considerably lower than white income, it was felt that the presence of such a large proportion of Negroes in the tract would invalidate the assumption that the white precinct's median income was identical with that of its parent tract. Therefore these two precincts were removed, leaving thirty-eight precincts that were in census tracts containing in most cases less than 1 percent and in no case more than 5 percent Negro population, according to the 1960 census.

(5) Up to this point, the racial characteristics of the precincts had been obtained by using both census data and information from the Harris County Council. As a final safeguard, the author drove slowly through all of the thirty-eight precincts remaining in the sample. The sorties into these widely dispersed neighborhoods were made on weekends in weather in which children would be prone to play outdoors. In three of the thirty-eight precincts a sizable number of Negro families were found to be living there, apparently having recently moved into previously all-white areas. Thus, these

2 United States Bureau of the Census, *Census Tracts, Houston, Texas,* Final Report PHC(1)–63 (Washington, D.C.: United States Government Printing Office, 1963), 1.

3 precincts were also removed from the sample, leaving a total of thirty-five.

(6) One purpose of the analysis was to obtain data from which generalizations about white Anglo-Saxon Protestant voters could be made. However, among the thirty-five remaining all-white precincts, three heavily Jewish and two Mexican-American precincts were to be found. As both Jews and Mexican-Americans have distinctive voting habits, the decision was made to remove the five remaining ethnic precincts, leaving a total of thirty in municipal Houston. Of these, twenty-four were within the Houston Independent School District.

The thirty precincts, listed by their identifying number, their rank according to income, the number of their parent census tract, the 1959 median family income of the tract, and the percentage and quantity of Negroes and Spanish-surnamed persons in the tract, are presented in Table A.2.

From the standpoint of sampling methodology, the selection of precincts has several shortcomings. First, the sample was not selected according to strict probability procedures. Second, at least one group of precincts has been systematically excluded and this exclusion has possible theoretical relevance. Mixed precincts were removed in order to exclude Negro voters from the analysis. Whites living in transitional areas may have somewhat different attitudes toward Negroes. Hence the sample may be biased if they are seriously underrepresented. It is virtually impossible to ascertain how many whites in Houston actually live in transitional neighborhoods. Part of this difficulty lies in the ambiguity of the term "neighborhood." Part lies in the lack of adequate research facilities. As mentioned in Appendix A, it was estimated that there were 44 mixed precincts in Harris County in 1964. Of these, thirty-six were in Houston. This represents about a fourth of all predominantly white precincts in the city. However, as the definition of a mixed precinct is very loose—one containing as low as 5 percent nonwhites—it is reasonable to assume that a minority of the whites in these precincts live in "fringe" areas. Moreover some of the precincts in the sample

Table A.2
DATA ON VOTING PRECINCTS IN SAMPLE

Precinct Number	Rank by Income Among 30 Precincts	Rank by Income Among 24 Precincts	Tract Number	Median Family Income 1959	"Parent" Census Tract Data			
					Negro Persons		Spanish Surname Persons	
					Number	Percent	Number	Percent
227	1	1	29	$21,102	270	5%	57	1%
234	3	3	66C	18,586	124	1	67	1
269	3	3	66C	18,586	124	1	67	1
135	3	3	66C	18,586	124	1	67	1
265	5	–	91D	13,728	32	1	0	0
232	6	5	67D	11,785	17	0	50	1
148	7	6	43	10,486	79	1	62	1
8	8	7	91I	8,601	7	0	16	0
41	9	–	91B	8,599	8	0	83	1
204	10	8	65A	7,828	235	3	220	3
43	11	–	91A	7,763	3	0	70	1
189	12.5	9.5	64A	7,621	109	1	422	3
244	12.5	9.5	64A	7,621	109	1	422	3
134	14	11	51A	7,523	3	0	251	2

142	15	12	52A	7,478	0	0	101	2
94	17.5	14.5	50	7,433	18	0	189	1
211	17.5	14.5	50	7,433	18	0	189	1
231	17.5	14.5	50	7,433	18	0	189	1
172	17.5	14.5	50	7,433	18	0	189	1
181	20	17	52B	7,311	5	0	191	2
203	21	18	48B	7,048	0	0	117	2
266	22	–	99A	6,940	0	0	70	0
139	23	19	41	6,904	7	0	89	1
115	24	–	97C	6,323	31	1	61	1
257	25	–	112A	6,183	17	0	52	1
105	26	20	95A	5,902	3	0	313	3
38	27	21	30	5,723	533	5	331	3
153	28	22	62	5,403	4	0	272	3
75	29	23	2	5,173	1	0	129	2
57	30	24	4	5,117	3	0	171	2

Source: Calculations based on data from United States Bureau of the Census. *U.S. Censuses of Population and Housing: 1960. Census Tracts, Houston, Texas*, Final Report PHC(1)-63 (Washington, D.C.: United States Government Printing Office, 1962).

border on Negro precincts, although they are not integrated. One would expect that if proximity to Negro residences changes white attitudes—and this is not a well-established finding—the voters in these border precincts would be affected in somewhat the same way as whites living in mixed precincts.

Third, the figures on income were relevant to 1959. As the elections analyzed were from 1960 through 1966, it is possible that enough population shifts occurred to change the relative economic positions of some precincts within that time span. Fourth, only precincts within the 1960 corporate limits of Houston were included. Yet our findings in some cases purport to apply not only to city precincts, but to county and school district ones as well. Both the latter contain residents outside of Houston. Fifth, the boundaries of Houston have expanded since 1960, and new precincts had been created by 1966 that may have had features different from those typical of the older city, though the chances of this are very small. Annexations between 1960 and 1966 were few in number and small in area compared to those between 1950 and 1960. The largest annexation, in terms of area, was that north of the city which includes the site of the new international airport and Lake Houston. This was sparsely populated land in 1966 and it fell entirely within two voting precincts formerly outside of the city. The addition of 15 precincts in the city between 1960 and 1966 was primarily the result of redrawing precinct boundaries which were within the 1960 city limits.

Despite these possible sources of error, there are reasons for believing that the sample is representative of all non-Negro precincts in the electoral units in question during the time span under analysis. First, sampled precincts, while not geographically random, fall in most of the areas of the city which are perceived by local politicians to have important socioeconomic peculiarities. For example, the "old rich" are represented by Precinct 227, that falls within the River Oaks area. The new suburban rich are found in Precincts 234 and 265, both wealthy residential areas in the southwest part of the city. The slightly older upper-middle-class areas are represented by Precincts 148 and 232. The precincts clustered in the southeast area of town, near the ship channel, are relatively old blue-collar districts, containing a sprinkling of labor union families. Precincts 75, 115, and 153 border on Negro precincts and may compensate for the absence of mixed precincts in the sample. Further, a number of precincts are in the core city, defined as that area encompassed by Tracts 1 through 50, while many others are in the suburbs. Fairly new subdivisions are represented, as well as old neighborhoods.

A comparison of the census tracts of the sampled precincts with all predominantly white tracts within the city in 1960 is useful. For our purposes we have defined predominantly white tracts as those having a nonwhite population of 10 percent or less. If the distribution of tracts according to median family income is similar in these two populations, we have the added assurance that the sample is adequate. The table below compares their medians and ranges. The range is slightly larger for all predominantly white tracts (N=76), and the median is about six hundred dollars higher in the sampled tracts (N=24).

Table A.3

COMPARISON OF MEDIANS AND RANGES OF MEDIAN FAMILY INCOME, 1959, ALL PREDOMINANTLY WHITE CENSUS TRACTS AND SAMPLED CENSUS TRACTS, CITY OF HOUSTON

Group	Median	Range
Predominantly White (N=76)	$6,870	$21,102–$2,977 = $18,125
Sample (N=24)	$7,455	$21,102–$5,117 = $15,985

Index